SECESSION AND THE UNION IN TEXAS

Secession and the Union in Texas

by Walter L. Buenger

UNIVERSITY OF TEXAS PRESS, AUSTIN

Requests for permission to reproduce material
from this work should be sent to:
    Permissions
    University of Texas Press
    Box 7819
    Austin, Texas 78712

LIBRARY OF CONGRESS CATALOGING IN PUBLICATION DATA
Buenger, Walter L. (Walter Louis), 1951–
    Secession and the Union in Texas.
    Bibliography: p.
    Includes index.
    1. Texas—Politics and government—1845–1865.
2. Secession. I. Title.
F391.B88   1984   976.4'05   83-19788
ISBN 0-292-77581-4

This book was a winner in the Mrs. Simon Baruch University Award contest, sponsored by the United Daughters of the Confederacy. A complete list of winners of the Baruch Award from 1927 through 1982 appears at the end of the book.

For Walter L. Buenger, Sr.

Contents

Acknowledgments

I first began thinking about a study of secession in Texas nine years ago. Along the way I have been helped by many people, and they have my thanks. Frank E. Vandiver encouraged and guided my early work on this topic. He has insisted that I write and publish ever since. Frederick R. Zuber must have at least once wished that I had not listened to Vandiver because, besides checking my translation of quotes from Texas German newspapers, Fred read and commented upon every version of this manuscript. Babs Willis typed and corrected many of those versions. What she did not type was typed by the secretaries in the Department of History at Texas A&M University. The staff of the University of Texas Press took that typed manuscript and made it more consistent and readable. Throughout the publication process Donald J. Pisani supported me with his friendship and advice. Publication was assisted by the United Daughters of the Confederacy. Liz Conrad deserves special thanks for her work on the maps. From time to time others have helped, and I hope they know that I appreciate their efforts.

My father was too ill to ever read what I have written, but his example of strength and courage in the face of adversity has kept me going whenever my own problems have discouraged me from continuing this project. I wish to dedicate this book to his memory.

SECESSION AND THE UNION IN TEXAS

Prologue: Demons of Anarchy

"Sam Houston! Sam Houston! Sam Houston!" Three times the officer of the Secession Convention of the State of Texas called for the governor to come up from his office to the legislative chambers overhead and take the prescribed oath of loyalty to the Confederate States of America. Three times Houston refused; according to legend he remained "silent, immovable, in his chair . . . whittling steadily on."[1]

That day, 16 March 1861, in Austin, Texas, marked the end of the long political career of Sam Houston. The roots of that career began in the War of 1812, and like so many others of his generation Houston emerged from the war a committed nationalist and a follower of Andrew Jackson. Houston's political skill aided the rise of Jackson in the 1820s, and it aided his own rise as well. In that decade Houston served as a U.S. congressman and as the governor of Tennessee. Coming to Texas in the early 1830s, he won fame by leading the Texans to victory at the Battle of San Jacinto. That battle made the Texas Revolution a success and Houston the first president, in 1836, of the Republic of Texas. After sitting out one term Houston again became president of the Republic in 1842, and in his second term as president he helped arrange the annexation of Texas. Elected as one of the state's first senators, Houston served in the U.S. Senate from 1846 to 1859, when he was elected governor of Texas. Little was constant in this long career except his devotion to Jackson and his commitment to the United States. This national perspective caused the loss of his seat in the Senate and, in 1861, finally ended his career.[2]

As governor from 1859 to 1861, Houston loudly opposed all threats to the Union. Even when Abraham Lincoln was elected president and other Texans called for secession Houston wrote his son: "The price of liberty is blood, and if an attempt is made to destroy our Union, or violate our Constitution, there will be blood shed to maintain them. The Demons of anarchy must be put down and destroyed. The miserable Demagogues & Traitors of the land, must be silenced, and set at naught." But one month later, in December, many unionists believed he had deserted their cause by calling the state legislature into a special session to consider "relations with the Federal Government and many of the States." Once in session, in January 1861, the state legislature quickly legitimized a secession convention organized without the authority of the state government, gave that convention the legislature's own chambers as a meeting place, and retired to await its actions. Also acting quickly, the convention voted by a large margin to secede, but agreed with the governor that such action would only become legal if it were endorsed by the public in a statewide referendum. Houston, however, refused to admit that the convention had any power either to acquire the federal goverment's property in Texas or to join Texas with the six already seceded states of the Lower South in the Confederate States of America. When the convention took steps to do both before the secession referendum, Houston balked and refused to continue to cooperate with the convention.[3]

Houston also refused to accept the idea that secession was necessary. He insisted that he had called the legislature into special session and had cooperated with the Secession Convention only to gauge the will of the people. As he said in a letter written a few days before the 23 February referendum:

> I still believe that secession will bring ruin and civil war. Yet if the people will it, I can bear it with them. I would fain not be declared an alien to my native home in old Virginia, and to the scenes of my early toil and triumph in noble Tennessee. I would not of my own choice give up the banner beneath which I have fought, the Constitution which I have revered, or the Union which I have cherished as the glorious heritage bequeathed to me by my fathers. Sixty-seven years of freedom, the recollections of past triumphs, and past sufferings, the memories of heroes whom I have seen and known, and whose venerated shades would haunt my footsteps were I to falter now, may, perhaps, have made me too devoted to the Constitution and to the Union, but be it so. Did I believe that liberty and the rights of the South demanded the sacrifice, I would not hesitate. I believe that far less concession than made to form the Constitution would now preserve it. Thus believing I cannot vote for secession.

Regardless of the views of their governor, on 23 February 1861 the voters of Texas approved secession by a count of 46,153 to 14,747.[4]

Houston, however, demanded that the public also vote on the issues of joining the Confederacy and accepting the Confederate

Constitution. The convention refused to put those issues to another popular vote, and continued to seize federal property, force the evacuation of federal troops, and take steps to join Texas to the Confederacy. As part of this process, the convention decreed that all state officials must swear an oath of loyalty to the Confederacy. When Houston refused to appear at the appointed time to swear his oath the convention declared his office vacant. Houston declined the pleas of his friends and supporters to forcibly resist what they termed an usurpation of authority and soon thereafter left Austin.

Among those urging Houston to resist secession and illegal usurpation of his authority was Abraham Lincoln. The president gave Houston a good opportunity to live up to his boasts to his son the previous November, but instead of spilling blood to preserve the Constitution he turned away from the fight. Some time in March or April 1861, the president offered the governor 70,000 soldiers to keep Texas in the Union. These troops, combined with Texas unionists and Houston's personal followers, might have allowed the hero of San Jacinto to bend Texans to his will one more time. Houston turned the plan down, claiming that he did not want to further divide the people of his state.[5]

All the spark and all the attachments to the Union had not completely faded in the old man. On Houston's way from Austin to his home at Cedar Point, near the city of Houston, men who had fought under the General in past days called upon him at Brenham to make a speech. He was reluctant to speak until a mob of young southern sympathizers angered him by threatening him with violence. Violence was averted when "Hugh McIntyre, a wealthy planter of the community and a leading secessionist, sprang upon the table and drew a large Colt revolver saying: I and 100 other friends of Governor Houston have invited him to address us, and we will kill the first man who insults, or who may, in any way attempt to injure him." After reminding the crowd that it was Houston who led the fight for Texas independence in 1836, McIntyre is reputed to have said, "Now, fellow-citizens, give him your close attention; and you ruffians, keep quiet, or I will kill you." With his old friends and comrades-in-arms standing guard with drawn revolvers, Houston went on to speak.[6]

After reminding his audience of San Jacinto, as was his custom in most major speeches, Houston warmed to his topic and addressed the difficulties of relying upon reason and maintaining personal integrity while serving as an elected official in a popular democracy. As he put it:

The Vox Populi is not always the voice of God, for when demagogues and selfish political leaders succeed in arousing public
prejudice and stilling the voice of reason, then on every hand
can be heard the popular cry of "Crucify him, crucify him."
The Vox Populi then becomes the voice of the devil, and the
hiss of mobs warns all patriots that peace and good government are in peril.

Houston then went on to reiterate his opposition to the Confederate government and his attachment to the United States.

But the hiss of the mob and howls of their jackal leaders can
not deter me nor compel me to take the oath of allegiance to a
so-called Confederate Government. I protest against surrender-
ing the Federal Constitution, its Government and its glorious
flag to the Northern abolition leaders and to accept in its stead
a so-called Confederate Government.

Houston predicted that since the Confederacy had been founded
by secession it could not endure because its member states could always secede if dissatisfied. He concluded his gloomy forecast by insisting that war between North and South was inevitable.

When the tug of war comes, it will indeed be the Greek meeting Greek. Then, oh my fellow countrymen, the fearful conflict will fill our fair land with untold suffering, misfortune
and disaster. The soil of our beloved South will drink deep the
precious blood of our sons and brethren. In earnest prayer to
our Heavenly Father, I have daily petitioned him to cast out
from my mind the dark foreboding of the coming conflict. My
prayers have caused the light of reason to cast the baleful
shadows of the coming events before me. I cannot, nor will I
close my eyes against the light and voice of reason. The die has
been cast by your secession leaders, whom you have permitted
to sow and broadcast the seeds of secession, and you must ere
long reap the fearful harvest of conspiracy and revolution.

With the cries of the ardent southerners hushed by Hugh McIntyre's
Colt and his words, Houston concluded his last public statement
against the disintegration of the Union.[7]

Soon after Houston's speech of 31 March 1861 in Brenham, the
firing started at Fort Sumter. Lincoln called for 75,000 troops to put
down an insurrection in the South, and Virginia, North Carolina,
Tennessee, and Arkansas seceded to join the Confederacy. The war
Houston had predicted had begun. Houston could side only with the
South, and by 10 May in Independence he was saying:

I was for preserving the Union. The voice of hope was weeks since drowned by the guns of Fort Sumter. It is not now heard above the tramp of invading armies. The mission of the Union has ceased to be one of peace and equality, and now the dire alternative of yielding tamely before hostile armies, or meeting the shock like freemen, is presented to the South.

In his speech at Independence Houston went on to capture the sentiment of many unionists when he declared:

The time has come when a man's section is his country. I stand by mine. All my hopes, my fortunes, are centered in the South. When I see the land for whose defence my blood has been spilt, and the people whose fortunes have been mine through a quarter of a century of toil, threatened with invasion, I can but cast my lot with theirs and await the issue.

From that May to his death on 26 June 1863, Houston insisted upon his loyalty to the Confederacy. He pointed proudly to his son serving in the Confederate army and loudly boasted that the shrillest voices calling for secession now skulked in the rear while his son fought at the front; his section was his country.[8]

So Sam Houston comes down to us a host of contradictions, a tarnished hero often misunderstood. He was neither clearly a secessionist nor a unionist, but he knew better than any other Texan what was to come. With what Congressman John H. Reagan later called "prophetic insight" he foretold the spilled blood, social anarchy, inevitable destruction of slavery, and ultimate defeat of the South that would result from secession. This end was all the more tragic because he felt the pull of the two nations he had helped build—Texas and the United States—and resented both for varying from the course he had so long prescribed. Identifying self with nation, feeling the emotional force of Unionism, and seeing the inevitable end to which secession would lead, he symbolized the paradoxical southerner Lincoln never understood. Sympathetic to the Union, and an opponent of secession, when the issue was decided he, nevertheless, went with his state.[9]

Quixotic but pragmatic, Houston's motivations and actions ran to extremes; so did his state's. He must have wondered that March day in Austin, while whittling in his office, just how his Texans had reached the point of joining the Confederacy. He thought he understood why the "demons of anarchy" were loose in the land, but his understanding gave him little solace. He blamed demagogues and incompetent leaders who performed such stupid actions as the passage of the Kansas-Nebraska Bill. While realizing the failings of individuals, he must have still wondered how his people could desert him. Looking back, he could recall the fight with Mexico, the establishment of an independent republic, and the desperate desire of most Texans to annex that republic to the United States. In his speeches during the secession crisis he pointed out how much Texas had prospered since annexation and how much the population had grown. People! That was one answer that might have come to him. The population of Texas after annexation in 1846 and until secession in 1861 had grown steadily, like that of Alabama or Georgia. Whites from the Lower South had moved into the state and brought with them a culture and an interest, slavery, that bound Texas to the other cotton-growing states. It is possible that by 1861 Texas was only a slightly altered extension of the Deep South and when the states of that region seceded they drew Texas with them.[10]

Yet Houston knew that even in 1861 Texas did not mirror Alabama or Georgia or any other lower southern state. After all, he was the governor and he was an avowed unionist. Texas was split into many factions. Some of these factions—Whigs, immigrants from the Upper South, frontiersmen, Texans who spoke Spanish or German—had little reason to combine in secession with Texans from the Lower South and with Democrats. This factionalism accounted for Houston's election as governor in 1859, and also accounted for the failure prior to 1861 of any attempt to disrupt the Union.

During his career in the Senate, however, Houston had seen that slavery and the passions it engendered could end the heterogeneity of the South and separate a united South from the North. Whether Houston would admit it or not, slavery let loose "the demons of anarchy." Once begun, this process of anarchy would lead even the best of human beings to rash and foolish actions that could not easily be undone. Such actions would force the sanest individuals along a path they had not wished for.[11]

Houston could not believe in the justness or necessity of such a course. While pointing to the irrational nature of human beings he continued to pin his hopes upon reason. He saw the pragmatic benefits of being part of a large and prosperous nation. He understood the multitude of ties that had bound him to that nation since his birth. Why could others not see and understand? How could they let their passions guide them?

Others, to a lesser or in some cases greater degree, did see and understand the value and importance of membership in the United States. At the end of 1860, Texans basically fell into four categories. A small minority had worked for secession for nearly a decade. A larger group perceived the worth of the nation and endorsed secession only after the election of Abraham Lincoln. Another group, almost as large, still opposed secession and clung to the Union, but would support their state in any event. A small minority, the equal in numbers of the ardent secessionists, would never abandon the Union. Texans fell into these categories because of the pre-1860 cultural and political factions to which they belonged, because of the destabilizing force of slavery, and because of the chain of events which Houston referred to as anarchy. Stilling the voice of reason in the late winter and early spring of 1861, however, did not occur easily, nor did it occur completely.

Houston symbolized his state. Texans were not simply secessionists or unionists. Ardent southerners retained a grain of Unionism. Militant nationalists called themselves Texans and southerners. The force of emotion and the delusion that war would not follow secession obscured these mixed feelings. Making the new nation much like the old and Texans' natural desire to go along with their community eased the transition from one government to the next. Yet the change in government did not instantly create those new associations that bound the citizen to the nation, nor did it cleanly sever the old ties to the Union. Reason still bred ambivalence to secession.

1

Antebellum Texas and the Plantation South

Texans stood on a balance beam between secession and the Union in 1860, a position that accurately reflected the nature of their state. Texans by and large were recent immigrants to the state; less than one-fourth of the population could claim to have been in Texas before annexation in 1846. Their newness to Texas meant that they often identified more strongly with their former homes than with their new one. These immigrants tended to cluster into homogeneous groups that preserved their native folkways and values. The cohesiveness of these group associations, the great variety of climate and terrain in Texas, and the lack of adequate transportation in many portions of the state made the economic interests of Texas almost as diverse as its population sources. Texans from the Upper South, the Lower South, Germany, and Mexico all had different interests and values. Frontiersmen in the semiarid west, cotton planters in the humid east, and merchants on the Gulf Coast differed in their respective points of view. Political opinion in 1860 mirrored this disjointed society. Culture, environment, and local self-interest all molded dissimilar attitudes toward secession. Even within the individual resident such things as partisan ties or future hopes might pull in opposite directions. Attachments to the ritual and significance of the Union and Constitution battled desires for tranquility and prosperity.

Complex individuals in a dissociative society, most Texans never seriously considered secession before 1860. They were too multifaceted to accomplish radical change. Inertia held them in the Union. Yet obviously something destroyed the habit of Unionism in 1860 and replaced it with the new direction toward secession. It was this process that Sam Houston called "stilling the voice of reason." In March 1861, the justification of secession seemed so slight and the mythology, prosperity, and stability of the Union so strong that Houston could only view secession as tragically irrational.[1]

From a viewpoint less immediate than Houston's, secession seems equally tragic and mistaken. Secession begat the Civil War, and the war, in addition to costing the nation a million casualties, forced Texans and southerners to abandon many of the old ways they had claimed to be defending when they seceded. If they seceded in defense of slavery, stability, and prosperity, then their actions destroyed all three. Perhaps it required tragedy and foolishness to end the evil of slavery. Still, human beings have seldom seemed so unaware of the cost of their actions as when this body of Americans moved toward secession. Houston might as easily have called secession the dance of fools.

Yet Houston himself came to support the secessionists. He would join in the dance. And the metaphor of dance is appropriate. Secession was a communal, almost primal activity, that had little to do with a rational assessment of alternatives. Secessionists danced, and the music and movement drew everyone on. The voice of reason was stilled because reason was irrelevant.

Perhaps, then, Texans were not so foolishly unaware of the cost of secession. Someone with the perspective of a Sam Houston could see where secession would lead, and even Sam Houston would eventually follow the secessionists. Secession and the war have a haunting aura of inevitability.

Whether irrational, instinctual, foolish, or inevitable, secession is comprehensible. It was a graduated process of dissolving the old ties to the Union and of unsettling the old balance of forces which kept Texans from acting. The old ties to the Union and the competing forces within Texas society did not instantly vanish, but caused Texans to fall into groups defined by the time at which they did accept secession, and by the tenacity of their feelings for secession. As previously stated, these groups can be characterized as those who were proponents of secession prior to 1860; advocates of secession because of Abraham Lincoln's election to the presidency; those who accepted secession only after the public referendum of 23 February 1861; and those who never accepted the destruction of the Union. While these groups did tend to modify the behavior of their members and to force consensus, individuals in all four groups remained ambivalent about or opposed to the dissolution of the Union until the spring of 1861. In the end, secession became acceptable to all individuals but the dogged group of militant unionists because the Confederacy served as a new focal point for the old hopes and feelings previously wrapped up in the Union, and because the war made it impossible to remain ambivalent. Understanding secession, then, requires an understanding of why Texans were initially unionists and why the old balance of cultures, environments, politics, ideologies, and interests that made deviation from traditional Unionism so difficult began to crumble. This understanding begins with the likeness of Texas to the plantation South.

In the early spring of 1861, when it joined the other states of the Lower South in the Confederate States of America, Texas must have seemed in strange company. Isolated by distance and poor transportation, threatened by Indians and banditos, Texas appeared to be too much a part of the western frontier to belong in the Confederacy. Climate, geography, history, population makeup, and regional characteristics all made Texas different from the South. Yet these differences failed to prevent its secession with Alabama, Mississippi, and the other cotton-growing States. They failed in part because, from annexation in 1846 to secession in 1861, the economy and culture of the eastern half of Texas had become increasingly like that of the plantation South. In other regions of the state and even in isolated eastern counties, Texas in 1861 remained a classic frontier region, with semisubsistence agriculture, daily struggle for survival, and egalitarian habits dominating the economy and molding a special culture. The influence of the plantation South, however, extended beyond the present reality of the 1850s. Even if they did not live in a region like the Lower South, antebellum Texans' vision of their society's future status, stability, and prosperity often came to depend upon slavery and building westward railroads that would allow the growth of a cotton-based market economy. Texans did not cease to be Americans or Texans, but to the degree that a plantation economy dominated their present and their future they became increasingly like the lower southerners. This likeness made secession possible.[2]

In two regions of antebellum Texas, East Texas and the Houston-Galveston area, the plantation economy was clearly dominant. It was only in these two regions that cheap transportation, fertile lands, and favorable climate combined to make the growing of cotton and to a lesser degree sugarcane highly profitable. In actuality not all of the counties in East Texas, which have been traditionally defined as counties east of the Trinity River, were plantation counties. In some counties, such as Angelina, poor sandy soil and thick pine forests limited the development of plantations. In other counties, such as Lamar, snags and sandbars in the Red River made transportation difficult and the marketing of cotton costly. The Red River, however, was navigable from near Bowie County to its juncture with the Mississippi, and for those counties with easy access to it, the

Red River provided a perfect artery for the shipment of cotton to New Orleans. To a far lesser degree the other major rivers of East Texas, the Sabine, Neches, and Trinity, also served as carriers of cotton. Snags and sandbars in all three, however, prevented their use except when swollen beyond their normal level.[3]

Geographically East Texas is an extension of the humid southeastern forests of the United States, and crops grown in the Southeast can be grown in East Texas. In this landscape and climate, so totally familiar to the Mississippians, Alabamians, and Georgians who came to Texas in increasing numbers after 1845, patterns of life soon became almost identical to those of the people of their native states.[4]

Cluster migration aided the growing similarity of East Texas and the Lower South. An adventuresome individual from the Southeast would come to Texas and seek out land well suited for his agricultural habits. Then he might write home of the marvelous opportunities available in this new area. Others quickly joined the initial pioneer, and life in Texas increasingly resembled life in the immigrants' former home. East Texas first attracted settlers from the Lower South because of its proximity to their native states and its suitability for their economic system. Once established, these settlements offered a further inducement to immigrate. More cautious souls were reassured that not only the physical but the cultural environment would resemble that of their homeland.[5]

Access to markets, suitable terrain and climate, and cluster migration also fostered the growth of a plantation society in the area around Houston and Galveston. In the 1850s Galveston was the most important port on the Texas coast. It offered deep and safe anchorage and was connected to inland areas by Galveston Bay, Buffalo Bayou, and the lower Trinity and San Jacinto rivers. Just down the coast from Galveston the Brazos River fed into the Gulf of Mexico, and like most Texas rivers in high water seasons it offered limited transportation. Railroads added to these natural arteries of trade. Houston businessmen were particularly adept at securing railroad transportation and by 1861 rail lines stretched from Houston up to Washington and Brazos counties and down into Brazoria County. A railroad also connected Houston with the port at Galveston, so when Buffalo Bayou was impassable goods could still flow in and out of Houston. This ease of transportation together with the fertile soil, plentiful rainfall, and long growing season of the area made the region ideal for planters, and from the days of the Republic on, immigrants from the Lower South dominated the countryside surrounding Houston and Galveston. In turn, familiar culture attracted still more settlers in the 1850s from the plantation regions of Louisiana, Georgia, Alabama, and Mississippi.[6]

Some portions of the Houston-Galveston region, however, lacked the homogeneity of East Texas. In the cities of Houston and Galveston at least a third of the population was German, and a much higher percentage than in the countryside was northern born. Colorado, Austin, and Washington counties contained sizable German communities whose beginnings dated back to the 1830s. The clustering of Germans in these three counties and their early arrival in Texas slowed, but did not totally prevent, the spread of a plantation society. Some Germans became planters and slaveholders while others raised cotton on a smaller scale, using free labor. Thrown into daily contact with Texans from the Lower South and living in a favorable environment with access to markets, it is not surprising that by 1861 Germans near the Gulf Coast did begin to assimilate the Lower South model.[7]

In one way, the rural counties near the Gulf Coast with a high percentage of Germans characterize the antebellum history of both the Houston-Galveston and East Texas plantation regions. Each year, no matter where the population originated, assimilation made both areas more like the plantation regions of the Lower South; by 1861, these areas were in the process of becoming replicas of older plantation regions.

Several pieces of evidence illustrate this growing resemblance to other plantation regions of the Lower South over the course of the 1850s. Recent studies of Harrison County (which had good access to the Red River) reveal that from 1850 to 1860 the number and size of the larger landholdings grew at a faster rate than did the landholdings of the yeoman farmer. Those who owned slaves and land were also the most active politically. In both the East Texas and Houston-Galveston regions reported increases in the number of slaves, amount of improved acreage, and quantity of cotton ginned indicate that plantations were increasingly prosperous and increasingly numerous. For example, in the sugarcane- and cotton-growing counties of Brazoria, Fort Bend, and Wharton, just to the southwest of Houston, lived eighteen of the state's fifty-four slaveholders who held more than one hundred slaves in 1860. In these same three counties could be found almost one-fifth of those Texans who owned over $100,000 in total property in 1860. These were also the only three counties in the state where slaves made up over 65 percent of the population. Harrison, neighboring Marion, and nearby Bowie counties were among the few in which slaves made up from 50 to 65 percent of the population. All six of these counties were moving in the direction of the more famous southern plantation regions in coastal South Carolina and Louisiana and along the Mississippi Delta.[8]

Even counties or portions of counties without plantations could be considered part of a plantation region if their inhabitants were economically interdependent with planters. Texas plantations typically produced their own food supplies; planters raised enough corn, hogs, and sweet potatoes to feed their families, hands, and draft animals. If they were not self-sufficient, however, nearby yeoman farmers who primarily raised corn and herdsmen who raised hogs and cattle could supply the planters with foodstuffs. Farmers who grew a specialty crop, usually fruit, vegetables, or tobacco, might also sell a portion of what they produced to neighboring planters. Many farmers in antebellum Texas, however, were just above the subsistence level, and they sold or bartered their meager surplus of corn, livestock, or some specialized product in urban areas. It was there they obtained the few utensils, tools, and supplies they needed or wanted. Such towns might never have existed or would have been much smaller had their growth not been stimulated by the outside world's demand for plantation crops. Certainly, the export of lumber, livestock, and hides from eastern Texas infused some cash into the economy, but in antebellum days cotton and in some areas sugarcane were the primary stimulators of economic and urban growth. Even lumber mills, the most prevalent form of industrial activity, often sold to local customers whose incomes derived directly or indirectly from plantation crops. This was even more true of merchants and lawyers who could not have existed in a semisubsistence economy. Thus, without plantations in eastern Texas, there would have been little growth and prosperity. Those who cared for such benefits were tied to a plantation economy even if they never owned a plantation.[9]

Such economic interdependence with the growers of plantation crops was traditional for most Texans east of longitude 96° west. It was part of their culture. Corn growers, stock raisers, lumber millers, lawyers, and merchants from the Lower South came to this region for the same reasons as sugar or cotton planters. The natural and cultural environment allowed them to duplicate their former lives, with one important exception: the move to the new region of Texas allowed the immigrant an opportunity to move up the economic and social ladder. These were traditional opportunities defined in traditional Lower South fashion—that is, they were interlocked with slavery and the growth of the plantation system. Most of these former southern residents shared social values, and their attitude toward slavery, their conception of the importance of the nation, and even their religious beliefs were very much the same. This area of Texas east of longitude 96° west, then, was the most homogeneous in the state and the most like the Lower South. Only in the cities of Houston and Galveston did any degree of economic or cultural diversity exist.[10]

Of course, even in 1861 there remained some portion of former president of the Republic Mirabeau B. Lamar's dream of creating a unique Texan, or Texian, as he styled his countryman. Just as Texas became southern, southern immigrants to eastern Texas became Texian. These new Texans acquired their state's conception of itself as somehow set apart from the rest of the country. Other Texans enjoyed not only these distinctions but also a new physical environment, a different economy, and a mix of cultures unique to Texas.[11] Despite this, it was no accident that Texas seceded with the Lower South. From the founding of the Republic on, Lamar's dream of empire and a special folk had slowly died; Texas was in the process of becoming more like the South. By 1861, economics and a slaveholding culture tied the eastern half of Texas to the Lower South. By that date, as well, both aspirations for and fears of the future bonded numerous other Texans to the Lower South.

Something more than economic interdependence and a common culture connected yeoman farmers to planters in antebellum Texas. Corn growers might dream of the profits and status to be achieved with cotton and slaves. Such dreams made them think of the future like planters, not semisubsistence farmers. Regardless of the cultural or subcultural group Texans had originated in, they came to the state to improve the quality of their lives. That did not mean that all Texans came to the state for profit. Some might have migrated because they wanted to preserve their traditional self-sufficient ways of life—lifestyles which forced each family to spin, weave, sew, hunt, farm, fish, and gather wood, only loosely tied to the wealth-producing market economy. Most new Texans, however, desired the security of wealth and the prestige of greater social status or political power. While these dreams were held in common, the paths to their fulfillment might be quite different. Each cultural or subcultural group tended to have a model for achieving wealth and power. An Upper South model, for example, was a farmer with a medium-sized farm who raised wheat and corn, invested in machinery to save labor, and aggressively marketed his wheat and the livestock he fattened on his corn. If this model did not prove viable in the new environment, or if another group's model demonstrated greater ability to bring wealth, status, and power, then the farmer

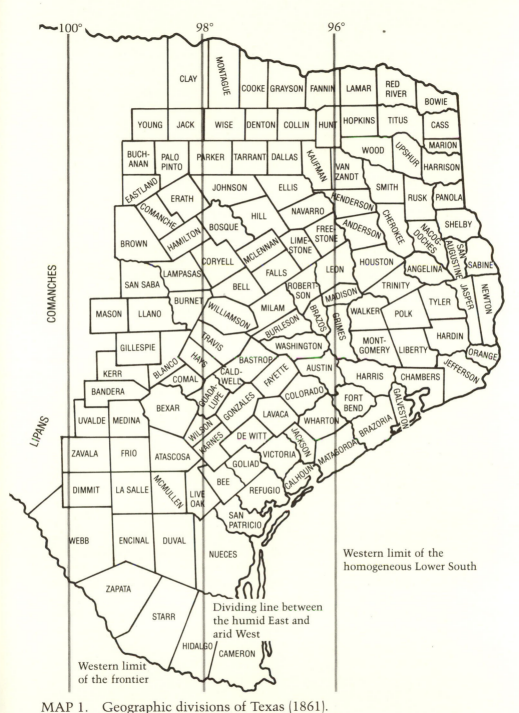

MAP 1.   Geographic divisions of Texas (1861).

Map by Liz Conrad. (County lines from map no. 13 in *Mitchell's School and Family Geography*, 1858.)

might abandon his traditional behavioral guidelines. The key to the process of assimilation was exposure to alternative patterns of living. Texans had to see other models of behavior in action before they would change their plans for the future. Of course, the large numbers of alternative cultural models surrounding them enhanced their willingness to change. That meant that if more Texans from the Lower South lived in a county than did Germans or Texans from the Upper South, and if climate, terrain, and transportation allowed it, over time wheat and corn growers became cotton growers and slave owners, or at least aspired to that level. The long hot growing season and fertile soils of Texas coupled with steady world demand for cotton made that crop and the cotton slave culture attractive wherever rainfall and transportation permitted. In effect, with the coming of the railroad, all of Texas as far west as about longitude 98° west, the point at which rainfall ceased to be adequate for cotton, was potentially the domain of the Lower South. That it was not so in 1860 can be attributed to the early settling of some regions by other cultural groups and continued isolation due to poor transportation.[12]

Texas was not totally like the Lower South, then, but Texans could view their state as progressing in that direction. They could identify their future with Alabama and Mississippi, and with the marketing of cotton and slave ownership. Thus either common present interests or common future dreams would incline some Texans to follow Mississippi and Alabama out of the Union.

Texas was the last of a series of states that emerged on the southwestern frontier from 1815 to 1860, and like those before it, the young state enjoyed flush times. No state in the South enjoyed a greater share of the prosperity of the 1850s than Texas. Agriculture dominated the economy. Land was cheap and abundant. Fortunes could be made in cotton. Slaves provided an able labor force. All that was lacking was an economical means of reaching the area and of transporting agricultural products from it. By 1855, just ten years after it became a state, Texas' assessable wealth had increased fivefold. From 1850 to 1860 the number of slaves increased from 58,161 to 182,566. In the same decade, the number of farms in Texas increased from 12,198 to 42,891, and improved acreage increased from 643,976 to 2,650,781. From these farms, 26,255 bales of cotton were received in 1850 at the port of Galveston. In 1856, considered a poor year for crops, over 90,000 bales of cotton were received. Sugar, cattle, molasses, and hides showed similar increases. Such growth was only the beginning for some Texans. Men like Willard Richardson, editor of the Galveston *News*, or Charles De Morse of the Clarksville *Standard* envisioned even greater material progress for the state. The key to this progress was railroads.[13]

Railroads fascinated Texas empire builders. They were to be the sinews which would bind Texas together and make it a self-sufficient and prosperous economic unit. They were also to be the means by which slavery was spread into the interior of the state. Despite the mania for railroads present since the time of the Republic, lack of capital to finance them and disputes over location and procedure delayed construction until the late 1850s. Still, the notable preoccupation with railroads evident in the newspapers and in the state and local governments of the time illustrates that Texans in the 1850s were intensely interested in economic expansion—expansion, as in the case of the Lower South, based on agriculture and commerce. Significantly, in East Texas, entrepreneurs designed railroads to further integrate the region with the economy of the Lower South. Texans like Willard Richardson thought of Texas as an empire unto itself, but still an empire closely resembling the Lower South. They looked forward to a day when railroads would facilitate the export of cotton, sugar, beef, hides, and flour, and at the same time help supply their state's own material needs through intrastate trade. With the vast cotton lands of the state opened up by railroads the potential for growth seemed unlimited. Railroads represented the reality of prosperity and economic growth. Railroads were linked with slavery. They represented dreams—dreams of a slaveholding empire based on agriculture and commerce—dreams that were common to the Lower South.[14]

Texans and southerners dreamed of territorial as well as economic expansion. During the era of the Republic there had been much talk of expanding Texas until it stretched from the Gulf of Mexico to the Pacific Ocean; in the time of antebellum statehood similar illusions of expanding southern territory into the Caribbean and Latin America were popular. In the view of John Marshall, editor of the Austin *Texas State Gazette* and chairman of the state's Democratic party, Manifest Destiny was closely linked to southern nationalism. While others dreamed of an ever stronger southern economy, Marshall dreamed of expanding southern territory. Nor were these the idle thoughts of one or two fanatics. The Knights of the Golden Circle, whose purpose, as far as can be understood, was to found a great slaveholding empire in the United States, the Caribbean, and Latin America, enjoyed modest popularity in Texas. Cuba was to be the geographic center of a circular empire whose radius stretched to the Mason-Dixon line in the north and down through

Brazil in the south. In 1857 John Marshall asked, "Shall we not go on in the attempt to acquire Cuba, and thus prepare the way for an inevitable decree of destiny in the final annexation of the rest of the Antilles?" A number of Texans would have answered yes.[15]

Economic and territorial expansion, then, were both tangible and intangible links with the Lower South. Slaveholders came to Texas at an increasing rate in the 1850s. Plantation crops increased in economic importance. Settlers from the Lower South spread into the western counties. The Lower South mix of planter, farmer, and herdsman became more common. In effect, the Lower South had extended its territorial borders to include the eastern half of Texas. Much of the rest of Texas was tied to the Lower South too, but it was a much more chimerical bond. In much of western Texas, slavery and the Lower South economy were not present, but the hope that the railroads would bring them there was. The belief in distant El Paso that the Southwest could be brought securely into the slaveholder's orbit helps explain that town's rabid support of secession.[16]

In a like manner but on a greater scale, the institution of slavery linked Texas and the Lower South in both a real and an ethereal sense. Slavery was one concept upon which Texans demanded conformity. From time to time there had been expressions of antislavery sentiment in Texas, but the exponents of such sentiment seldom remained in the state for long.[17] Rip Ford, editor, Texas Ranger, and later confederate general, probably summed up most Texans' attitudes toward slavery when after the war he wrote: "Slavery came to the Southern man authorized by the supreme Law of the Land. It came to him authorized by time, and custom, and law. The assumption in the Declaration of Independence that 'all men are created equal' was not intended to include [the] African race, or was a falsehood on its face. It was an institution sanctioned by the Bible, and it had all the authority of time to uphold it." In the 1850s, Charles De Morse, the talented editor of the Clarksville *Standard*, echoed the common southern lament that it was the master who bore all the responsibilities and burdens of life, while the slave lived a happy and carefree existence. Willard Richardson, the editor of the widely circulated Galveston *News* and the creator of the *Texas Almanac*, expressed another common belief of that decade when he lauded the increase in the number of slaves in Texas. Richardson viewed slavery as essential to the economic growth of the state. John P. Osterhout, a transplanted Pennsylvanian, considered slaves both a good investment and a necessary prerequisite to a higher social status.[18] William P. Ballinger, a prominent Galveston attorney, held some reservations about the economic value of slavery, but he noted that slavery civilized the Negro, and was "the only relation that can exist where the African is in any considerable numbers, and it seems to me if the hand of Providence be visible in anything in this world it is in American slavery."[19] In the eyes of antebellum Texans, slavery was just, moral, and beneficial to both slave and master.

Only one aspect of slavery aroused much dissension in Texas: the competition between slave labor and free labor. John Marshall combined nascent populism and slavery by arguing that every man should be a slaveholder so that the wealthy planters would not have a stranglehold on this important facet of the economy. He hoped, too, that widespread slaveholding would strengthen slavery in Texas.[20] Others were not so willing to see slave labor replace free labor. Jacob De Cordova, one of Texas's primary propagandists in the 1850s, declared slavery a "wise provision," but he argued that profit and loss should determine whether slave labor or free labor was used. In the classic tradition of liberal economics he wrote: ". . . labor, like every other marketable commodity, will always regulate itself; and there are few men indeed who, when they find out what description of labor is most profitable, will not employ it, if they can command it." Willard Richardson did not share De Cordova's opinion that white labor could be used to grow cotton; his disagreement with De Cordova was centered upon which labor force was the hardiest and most efficient. In effect, it was similar to the argument over whether it was best to plow with horses or mules.[21]

Slaves were scarce and expensive in Texas, and since Richardson and Marshall viewed the expansion of slavery as essential to growth they became outspoken advocates of reopening the African slave trade. In doing so they attracted the wrath of Ferdinand J. Lindheimer, one of the most influential Germans in Texas and editor of the staunchly Democratic *Neu Braunfelser Zeitung*. Lindheimer made it clear that he, as well as most Germans, did not oppose slavery. They did oppose reopening the African slave trade because it would take jobs away from Germans, who were one of the major sources of free labor in Texas. Lindheimer further argued that the African slave trade, instead of allowing more whites to own slaves, would allow the concentration of even greater numbers of slaves in the hands of those who had the most capital. Economic, political, and social power would thus be further concentrated in the hands of the large slaveholders. Other Texans with already large investments in slaves opposed Richardson and Marshall's plan because it would drive down the value of their slaves. The attempt to reopen the African slave trade, which came to be identified with the Democratic party in 1859, cost the party dearly when Sam Houston

pounced upon this issue and used it to help him win the gubernatorial election. That and the question of slave labor versus free labor were the only disparities in Texans' otherwise united stand on
slavery.[22]

Despite the acrimonious dispute in 1859 over expanding slave
labor, during the secession crisis unionists seldom attempted to take
advantage of some Texans' commitment to free labor. Perhaps they
did not want to risk being branded abolitionists, but it was also possible that this commitment existed only temporarily. Certainly slavery, like expansionism, concerned future hopes and fears as much as
present realities. R. W. Loughery expressed these hopes in the *Texas
Republican* when he wrote in 1856: "From the immense extent and
extraordinary fertility of her lands, [Texas] is destined to become the
recipient of most of the slave population of her sister States of the
South. She ought, therefore, to feel a more lively interest in every
question pertaining to the institution, and to its perpetuation, than
any other State in which it exists." Many Texans envisioned their
state as becoming a great slaveholding empire. To threaten slavery
was to flout destiny. Once again, Texans' conception of what they
were to become was a strong bond to the Lower South.[23]

Fear of the consequences of abolition proved to be an equally
strong bond. The summer of 1860 witnessed many unexplained fires
and other acts labeled terrorism in Texas which many believed to be
the fruit of abolitionist plots similar to John Brown's raid on Harpers
Ferry. This was final proof to Texans that the end of slavery meant
social, economic, and political anarchy. Fear of social discord has
motivated the body politic since Aristotelian times, and it was no
less so in antebellum Texas.[24]

John Marshall's *Texas State Gazette* most adeptly played upon
these fears, and spearheaded a drive to convince all Texans, slaveholders and nonslaveholders alike, that the defense of slavery demanded secession once the black Republicans were in control of the
federal government. On 17 November 1860, just a few days after
Abraham Lincoln was elected, a *Gazette* editorial read: "The negro s
would of course be set free, and like all emancipated African slaves
would prey, an idle, filthy, vicious, and worthless class upon the industrious white population." Even the frontier was threatened by
those who wanted to end slavery if abolitionists released either Kansas ruffians or vicious Indians on northwest Texas. In summing up
his position, the *Gazette*'s editorial writer insisted: "We are all vi-
tally interested in defending and maintaining slavery. It cannot be
destroyed without ruining and dishonoring every cotton State mate-
rially, morally, socially, and politically." Recent scholars have argued

that it was these fears that convinced the majority of Texans to abandon the Union. Certainly, in the case of U.S. Representative John H. Reagan, a man who ably expressed the moderate views of most Texans, this fear of anarchy, strengthened by Republican threats to property, moved him to support secession.[25]

More than anything else, slavery linked Texas to the Lower South. The attitude toward blacks was common in both the Upper and Lower South, but Texans' conception of the role slavery was to play in their own future was identical to the role of slavery in the Lower South. Furthermore, racial fears proved as potential in some parts of Texas as they were in South Carolina. Nor did the density of slavery in an area need to be high in order to provoke these fears. Secession was as hysterically discussed in Dallas, where few slaves lived, as it was in Brazoria County, where over 65 percent of the population were slaves. Slavery cemented the alliance between Texas and the Lower South.[26]

This alliance between Texas and the plantation-dominated Lower South had grown more close in the years between annexation and secession. Antebellum Texas shared the economic prosperity of the cotton states. Lower South whites and blacks came to Texas in increasing numbers in these years and their influence spread throughout the state. In their attitude toward slavery Texans were in consensus with the Lower South. Still, not just the social and economic realities of 1861 tied Texas to the Lower South. Texans' conception of their future prosperity, the future of slavery, and the awful potential of freedom for the blacks bound Texas to Alabama. These changes in interests and dreams altered traditional politics and set the stage for secession.

2

Partisanship and Ideology

Once Texans' future prospects, present interests, and cultural perceptions became more like those of lower southerners, they became increasingly similar politically; similar but not the same. Politics was more than an extension of economic opportunities and regional culture. Partisanship and local political feuds often overrode economic interests and cultural ties. By the same token, Texans held a common American ideology, an ideology shaded differently in every part of the United States. Secession was a political event, an event shaped not just by regional culture and interests but by the history of partisan politics in Texas and by the evolution of American ideology in Texas.

As Democrats or as members of the many successive opposition parties which competed for power and position within the state, Texans developed loyalties which split them from their neighbors and tied them to Americans in distant counties and distant states. Party affiliation could make a man more of a Texan and it could make him more of a southerner, but it could also make him more of an American. Affiliation, though, was not just something inherited, or assumed because of a single particular issue. Antebellum parties, through their spokesmen on the stump and in the press, were the articulators and major carriers of ideologies from generation to generation. A two-party system was surprisingly persistent in antebellum Texas. It was persistent not just because of competition for political office and influence, but because Texans had marked ideological differences. Like political parties, ideology cut across many boundaries: Texans could be Germans, Lutherans, Democrats, and romantic nationalists. They could be planters, Baptists, Whigs, and romantic nationalists. If they met on no other level, ideologically Texans could be kin.

Without political parties, however, these kindred spirits might never act in concert. Parties muted ideology for political gain. They combined for a common purpose factions with often diverse ideologies. Still, only through parties could individuals' ill-defined values and beliefs find effective political expression. Parties, despite the blurrings required of practical politics, attracted adherents because of the values and beliefs they represented. As long as such institutions that could express collective Unionism existed the nation would have a strong protector. When such an institution vanished, secession would be simpler.

Texas certainly had its share of political rivalries in the 1850s. The state was governed in the main by the Democratic party, a party which became increasingly aligned with the militant secessionists of the Lower South. The Democracy (as the party was called), however, did not rule unchallenged. First the Whigs, then the Know-Nothings, and finally the Opposition or Union Democrats competed with them. More than simple competition for office separated the Democrats and their opponents; the principles of those challenging the Democrats changed with the situation. A Whig was not necessarily a Know-Nothing, nor was the Know-Nothing always a member of the Opposition. Increasingly, however, the Democrats' opponents were distinguished by devotion to the Union and belief in its God-given greatness, while the Democrats—although still believing in the goals of an American nation—became increasingly militant in their defense of the South's place in that nation. As distinctions between parties and ideologies became clearer, it was the Opposition that defended the Union and the Democrats who attacked it.[1]

A Whig party in Texas existed only briefly, but it left an important legacy. In the presidential elections of both 1848 and 1852 Whig candidates drew a surprisingly large vote despite being personally unpopular in Texas. During the same period Whigs competed successfully with Democrats in local elections, but only once, in 1853, when William B. Ochiltree ran for governor, did the Whigs achieve any degree of success in a statewide race. Most Whig support in Texas was localized in East Texas, North Texas, and in the urban and commercial areas, and although opposition parties in Texas became more broadly based, there would always be a clear distinction between Know-Nothings and Union Democrats from the old Whig areas and those from the other regions of the state.[2]

These Texas Whigs brought as well the particular values and flavor of southern Whigs to any opposition party they joined. The Whig party of the South attracted prosperous planters, merchants, and professionals. The party stressed stability, economic growth, and an adherence to traditional American and Protestant values. In Texas, Whigs also tried to appeal to what their leading editorial mouthpiece, the Galveston *Journal*, called "the hard fisted yeomanry of our country," and they often attacked the Democrats as being undemocratic.[3] Nor did Texas Whigs have the overwhelming support of the largest slaveholders, as was true of Mississippi Whigs. Still, on the whole Texas Whigs followed the southern pattern. Besides their definite economic interest in banking and internal improvements, Whigs had in common certain class ties. While not above appealing to the yeoman at election time, the bulk of Whig leadership and support came from the agricultural elite and from the commercial classes of the towns and villages across the state. Whigs, too, were often Protestant reformers who desired to uplift society and force it to conform to the Whig model of proper behavior. Even their interest in banks stemmed in part from their desire to impose order on a chaotic financial system. At any rate, all Whigs felt more at home in their own party than among the licentious Democrats. Most Whigs, after years of association with their party and competition for office with the Democrats, viewed their opponents with the same loathing modern sports fans reserve for their favorites' archenemies. Politics was in many ways the "great game" of the nineteenth-century South, with each party struggling to secure victory for its candidates. Prominent speakers always drew a crowd, and the hostility aroused by flamboyant oratory often erupted into violence. Duels between rival editors and gunplay on the speaker's podium were common enough in antebellum Texas to prove the seriousness with which Texans took their politics. This sense of competition and of being set apart persisted and, combined with differences in ideology and interests, ensured that a hard kernel of opposition to the Democracy remained after the Whig party in Texas, the national party having split apart in 1854 over slavery and the Kansas-Nebraska Act, began to wither.[4]

Perhaps the most crucial ideological legacy of the Whigs was the concept of nationhood. Almost all Texans placed some degree of value on the Union before 1860. Whigs, however, favored a stronger and more active central government. This did not mean that they opposed the federal system. It was a question of degree. Whigs placed more emphasis on an active and authoritative national government and less on the freedom of the individual states. Whigs, too, were often romantic nationalists and had deep emotional ties to the Union. Men like James W. Throckmorton had as deep a loyalty to their country as they did to their region and state. Such a commitment was not typical of all Whigs, though, and in 1850 and 1860 many southern Whigs loudly advocated secession. Still, Whigs as a whole held a broad national perspective and did not view each new crisis strictly through the eyes of a Texan or a southerner. During the crisis of 1850, in which Texans took a special interest because their claim to eastern New Mexico became a southern cause, the Galveston *Journal* was even willing to sacrifice the Whig party for the Union and declared: "In other states the terms Whig and Democrat have almost been forgotten in the absorbing question of union or disunion. The Whigs of Texas are for the Union, and, therefore, from the highest motives that can prompt men in their political views, desire no strict organization until the Union is safe from the agitation which at present threatens it."[5]

Unfortunately for the antisecessionists, the Whigs left behind several political liabilities which hampered any opposition parties to which they later belonged. Among these liabilities were Whig opposition in the United States to the annexation of Texas and later to the Mexican War. Also important was the opposition of the Taylor-Fillmore administration to the Texas border claims in New Mexico. Most important in the long run, however, was the identification of the Whig party on the national level with abolitionism. In 1852 Texas Whigs reacted angrily to the nomination of General Winfield Scott for president. John B. Ashe of Galveston County, a delegate to the national convention and former Whig congressman from Tennessee, had been nominated by an earlier Whig state convention as a presidential elector but resigned from that position when Scott was nominated. He declared: "We thoroughly understand the temper and wishes of the abolitionists of the North, to whom General Scott owes his nomination. The same power which could procure his nomination could control his administration, and then where would we be?" Such sentiments account for the precipitous decline in the Whig party's vote in East Texas counties. Here, where slavery was the most firmly established, threats to that peculiar institution were more important than party loyalty. Thus, by 1854 Texas Whigs carried with them into any new political organization a number of serious political handicaps.[6]

In 1854, with the Whig party rapidly vanishing from the political hustings, the Democratic party showed few signs of life itself. Texas politics had lacked organized political parties before 1848, and while most Texans considered themselves Democrats, it was only in regions or elections in which organized competition existed that the Democratic party as an institution had come into existence. The party had no regular convention system and very little statewide organization. Especially in the more recently settled regions of the state, local commentators would have agreed with the Austin editor who wrote in 1855: "Hitherto a campaign could hardly be said to wear anything of a political color, and in many instances the predilections of those who offered themselves for office were not investigated, and men were chosen in consideration of services rendered in the dark and troublesome times, when side by side Democrats

and Whigs struggled for the rights of many regardless of anteced-
ents." Men called themselves Democrats when they ran for office,
but what mattered most were personality and reputation.[7]

This did not mean that the Democratic party was not without
considerable strength within the state. The dominant personality in
Texas politics had long been Sam Houston, and like Houston most
Texans identified with Andrew Jackson and his political party. While
Whigs might still rail against "King Andrew," the majority of Texans
in 1854 espoused Jacksonian ideology and deeply admired Houston
and Jackson. They believed that all free males should vote, that political office should not be reserved for the elite, that all offices
should be filled by popular elections, and that banks were evil. It
was wrong for internal improvements within the states to be financed by the federal government. Corporations were to be bound
by legislative restrictions because they represented concentrations
of wealth and power that could corrupt the democratic system. For
Democrats this did not mean that prosperity should not be encouraged by government, but that prosperity should be promoted for all
men, not just the privileged few. In Houston and the legendary Jackson, Texans saw protectors of the people and defenders of the ideology of the common man. In war and in peace—by their military and
political leadership—Houston and Jackson sheltered and directed
their people. Fealty was owed these chieftains, and fealty meant that
when the choice was clear Texans voted for their chieftain's Democratic party. The strength of the Democratic party in Texas prior to
1854 was twofold: the party represented a loosely knit collection of
ideas, and it bore the stamp of the major public personalities in Texans' lives.[8]

After 1854 the Democratic party would begin a period of evolution that would last about four years. The party would never totally
lose its Jacksonian base, but it would change greatly. This change
was caused by the high level of political turmoil within the nation
itself, the increasing strength of a Lower South culture in Texas, and
the statewide competition of the Know-Nothing party. Of these
three, the Know-Nothing party was the clearest and simplest cause
of change.

Like the Democratic and Whig parties, the Know-Nothing party
was an import to Texas. It began as a semisecret organization dedicated to reform, but it quickly changed into a full-fledged political
party. Appealing to nativists, nationalists, and Democrat-haters, the
Know-Nothings achieved considerable success in the state and local
elections of 1854–1855.

Since over 15 percent of the free population in Texas during the 1850s could be considered "foreign" and since this was a rapidly growing group, the nativist planks of the Know-Nothing platform had great appeal among the American born in the state. Judging from the Know-Nothings' newspapers, nativism was based upon a closely connected series of impulses: anti-Catholicism, racism, resentment of economic competition, fear of foreign radicals, and a fear of the debasement of Anglo-Saxon institutions. Catholicism's danger grew from its undemocratic nature and the subversive influence of the Pope. According to the Know-Nothings, priests controlled the voters and the Pope controlled the priests and manipulated Catholics for his own purposes. Since all Mexicans and about half the Germans were Catholics, this meant other Texans could easily associate foreignness and Catholicism with danger. The threat to democracy was all the greater because Mexican Catholics were considered inferior beings whose genetic makeup would pollute the Anglo-Saxon bloodline. Germans as Western Europeans were not considered racially inferior, but both groups competed with Americans for jobs. This allowed the Know-Nothings to attract urban workers and craftsmen who believed their economic position threatened by foreigners. Other Texans saw the foreigners not as an economic threat but as a threat to the stability of their society. Mainly because of their alleged opposition to slavery, Germans and Mexicans had to fight the charge of being radicals and anarchists. Since some German intellectuals did criticize slavery and some Mexican abolitionists did help slaves escape, there was enough truth in the charge to keep rumors flying for years about the dangerous nature of the foreign element in Texas. In essence, the Know-Nothings considered foreigners a threat to Anglo-American society and government.[9] As an editorial in the La Grange *True Issue* put it in 1855, "indiscriminate immigration, a universal amalgamation of all the schismatic Red Republicans, tumultuary propagandists, all the hyferlutin odds and ends of all the world and the rest of mankind must and will assuredly, certainly and inevitably overwhelm in dire discord and bloody wreck, the sacred citadel of liberty, and light the funeral pyre around its ruins."[10]

This concern with the integrity of American institutions and with the ethnic purity of the American people was in some ways simply another side of the Know-Nothings' commitment to the nation. Nationalists and nativists alike were concerned with maintaining the purity and integrity of the United States. The events of the mid-1850s threatened the nation as deeply as did foreign immigration, and the clearest source of Know-Nothing strength grew from

dissatisfaction with the Kansas-Nebraska Bill of 1854 and from sub-
sequent events in Kansas. The Kansas-Nebraska Act had been a
Democratic measure, endorsed by President Franklin Pierce and
passed by the votes of Democratic congressmen. In 1855, when it began to seem to some southerners that the Kansas-Nebraska Act
threatened the Union by dividing it along sectional lines and by
leading to the bloody fighting between northerners and southerners
in Kansas, the Democratic party was blamed for the course of events.
In Texas those dissatisfied with the Democrats often joined the
Know-Nothings more out of concern for the stability and safety of
the Union than because of nativism. Know-Nothings accentuated
this commitment to the nation by calling themselves the American
party, and it became a standard argument of the Know-Nothing campaign that the Democrats sought the disruption of the Union.[11]

Sam Houston was one of those who moved toward the American party because of the Kansas-Nebraska Act. Almost ousted from
the Democratic party because of his vote against the measure, Houston never actually joined the Know-Nothings but did support many
of the party's views. In a public letter of 24 July 1855, he maintained
that the old Democratic party of Jefferson and Jackson had grown de-
based and that the Know-Nothings represented a return to the principles of his mentors. While not condoning any restrictions on the
civil rights of immigrants, Houston endorsed the extension of the
naturalization period to twenty-one years and voiced anti-Catholic
sentiment. He also condemned the modern Democratic party for
being under the sway of John C. Calhoun and argued that its support
for the Kansas-Nebraska Act had "built up a freesoil and abolition
party." For these reasons he declared, "I believe the salvation of my
country is only to be served by adherence to the principles of the
American Order."[12]

Nationalism was not simply a direct response to immediate
events. Long-term commercial and economic interests had led many
to support the nation and the party. With their prosperity threatened
by sectional strife, the commercial centers of East Texas gave consistent support to the Know-Nothings. Here the Whig party had
been strong, and the Know-Nothing party was a direct descendant.
Prosperous planters, lawyers, and merchants who favored federally
financed internal improvements, state banks, and a maintenance of
the status quo, all of which would have enhanced or perpetuated
their profitable market economy, transferred their allegiance to the
Know-Nothings. Businessmen in San Antonio, where the U.S. Army
made a major contribution to the economy, were another source of

Know-Nothing strength. Those most concerned with preserving the relationship among the states as well as expanding the economy were often Know-Nothings.[13]

An emotional or ideological attachment to the Union also played a part in the origin of the Know-Nothing party. Many Know-Nothing adherents, like Sam Houston, claimed to be old Jacksonian Democrats—opponents of nullifiers and secessionists, proponents of a strong national government. Other conservative old-line Whigs added their own nationalism to the Know-Nothing party's and attempted to portray Know-Nothings as citizens "that love the Union, that have the good of the country at heart, and will support the constitution."[14]

Many Know-Nothings joined the party not for nativism or nationalism but because of traditional dislike for Democrats and Democratic measures or because they saw the party as a means to gain office and influence. In this sense, then, the Know-Nothing party was a natural outgrowth of the competitive nature of southern politics. Many traditional Whigs swallowed their dislike of nativism and supported the Know-Nothing party as a conservative and beneficial force—a force much preferred to their traditional Democratic enemies.[15]

Out of these complex origins—nativism, nationalism, and a sense of competition—sprang the Texas Know-Nothing party in 1854. Catching the Democrats by surprise and at first attracting nonpartisan support, the Know-Nothings made an impressive showing during their first year in Texas, with party members elected as the mayors of Galveston, Austin, and San Antonio. They went on to field a full slate of candidates for the 1855 state election.

Know-Nothing success spurred the Democrats into action, and in their state convention of 1855 they demonstrated that, when threatened by an outside force, they could act in concert. Despite the fact that E. M. Pease's state plan for railroad construction was a divisive issue among Democrats, they united behind the incumbent governor and attacked the Know-Nothings for their secrecy and nativism. Many Democrats who had originally joined the Know-Nothings, such as W. S. Oldham, now renounced the party when it became apparent that it was competing with the Democrats for official positions. Earlier, the Know-Nothings had seemed like a club or fraternal organization with an interest in politics. By mid-1855, however, they had assumed all the trappings of a political party. By the August elections of that year the contest was, in most cases, between Know-Nothings and Democrats and not between personalities operating within a vague and amorphous Democratic party.[16]

Know-Nothing successes in 1855 were mildly encouraging to the party faithful. Lemuel D. Evans's victory in the eastern congressional district was highly touted as a portent of future success. Sam Houston's flirtation with the party was also considered noteworthy. Added to this was the election of a political neutral, Stephen Crosby, as state land commissioner, and the election of several Know-Nothings to the state legislature. Democrats, however, swept every statewide office except that of state land commissioner, and they remained in solid control of both the House and the Senate. They, too, had cause for rejoicing. They could claim to have beaten back the Know-Nothing challenge, and they had laid the groundwork for a highly organized party.[17]

Know-Nothing successes after 1855 were few; that year was the high-water mark for the party in Texas. Presidential elections were the mortar which held antebellum parties together, and when the Know-Nothings' candidate, Millard Fillmore, failed miserably in 1856, the party declined in strength across the country. In Texas, the 1856 presidential campaign centered upon accusations by the Democrats that the Know-Nothings were un-American because of their nativism and secrecy, that the northern wing of their party was dominated by abolitionists, and that a vote for the Know-Nothings only aided the cause of the Republican party. Know-Nothings in turn stressed that they were moderates with a grave concern for the Union.

Such appeals by the Know-Nothings swayed only limited numbers of Texans, and the party suffered a two-to-one defeat in the state. Know-Nothings carried only eight counties in 1856, and their strength, like that of the Whigs before, was highly localized. Traditional Whig counties east of the Brazos and Trinity rivers gave the Know-Nothings a sizable portion of their votes. Counties between San Antonio and Corpus Christi, where there was a lingering resentment of Mexicans among the Anglos, also either chose the Know-Nothing ticket or gave it a sizable minority. Central Texas, between Austin in Travis County and Waco in McLennan County, where there were many promising young Know-Nothing leaders, was another area which cast a large vote for that party. Voters along the southwestern frontier, in Uvalde and Bandera counties, also voted for the Know-Nothings. Judging from these returns, Know-Nothing success can be attributed to the two-party tradition in the east, the ability of the Know-Nothing leaders and the appeal of the unionist platform in central Texas, and Anglo resentment of Mexicans in the counties between San Antonio and the Rio Grande Valley.[18]

Other weaknesses besides the loss of the 1856 presidential election speeded the Know-Nothings' demise. Slavery split the Know-Nothing party on a national level, as it had split the Whigs, and after 1856 the party in Texas lost all outside impetus for growth. Discouraged by their lack of victories and by the effective assault of the Democrats on their nativism and secrecy, local organizations began to wither, and in 1857 few candidates claimed to be Know-Nothings. Instead they adopted the old Whig policy of claiming to be Democrats when speaking before Democratic audiences and acting like Whigs in front of Whig constituents. This policy had been successfully applied by Lemuel Evans and Stephen Crosby in 1855, and Know-Nothing candidates hoped that it would bring them success once again in 1857. It necessitated, however, the abandonment of a state platform, a party ticket, the convention system, and a centralized party structure; in effect, it meant the deinstitutionalization of the Know-Nothing party.

Even with their efforts to shed the label of Know-Nothingism, the opponents of the Democracy fared badly in the 1857 state elections. Sam Houston, estranged from the Democrats by his vote against the Kansas-Nebraska Bill and his endorsement of the Know-Nothing party, lost his bid for the governor's chair to Hardin R. Runnels, the nominee of the Democratic convention, and the well-organized Democrats swept almost every office in the state. Even the incumbent Lemuel Evans, despite his strong stand in favor of the Union, was defeated by Judge John H. Reagan in the First Congressional District. That year marked the high point of the antebellum Democratic party in Texas; at no time was it more harmonious, more united, or more effective. That year, too, marked the virtual end of the Know-Nothing party on a statewide level. It shrank to a few remaining bastions of strength in East Texas.[19]

In some ways the Know-Nothings continued the Whig legacy. Both groups held a national orientation, both favored moral reform. Both parties were strong in East Texas, North Texas, and the urban-commercial areas. Both groups drew strength from opposition to the dominant political party in the state. Know-Nothings, however, narrowed and intensified their drive for moral reform by concentrating on nativist issues. At the same time, their economic policies were less clear-cut than the Whigs. While their regional strength was roughly the same as the Whigs, the Know-Nothings also drew support in the south-central portion of the state. Here there was no tradition of opposition to the Democratic party, or no real history of party politics for that matter. This resulted in an east-west division in the state's Know-Nothing party. Those in the eastern portion of the state were more like their Whig predecessors and opposed the

Democrats as much out of habit as anything else. Those in the west were drawn by the Unionism and nativism of the party.

Despite its brief existence the Know-Nothing party contributed greatly to the political climate of the secession years by helping to remake the state's Democratic party. For the first time it could be said that Texas had an organized party with local, district, and state committees carrying on the work of the party between elections. Also for the first time the state's Democrats had a convention system that worked. Because their opponents often claimed to be Democrats, it became increasingly important to party regulars that a candidate be endorsed by a convention. These conventions and committees were usually controlled by a stable group of party leaders. Prior to 1858 some of these leaders, like Ferdinand Flake, a Galveston businessman and editor of a German-language newspaper, and George W. Paschal, a lawyer and editor of the Austin-based *Southern Intelligencer*, were highly vocal unionists, but after Sam Houston was ostracized from the party for his support of the Know-Nothings, the bulk of the party leadership was closely identified with the militant states' rights party of the Lower South. Ironically, the Know-Nothing party, which drew much of its strength from its conservative stand on the Union, contributed to its destruction by forcing the solidification of an institution controlled by men less interested in preserving the nation and more culturally kin to the Lower South.

It was equally ironic that Know-Nothings linked nationalism and nativism and, by reconfirming the Democrats' traditional defense of individual freedom and personal liberty, helped make secession palatable to nonsouthern cultural groups. The Know-Nothings' brand of nationalism implied conformity, a conformity that insisted that the American people move forward with common cultural memories toward a common national purpose. This idea of being part of one folk might appeal to some Germans and Mexicans, but when the price of being part of that folk meant giving up traditional religious practices or the drinking of lager beer, then the price seemed too high for most. It would not be difficult for the Democrats to hold the lines of party loyalty firm in the secession crisis if they could portray that crisis as another example of the Democratic party defending its supporters from the anti-individualistic ideas of the Know-Nothings recast as Republicans and unionists.[20]

Not just the challenge of the Know-Nothings within Texas remade the Democratic party between 1854 and the beginning months of 1858. The party also responded to the intense distress of the nation—troubles which cast the old Jacksonian ideology in a new light and helped weaken the symbolic impact of Houston and Jackson. The existence of the nation had been vital to Jackson and Jacksonians. Jackson had a deep emotional commitment to the nation, and Jacksonians regarded national unity as essential to the achievement of their goals. Beginning with the dispute over the Kansas-Nebraska Act in 1854, events occurred in rapid succession which made the nation seem more a burden than a help. In 1855 and 1856 the turmoil in Kansas showed Texans that the North was growing more militant. As southerners, Texans felt under attack. The evolution of the Republican party and its strong showing in the elections of 1856 and 1857 also caused alarm. Republicans were not just abolitionists; to Texans theirs seemed a sectional party determined to promote the economic and political interests of the North no matter what the cost to the nation. Vehement Republican criticism of the Dred Scott case in 1857 suggested to Texans that even the courts and the law were not safe from Republican attack. Actions of Republican-controlled states that negated or avoided compliance with the Fugitive Slave Law reinforced the belief that not even the law would protect the South from the attacks of the Republicans. Feeling threatened, Texans were more willing to accept the Democratic party's increasingly militant defense of their rights even though this defense might threaten the existence of the nation.[21]

Nationalism or commitment to the Union, though, was always more than a pragmatic concern for what the nation could or could not do for the individual. For Democrats in Texas, attachment to the nation was wrapped up in their loyalty to Sam Houston and Andrew Jackson. Sam Houston was one of only two southern Senators to vote against the Kansas-Nebraska Act, and his action was condemned in Texas as both a betrayal of the Democratic party and the South. In 1855 and 1856 he moved further from the Democratic party by all but officially endorsing the Know-Nothing party. His vote against the Kansas-Nebraska Act and near endorsement of the Know-Nothings caused a loss of public esteem. Democratic party regulars were particularly incensed and censured his actions in the state legislature, which they controlled, and at the state Democratic convention of 1856. Knowing that he would have difficulty being reelected to the Senate by the state legislature, Houston decided to run for governor in 1857. The Democrats mounted an extensive campaign against Houston, and their candidate, Hardin R. Runnels, defeated him by a slight margin. When the legislature did indeed fail to send him back to the Senate Houston seemed doomed to retirement and oblivion.

With his defeat and discredit came not just a fall in his personal fortune but also a decline in his impact as an ongoing symbol of the nation.

Andrew Jackson, of course, could no longer lose or gain popularity by his stand on the issues of the day. His death and the death of most of his contemporaries had removed from the scene the generation that had grown up during the American Revolution, had fought in the War of 1812, and had worked for the expansion of the nation through the close of the 1840s. The emotional commitment to the nation which he invoked so well in the Nullification Crisis of 1832 had less appeal to a later generation, but Jackson still remained an ongoing symbol of the nation. In the turbulent days of the 1850s, however, his stand in favor of the nation at the expense of the minority rights of South Carolina seemed less ideologically sound to Texans. Not only were they a later generation, but their experiences had shown them that the nation was not unqualifiably good. Jackson's voice and presence, which had been so strong in the 1840s and early 1850s, began to ebb with the passage of time and the impact of events. Like Sam Houston, his potency as a symbol of the nation decreased.[22]

By the start of 1858 an increasing number of Texas Democrats viewed John C. Calhoun and not Andrew Jackson or Sam Houston as a more proper hero. Not only did Calhoun defend minority rights against the encroachments of the federal government and the North, Calhoun symbolized the plantation South. The willingness of the Democrats to move to a more radical defense of slavery and southern rights in 1858 was directly related to the increasing importance within Texas of an economy and a people like that of the Lower South. The growing importance of commercial agriculture based upon slavery, cotton, and the plantation system made it in the interest of Texans to align themselves with the Deep South. The increasingly high percentage of Texans who emigrated from this region reinforced the ties of economic interest with those of friendship, kinship, and common culture. As the Democratic party of the Lower South became more radical and sectional, inevitably the party in Texas was drawn into a common orbit.[23]

Texas in 1858, though, was still not South Carolina. Its people, economy, and landscape were more diverse, and so were its politics. Within the Democratic party, the process begun by opposition to the Know-Nothings and accelerated by the events of the 1850s and the growth of lower southern influence in Texas could not be easily reversed. A high degree of organization, reliance upon the convention system for the selection of candidates, and an increasing identification with the states' rights Democrats of the Lower South seemed to be permanent characteristics of the party. This conduct was to be the midwife of a new political organization. Without the threat of external competition to keep the party united, estranged Democrats alienated by the convention system, worried by the radicalization of their party, or denied a place in the party hierarchy abandoned it. By January 1858, less than six months after its victory over Sam Houston, the party's unity had begun to crumble.

Judicial nominations by political conventions were the wedges which began to cleave the Democratic party. John Marshall, now the state party chairman, was determined that his party should nominate candidates for all elected positions. Nonpartisan judicial elections, however, had long been a tradition in Texas, and Marshall's drive to secure the nomination of a Democrat to fill an opening on the Texas Supreme Court drew fire from many leading Democrats. Nonetheless, Marshall had enough support among party regulars to secure the selection of Judge C. W. Buckley as the Democrats' nominee. Other Democrats, led by George W. Paschal, joined with former Whigs or Know-Nothings like lawyer William Pitt Ballinger and editor and lawyer J. W. Barret of Marshall in support of Judge James H. Bell. They campaigned for judicial integrity and against allowing politics to corrupt the law. Buckley was the only nominee of the Democratic party opposed in 1858, but the strength of the party name did not save him. Bell won a narrow victory in August 1858, and a new political coalition began to take form.[24]

This coalition's strength was unwittingly aided and abetted by the actions of Governor Runnels and his ideological twin John Marshall. Throughout 1858, both warned of the dangers to the South posed by the North. Both worked to weed moderate men from the Democratic party hierarchy. Both took strong stands in favor of Kansas's Lecompton Constitution and threatened secession if the balance between North and South were not preserved by the admittance of Kansas as a slave state. Both favored the radical step of reopening the African slave trade. By the late fall of 1858, their actions had convinced many Union-loving Democrats that their old party was no longer a suitable home.[25]

Already alienated from the leaders of the Democratic party by opposition to judicial nominations or fire-eating rhetoric, men like George Paschal were driven by still another force to abandon the party. Throughout the 1850s Democratic newspapers would accuse members of the "Opposition" of being "dissatisfied office seekers." There was something to this argument. When George Paschal was denied a place on the Travis County delegation to the Democratic state convention in 1858, he was undoubtedly angered. After all, he had been on the party's central committee the year before. As ortho-dox southern views or orthodox views on the convention system be-came increasingly necessary for a position within the party, those who held different opinions were driven into the new coalition.

During the fall of 1858 and the first part of 1859, as John Mar-shall and George Paschal engaged in a bitter controversy over public printing, the split within the Democratic party widened. Some of the backers of Judge Bell returned to the regular Democrats, but many joined former Whigs or Know-Nothings in a contravening party. In the August election of 1859 these self-styled Independents or Union Democrats achieved a stunning victory over the Democracy and elected Sam Houston as governor and Andrew Jackson Hamilton as a congressman from the Second Congressional District.[26]

General Houston's skill and popularity obviously aided this dra-matic rise in the fortunes of what came to be called the Opposition party.[27] In his loss to Runnels in 1857 Houston had been hurt by his association with the Know-Nothings. Even so he had run a strong race and demonstrated that he still had tremendous personal appeal. In 1859 Houston changed his tack. Once again running against Run-nels, he disassociated himself from the Know-Nothings and claimed to be a supporter of the national Democracy as opposed to the states' rights Democracy. As politician and rancher Francis R. Lubbock put it, "'Old Sam' was now out-Heroding Herod in his devotion to Democracy." Houston and his supporters combined this devotion with a brutal attack on Runnels's frontier policy, the convention sys-tem, and the attempt of Runnels and other Democrats to reopen the slave trade. Evoking memories of the glorious victory at San Jacinto, Houston's record of service to his state, and his constant advocacy of the Union, the Opposition threw the Democrats on the defensive in every political debate. Thus in 1859, Houston added to his hard core of personal followers many Democrats who believed in his adher-ence to the "old" party and shared his worries concerning the course the official Democratic party had followed in Texas.[28]

Partisanship also helped the Opposition. Former Whigs and Know-Nothings like Ben Epperson and James Barret continued their almost lifelong opposition to the Democrats. Newspapers like the San Antonio *Herald* and the *Harrison Flag* moved effortlessly from the camp of the Know-Nothings into that of the Opposition. Re-peated insistence by the Opposition that they were the true descen-dants of the party of Andrew Jackson might have repelled a few old-time opponents of the Democracy, but the principles of this new group had much in common with those of the Whigs and Know-

Nothings. In reality, the Opposition was their only viable alternative. Those who opposed the traditional Democratic platform or who harbored a deep-seated antipathy for the Democrats could either remove themselves from the political forum or support the Opposition. Furthermore, in 1859, with the strength of both the sectionally oriented Republican party and the sectionally oriented states' rights Democratic party on the rise, the Union was imperiled. In Texas, the Opposition continued to be more attuned to national interests than the rival Democrats. Despite features disconcerting to the Whigs and Know-Nothings who joined it, this new hybrid carried on the legacy of the minority parties in Texas.[29]

Unlike its predecessors, however, this new party won elections, and the primary reason for this success was the support of disaffected Democrats. A coalition only of Houston's personal supporters and former Whigs and Know-Nothings would not have brought victory. The addition of influential and everyday Democrats was needed to push the party to victory at the polls. A twofold force moved Democrats to abandon their party. First, the organization and regularization that had occurred in the Democratic party as a result of the competition from the Know-Nothings alienated many individualistic Democrats. Democrats in the state had long resisted the convention system and had been content to allow politics to follow a more informal pattern. This arrangement suited the frontier status of most Texas counties. Candidates announced they were running for office in the local newspapers. Claiming some form of Democratic affiliation, they ran on their own personal merits rather than on their party ties. As candidates on both a statewide and local level began to be picked by conventions and as devotion to a southern-style Democracy became increasingly pronounced, talented and articulate Democrats were excluded from office and influence by the party machinery. Men like Ferdinand Flake, George Paschal, and A. J. Hamilton had played prominent roles in the Democratic party from 1854 to 1858. By 1859 they were among the staunchest supporters of the Opposition's ticket, or as they often preferred to call it, the Union Democrats' ticket.[30]

They linked the words Union and Democrat with good reason because a second, almost inseparable explanation of this shift in loyalties concerned devotion to the Union. Flake, Paschal, and Hamilton shared a commitment to the Union and a disdain for anything that threatened to disrupt it. As a result, they became increasingly alienated from the states' rights faction of the Democratic party. The trio was particularly disturbed by the discussion of reopening the African slave trade. Flake left the 1859 Democratic state convention when this issue was brought up for discussion and in effect left the party. All three men attacked the Democrats' position on the slave trade throughout the campaign. For them it represented both an unworkable scheme and unnecessary agitation of the slavery question. Unfortunately for the unionists among the Democrats, the willingness even to consider reopening the slave trade was but the most obvious indication of the increasingly sectional perspective of the Democrats. Denied office and influence by the states' rights leadership of the party and estranged philosophically from the party in Texas, these unionists had little choice but to move into the camp of the Opposition. Thus, men like George Paschal, who had vigorously opposed Houston in 1857, just as vigorously supported him in 1859.[31]

In some ways the campaign of 1859 was less desperate and hard fought than that of 1857. In 1857 Sam Houston had sold some of his property to finance the campaign and had toured the state speaking wherever possible, In 1859 he spoke less often and relied heavily on the efforts of his friends. Hardin Runnels repeated his tactics of 1857 and also stayed at home, leaving the campaigning to other, more competent, speakers. It was a measure of the resurgence of Houston's support that in 1859 he attracted a number of very able supporters who, in their speeches and newspaper columns, carried his campaign messages to the public. In 1859, too, Houston was part of a consolidated ticket. Newspapers across the state carried Houston's name at the top of an entire slate of candidates. In 1857 Houston had run as an individual. In 1859 he ran as a part of an organization, and his party triumphed as much as Houston did.[32]

Besides the contest for governor in 1859, the Opposition also competed for both of Texas's seats in the U.S. House of Representatives. In the Second District, composed of counties west of the Trinity River and south of Dallas and Tarrant counties, A. J. Hamilton opposed Thomas N. Waul. Waul was a Democrat of long standing who had campaigned vigorously against the Know-Nothings. Party lines were well defined, and a clear choice existed between the two candidates. Waul defended his party's record of frontier defense, its efforts to reintroduce the slave trade, and its increasingly sectional attitude. Hamilton basked in the reflected glory of Sam Houston and eloquently expressed his love for the Union. The result was a narrow victory for Hamilton in an area in which the Democrats had been tremendously popular and in which there was only a short history of two-party politics.[33]

In the First District (also called the Eastern District) the incumbent John H. Reagan was challenged by William B. Ochiltree. Ochiltree had previously run for office as a Whig and had been a member of the Know-Nothing party. After 1857, however, alarmed by what he viewed as northern aggression against southern rights, Ochiltree had moved toward an extreme states' rights position. Reagan, in contrast, had always been part of the moderate faction of the state's Democrats. In fact when he openly opposed the party's discussion of the slave trade and voiced his own support for the Constitution and the Union, he alienated the more extreme members of the Democratic party in his district. Prominent Democrats such as R. W. Loughery, a lawyer and editor of the Marshall *Texas Republican*, refused to back Reagan at the nominating convention of the Eastern District. The majority of the convention, however, renominated the incumbent. At that point the extremists in the convention broke away and later convinced Ochiltree to run. So it was that in the east the candidate of moderation was a Democrat nominated by the Democratic convention, and the more radical candidate was a former Whig nominated by a splinter group of the Democratic party. Ochiltree was an experienced and able politician. Reagan was equally experienced and able, and his record of fidelity to the party, his conservative stand in favor of the Union and the Constitution, and his service as both a district judge and congressman won him plaudits from all but the most vociferous exponents of southern rights. As the campaign wore on, Democrats closed ranks as Reagan attempted to mollify the extremists and retain the support of the unionists. The result of his efforts was a smashing victory in August.[34]

These victories were interpreted as overwhelming endorsements of the Union. Certainly Houston's personal magnetism, Whig and Know-Nothing dislike for the Democrats, the defection of disenchanted Democrats, and a smooth-running organization helped the Opposition. Even those things cannot explain why it won all but two of the major races, and the two it lost were won by Democrats who took decided and vocal stands for the Union. In fact, George Paschal, a major leader of the Union Democrats, backed both successful Democrats, endorsing Reagan for the U.S. House and Frank M. White for commissioner of the General Land Office. Unionists had cause for rejoicing in August of 1859, and most agreed with Charles De Morse of the Clarksville *Standard* that the Democratic defeat had been "brought about by the votes of Union-loving Democrats; a class sometimes sneered at by the Ultraists; but that class composes all that is valuable in the Democratic party—its bone, sinew, and members."[35]

After the election, conditions looked good for the formation of a strong and permanent second party in Texas based upon devotion to the Union. Gaining the support of Congressman Reagan for this new party seemed a vital necessity. Not only was he a popular and influential individual, he was the most clearly visible unionist left among the Democrats. His open alignment with Houston, Hamilton, Throckmorton, Paschal, and other like-minded souls would have been a major public relations coup for the new party and would have attracted many more former Democrats. The new party could then legitimately claim to represent the best facets of the old Democratic party as well as devotion to the Union.[36]

During the 1859 campaign Reagan had precariously balanced his Unionism with his commitment to the Democratic party. Party leaders Hardin R. Runnels and Guy M. Bryan spoke in the strident tones of southern extremists and placed the interests of their state and their section far above the future of the nation. Reagan had often clashed with Bryan when the two had served together in the Thirty-fifth Congress. Runnels believed Reagan's unionist pronouncements had weakened his own gubernatorial campaign against Houston, and he was particularly bitter about Reagan's condemnation of reopening the slave trade. Runnels's alleged support for this issue had been used with telling effect by the Opposition, and in Runnels's eyes Reagan's speeches and circulars were additional nails in his political coffin. Reagan, however, while not actively campaigning for Runnels, had endorsed the entire slate of Democratic candidates. When Paschal, whose ideas about the Union resembled Reagan's, tried to solicit his support for Houston, Reagan replied that while he did not agree with the party's choice of candidates, he did support their platform and principles. Furthermore, as a candidate on the party ticket and a nominee of the convention, he had little choice but to back the whole slate of party candidates. Finally, he offered to Paschal the telling argument that for his entire life he had fought to maintain the principles of the Democratic party. How could he separate himself from the organization and still maintain his principles? For the man who had tried to promote the interests of an organized party since 1852, who had advocated the convention system, and who had fought against the Know-Nothings, it was difficult to break with the party simply because one slate of candidates did not meet with his full approval.

After the election, James W. Throckmorton embarked on a crusade to win Reagan's backing for the Union Conservative party he hoped to form. In an 18 August 1859 letter to Ben Epperson, Throckmorton pointed out the impossibility of a Houston supporter or an old-line Whig being selected by the state legislature to fill the Senate seat held by Matthias Ward. He believed the best course was to support a Democrat whose views were closely in accord with their own.

Reagan was such a man, but as Throckmorton wrote, "I wish to do more, I am for taking Reagan and with him for a leader building up a Union Conservative party in Texas." He went on to counsel Epperson that, while it would be a difficult pill to swallow, former opponents of the Democracy like themselves would have to stay in the background and let prominent Democrats like former Governor E. M. Pease or Congressman Reagan be the most visible members of the new party. He clearly realized that a successful party depended upon the ability of such respectable Democrats to draw to the party other unionist Democrats.[37]

Throckmorton also wrote to Reagan, pointing out that Runnels and the faction of the Democratic party he represented blamed him for their defeat. This enmity threatened Reagan's political future and in particular his ambition of becoming a senator. Throckmorton further argued that the failure of unionists to combine in one strong organization gave the less numerous but better-organized opponents of the Union a tremendous advantage. Throckmorton tried to persuade Reagan that he and Houston had more in common than he and Runnels and that both Reagan's future and the future of the Union would be best served by joining the Union Conservative party.[38]

Reagan, however, remained unconverted and resolved to work for the reform of the Democratic party from within. He admitted being uncomfortable in the company of some fellow party members, but blamed indifference on the part of the majority of Democrats for the control of the party by extremists. Neither he nor the public, he asserted, had worked hard enough to ensure that the delegates to the nominating convention reflected public sentiment. Next time it would be different. Control of the party would pass back into the hands of the "national and conservative school."[39] Reagan did not want to choose between the Democracy and the Union. He hoped to cling to his party and the principles he cherished and at the same time preserve the Union.

Reagan's failure to join their ranks was disheartening to the Opposition leaders, and so was their failure to secure the election of a moderate to the U.S. Senate. The Democrats had lost almost every statewide office, but they still had a slim majority in both the state Senate and the state House of Representatives, and these two bodies, meeting in joint session, elected the senators from Texas. The Democrats were determined to elect one of their own to the U.S. Senate, and the extreme states' rights advocate Louis T. Wigfall, a former South Carolinian, was the most available candidate. Wigfall had been working toward the nomination for over a year. He had campaigned for Democrats of all shades of opinion, including Reagan.

Unlike Reagan, he had few bitter enemies within the party, and although he had less than enthusiastic support from moderate Democrats, when the legislature convened in November of 1859 he received the backing of the Democratic caucus. The Opposition was poorly organized and unable to unite behind a candidate that could attract enough dissident Democrats to win the election. Reagan was unwilling to run because he had become convinced that his outspoken condemnation of the slave trade, filibustering, and other radical ideas had cost him the support of many Democrats in the legislature. Failing to find a suitable candidate, the Opposition split their votes among several candidates who attracted enough Democratic votes to prevent Wigfall's election for several ballots. With the legislature voting on strict party lines, Wigfall was eventually elected. Less than a year after its birth and just a few months after its triumph in the election of 1859, the Opposition party suffered a severe setback. Like the Know-Nothing challenge of the mid-1850s, the challenge of the Opposition in 1859 convinced Democrats to forget philosophical differences and unite for the good of the party.[40]

Probably the major reason they could reunite was that the philosophical, or more precisely the ideological, differences among Democrats were not as great as they seemed. Ultimately, not just the institutional strengths and weaknesses of the political parties in Texas, but also the ideologies which they expressed defined the roles the parties played in the secession crisis.

At the heart of political ideology in antebellum Texas were ideas about the Union and nationhood. These concepts fell into two general categories. The first concept derived from internalized values. The Union, the nation, was a thing of the heart. It was of great value in and of itself. The Union and the Constitution were the creations of the revered founding fathers. The United States had been created by the blood and sacrifice of the Revolution, the War of 1812, and the Mexican War. In an age of romantic nationalism, the nation was the ultimate expression of a people's worth and character, and weakening the nation revealed a flaw in the spirit of the people. The second category concerned the functional purposes of the Union or any other nation of American people. Americans shared a common sense of mission: to spread Anglo-American civilization across the wilderness, to preserve the benefits of that civilization, and to act as an example to the rest of the world. The rewards of this mission would be not only spiritual satisfaction but also great material prosperity. Through its stabilizing laws, through its mandate to organize and direct the energies of the people and resources of the land, and through its role as protector of a united people from foreign powers, the Union was expected to aid in this quest and enhance its rewards. The Constitution, almost always associated with the Union, provided a rationale and a knowable framework that regulated the place of individuals and communities within the nation. Together with the other laws of the national government, the Constitution was supposed to prevent social discord and protect the rights of individuals and their communities. Unthreatened by anarchy, Americans would be free to move west, to reach toward new goals where they already lived, and to achieve and hold on to material prosperity. Not only would the Union and the Constitution balance stability and freedom, they would actively aid Americans by insuring democracy, providing internal improvements and other boons to commerce, and by protecting citizens from Indians, the British, Mexicans, and any other foreign competitor for control of the American continent. For Texans, as for all Americans, the Union was both a thing of importance in itself and the best vehicle to achieve their goals and abolish their fears.

Political parties emphasized different facets of this ideology. While Whigs and Know-Nothings were well aware of the pragmatic value of the nation, they were also much more prone to speak of the nation in reverential terms. Democrats had emotional ties to the nation, but they were more concerned with the tangible benefits of nationhood for the individual than were the Whigs and their heirs. Whigs talked of community, tradition, and stability. Democrats emphasized progress for the individual and for the nation. Much of the success of the Opposition party in 1859 lay in its timely ability to attract Whigs and Know-Nothings who feared chaos and had extremely deep emotional ties to the nation as well as Democrats who still valued the Union for both what it meant and what it could do. When the Union began to seem less threatened to some and to others a threat itself to the traditional goals and purposes of the American nation, this rather fragile coalition dedicated to the preservation of the nation was bound to lose strength.[41]

That strength would be transferred to the Democratic party. When the Union was no longer a pressing issue, Democrats would return to the party they felt most comfortable in—a party they had long supported by habit and a party which best reflected their own ideological shading. When they began to see the Union as a great danger to law, order, prosperity, social stability, and slavery, former Whigs and Know-Nothings, lacking a long-standing commitment to the Opposition party, would join the Democrats in arguing for secession. Because of its institutional strength and ideological orientation, the Democratic party would be the primary creator of the secession movement in Texas.

Between the fall of 1859 and the fall of 1860, though, both parties would be tossed about by events. The political situation in Texas was in a state of extreme flux. During this year's time, parties, ideologies, the impact of culture, and regional interests within Texas all became secondary to the events themselves. They were shaped by rather than the shapers of those events.

3

Public Prejudice

For most of the antebellum period, once immigrants brought their party ties and ideological commitments with them to Texas, ideology and partisanship developed as they did because of competition between parties within the state and because actions of state party leaders, such as attempts to reopen the slave trade, threatened traditional ideology. Essentially, until 1859, partisanship and ideology evolved because of reasons internal to Texas. Of course, Texans had been influenced by the events surrounding the Compromise of 1850, the dispute over Kansas, the rise of the Republican party, the importation into Texas of the Know-Nothing party, and the growing acrimony in Congress over slavery. Texans' interests in these outside events, however, took on a peculiarly local cast. Their primary interest in the 1850 Compromise, for example, stemmed from their claim to eastern New Mexico. The Know-Nothing party grew as fast as it did in the state because it fulfilled the needs of former Whigs and because there were enough foreign-born in Texas for the foreign threat to seem serious. Beginning in the fall of 1859 and lasting through November 1860, however, events not of their making battered Texans. At the close of this year of trauma, "public prejudice" in favor of secession did not spring only from the mouths and pens of reckless militants.[1] That year's experiences had frayed many nerves, redefined political loyalties, and convinced many moderates that their interests and culture were threatened. Militants had long talked of secession, but had been little attended. In December of 1860 they were not only listened to, they were pushed forward to speak. The public led the leaders. That they did so cannot be separated from what happened during the previous year.

John Brown's raid on Harpers Ferry was the first of the psychological and physical shocks that would cause Texans to doubt the value of the Union or to express their old Unionism in new ways. As news of the raid spread, it became a popular propaganda tool for the states' rights wings of the Democratic party in Texas. Through their editorial and oratorical spokesmen, these Democrats vividly portrayed the awful implications of Brown's attempt to incite a slave uprising—homes burnt, property destroyed, wives and children murdered. Brown's raid illustrated just how vulnerable the South was and how determined northerners were to destroy slavery. Even the most moderate newspapers could not deny that Brown's "conspiracy" received widespread backing in the North. Nor could they deny the apotheosis of Brown by some abolitionists. Harpers Ferry put opponents of the more militant southerners in Texas on the defensive and made it more difficult than ever to explain the value of a union with northern extremists.[2]

Events along the Texas frontier also called into question the worth of the Union. About the same time that John Brown attacked Harpers Ferry, Juan Cortina seized the city of Brownsville at the mouth of the Rio Grande. When he held Brownsville for several days, and threatened South Texas counties for months, militants challenged the good of a Union that could not protect its borders. They even hinted that Cortina's activities might have been inspired by abolitionists.[3]

Adding to the turmoil, in the fall of 1859 Indian attacks on frontier counties increased. The undermanned, often inadequately trained, and poorly led United States forces along the frontier failed to protect the area adequately, and the Texas Rangers and local militia groups were forced into action. When the U.S. Congress, embroiled in a bitter dispute between Republicans and Democrats, failed either to pay for the state troops or to reinforce the frontier defenses, disunionist propagandists had another argument.[4]

Congressional disputes were common enough in the 1850s, but the one that took place in the winter of 1859–1860 was of special significance because for almost two months the House of Representatives was unable to organize itself and elect a Speaker. In the Thirty-sixth Congress neither the Republicans nor the Democrats had a clear majority. The Republicans had a plurality of representatives, but because there were still over twenty southern representatives aligned with the American party, as the Know-Nothings were officially known, neither major party could command a majority. This problem was exacerbated by the fact that the Republican choice for Speaker, John Sherman of Ohio, had endorsed Hinton R. Helper's book *Impending Crisis.* Southerners considered Sherman's endorsement to be another example of the Republicans' determination to end slavery by legal or illegal means. As the debate dragged on, it became more heated, and weapons were observed under the coats of distinguished congressmen. Eventually violence was avoided and the House organized when the Republicans substituted an unknown new member of moderate stance for Sherman. William Pennington managed to attract enough Democratic and American support to be elected 1 February 1860, but by then, Congressman John H. Reagan and other leaders of the Democratic party in Texas had begun to despair for the future of their government and their nation.[5]

Brown's raid, the Cortina affair, unchecked Indian attacks, and a wrangling U.S. House of Representatives ushered in 1860 on a highly emotional note. The importance of Brown's raid in shaping the political minds of Texans has perhaps been overemphasized in the past, but together with the other events it created an atmosphere of tension and stress. Most Texans at the start of 1860 were still more concerned with their personal endeavors or affairs within their state, but few were totally immune to the persistent worries about their nation which the events of the fall of 1859 and the first months of 1860 began to bring into focus.

These events brought worries into focus because they served as evidence of the decay of the nation. Brown's raid showed that at least some militants in the North were ready to resort to violence in order to have their way in the South. Cortina's attack on Brownsville and the Indian menace demonstrated the ineffectiveness of the national government in protecting the borders of Texas. The squabbles in the House of Representatives over who was to be the Speaker not only delayed adequate defense measures for the Texas frontier but proved to many Texans that the Republican party, strictly a northern institution, had only its own section's interests at heart. Such sectional interests would cause the national government to cease to function as smoothly and as fairly as it once had.

Evidence of national decay and heightened emotions combined in Texas to create a feeling of crisis. It was not an acute sense of crisis. Texans were not yet at the point where any action to relieve tension was acceptable. Nor were they yet at the point of perceiving the North and the Republicans as truly aggressive threats to their existence. The building of a siege mentality, though, had begun. Unless events of the future demonstrated otherwise, Texans at the close of 1859 were more willing to accept arguments that the Union was obsolete than they had been just a few months before. They were also becoming more willing to accept a novel solution to their dilemma.[6]

Ultimately it would be the selection of a president of the United States that would change the glimmer of discontent with the old Union at the close of 1859 into growing acceptance of the novelty of secession. Even before the events of the fall of 1859, indeed before the sparks generated by the state elections of 1859 had cooled, Texans began to argue about presidential politics. The argument about who would be the Democratic party's candidate was particularly fierce. In late August and September, George Paschal, the leading spokesman of the numerous Democrats who had supported Houston the previous summer, exalted in the defeat of "the whole family of Mississippi barnacles," as he called John Marshall, Governor Runnels, and their supporters, and he called for Texans to begin to remake the Democratic party into a party with universal appeal. He envisioned a party of "national men, Union men, States' Rights men, and friends of the Constitution." Paschal hoped to see Sam Houston as this remade party's nominee for president in 1860, and he forecast that as president Houston, like his mentor Andrew Jackson, would preserve the Union and elevate the Democratic party to new heights of glory.[7]

John Marshall, Paschal's journalistic and political rival, scoffed at the idea of Houston as the candidate of the Democratic party. He asked how a man who had abandoned the party could be the presidential nominee of that party. He wondered how Texans, as southerners, could support a man who had abandoned the South when he had been a senator. Marshall was right, and by early 1860, Paschal could see the handwriting on the wall.[8]

In a letter written in February, Paschal described how unionist Democrats in the state legislature had gone along with their brethren out of party loyalty. He still hoped that Texas unionists could gain political control of the state, but he realized that this control would have to come from outside the Democratic party. In such a situation it was impossible to expect Houston, the enemy of the Democrats within his state, to be the national party's nominee for president.[9]

By April 1860, when the state party convention assembled, the party had indeed closed ranks in preparation for that year's state and national elections. Moderate Democrats accepted the continued leadership of radicals like John Marshall out of loyalty to the party, but it is also probable that the events of the past few months had made them more radical themselves. All the delegates were particularly incensed with the Republican party, and a delegate from Karnes County on the Texas frontier was expelled from the convention because he admitted having been a Republican supporter before migrating to Texas. Delegates next showed they had neither forgiven nor forgotten Sam Houston when they lambasted his frontier policy. With those two preliminary actions out of the way, the assembled gathering moved on to draft a platform attacking Stephen A. Douglas and "squatter sovereignty," and declaring that society was best served by the "happily existing subordinant condition of the negro race." Underscoring their treatment of the Karnes County delegate, the conventioneers made condemnation of the Republican party the keystone of their platform. Labeling Republicans selfishly sectional, in near hysterical terms the Democrats decried that party's attempts to disturb race relations in the South. With the platform drafted, the convention went on to select Guy M. Bryan, still a leading spokesman of the radical southerners, as chairman of its delegation to the Democratic National Convention at Charleston, South Carolina. Among the five other delegates were former Governor Hardin R. Runnels, whose extremism had just been rejected at the polls, and Francis Richard Lubbock, who became one of the Confederacy's and Jefferson Davis's most ardent Texan supporters.[10]

In Charleston later that April, the Texas delegation followed the lead of William Lowndes Yancey of Alabama in attempting to block the nomination of Stephen A. Douglas for president and in forcing into the platform a specific guarantee that slavery could not be excluded from any territory of the United States. When the guarantee was deleted from the platform, the Texas delegation joined other delegations from the Lower South and withdrew from the convention. The convention, unable to agree upon a presidential candidate, then adjourned.[11]

Insistence upon the right of slavery in territories where the climate precluded it from flourishing and the resulting breakup of the Charleston convention drew fire from moderate Democrats in Texas. Charles De Morse, in his editorials in the Clarksville *Standard*, urged Democratic leaders to remember the rejection of extremism by the voters in the state elections of 1859 and expressed the hope that the national Democratic party could be restored. On the whole, however, between 3 May when the Charleston convention adjourned and 18 June when the party reconvened in Baltimore, the distance of Texas from the scene of events, and the inclination of most Democrats to wait and see what happened at the reassembled convention prevented any attempt on the part of party members in Texas to send a more moderate delegation to Baltimore.[12]

In the meantime, members of the Opposition party in Texas were working to secure the nomination of Sam Houston as the presidential candidate of the Constitutional Union party. It had proven impossible to secure for him the Democratic nomination, but Houston still appealed to a wide cross section of Texans. His backers hoped that a party formed in part out of fear that the destruction of the Whig and Democratic parties on a national level would lead in turn to the dissolution of the nation would enthusiastically nominate a man of Houston's proven vote-getting ability. The Constitutional Unionists, however, were dominated by former Whigs from the border states, and they were unwilling to nominate an old Jack-

sonian Democrat. Instead, in mid-May the delegates to their convention selected John Bell of Tennessee as their candidate for president.[13]

In June the Democrats failed to reconcile their differences at
Baltimore. They argued not only about slavery in the territories but
about the seating of several new delegations from southern states.
Once again the convention broke apart. The Texas delegation, along
with most other southerners, retired to Richmond. There was no
further attempt at reconciliation, and both factions of the Democratic party nominated presidential candidates. Southern Democrats
together with a scattering of northerners and westerners nominated
John C. Breckinridge for president. What was left of the national
party nominated Stephen A. Douglas.[14]

While the Democrats and the Constitutional Unionists were arguing about candidates the Republican party met in Chicago and
nominated Abraham Lincoln for president. By the middle of June,
four candidates—Lincoln, Douglas, Bell, and Breckinridge—were in
the race for president.[15] When news of these events drifted back to
the state at the end of June, Texans found themselves awash in a political storm that few of them had wanted or helped create. Nonetheless, their reactions to this storm and the furies that it unleashed in
other portions of the nation proved to be the catalyst for secession.

At first, none of the presidential candidates excited Texans. Lincoln and the Republicans were distant bogeymen. Douglas's supporters were vocal, but few in number, and they had no organized
party. For a time, Houston and his supporters considered running
him as an independent candidate. Texans liked the idea, but few outside the state encouraged the hero of San Jacinto, and the majority of
the Opposition party's leaders reluctantly endorsed John Bell. Their
reluctance came from a correct reading of the public mind. As a former Whig and a man with continued ties to the Know-Nothing or
American party, Bell alienated many moderate Democrats who had
supported Houston's party in 1859. Besides, there was some truth to
the Democrats' claim that Bell was "an old fogey" who lacked the
dynamic qualities and charisma a president would need in 1860.[16]
Nonetheless, Bell was a better choice for many than Breckinridge.
No matter how much Breckinridge's campaign managers tried to
disassociate him from Yancey and disunion, the very earnestness of
their appeals showed the difficulty of their task. Eventually, though,
party lines hardened, and Texans took part in a vigorous presidential
campaign.

During June and July it looked as if the Democrats, who had
been beaten in 1859, would win by default in 1860, because their opponents could not decide between Douglas, Houston, or Bell and

spent more time arguing among themselves than organizing their campaign. Houston's supporters clung idealistically to the man they considered the representative of the best tradition of American politics, and Houston himself did not officially withdraw from the race until 18 August. Douglas's foes in the Democratic party had painted him as an enemy of the South long before 1860, but some Douglas supporters, like Ferdinand Flake of Galveston, never gave up on their candidate. Across Texas there would be a scattering of votes for the only candidate who attempted a nationwide campaign. In the face of such staunch support the lackluster Bell made little headway in gaining the endorsement of those who feared the Democrats were secessionists. Finally, on 6 July the *Harrison Flag*, the state's most consistent advocate of the American party, gave up on Houston and urged the election of Bell. Other supporters of Houston drifted into the Bell camp, and most former Whigs or Know-Nothings also came out for Bell in mid-July. Still, Douglas Democrats seemed more concerned with the integrity of their candidate than with the necessity of defeating the regular Democrats in Texas. The Opposition party had won in 1859 by putting together disparate political factions, and by relying on the leadership of the dynamic Houston. In 1860, however, the election was a national one, and each candidate carried into the state strong ties with clearly defined political parties. Such clear definition of partisanship together with the absence of a viable candidate made the task of the Democrats all the easier. All they had to do was call home the disaffected moderate Democrats of 1859 and the election in Texas would be theirs.[17]

Moderate Democrats grumbled about their party's candidate in the early summer, and it was probably true that rank-and-file Democrats remained far less committed to southern rights than their leaders. Charles De Morse, for example, continued to consider Douglas a stronger candidate than Breckinridge well into June of 1860, and he and many other Democrats expressed fears about the breakup of the party. The moderates knew that their party's split would make it easier for the Republicans to win and they realized a Republican victory might result in secession. They suspected this had been the intent of Yancey and his followers, and they were reluctant to associate with a candidate who bore the Yancey stamp. Nonetheless, by the end of July most prominent moderates had joined the Breckinridge camp.[18]

Support for Breckinridge grew over the summer among these active political leaders because of traditional party loyalty, because no other candidate proved to be a viable alternative, and because, as always, they wanted their side to win. Democrats in Texas might feud in off-years, but the highly competitive nature of presidential elections demanded that if they were to exist as an effective party, they must bury divisive issues and work together for their candidate's victory. Antebellum political parties developed out of a desire to win presidential elections and control Congress, and even on the eve of the Civil War, this original reason for being had not lost its force. In order to placate the moderates, staunch Breckinridge men went to great pains to prove that Yancey had no influence with Breckinridge. They argued loudly that their candidate loved the Union, and called for a united party to give Breckinridge the support he deserved. Moderates listened and began to fall in behind their delegates to the national convention and their party's state executive committee.[19]

In midsummer of 1860, Breckinridge was the only realistic choice for moderate Democrats. He could win, and he was a Democrat. The same could not be said of Douglas, Houston, or Bell. Texas editorial writers made it clear that Douglas might get a larger popular vote but stood little chance of obtaining the electoral votes he needed to win. Houston, spurned by both the Democrats and the Constitutional Unionists, had no chance of gaining any electoral votes outside of Texas. Breckinridge men, though, could make a strong case for the probable victory of their candidate. All he needed to do was secure the votes of the fifteen slave states, plus Oregon, California, and Pennsylvania or New York. Bell, who had strong support in the border states, could have been projected as a victor as well, but until August, Bell and his supporters in Texas acted like Whigs and Know-Nothings in new costume; as such he was anathema to Democrats with deep-seated partisan prejudices. Since Lincoln was an unthinkable alternative, only Breckinridge was left. Realizing that Breckinridge was the only pragmatic choice and feeling the tug of partisan politics, moderates like Charles De Morse abandoned Douglas in July and began to support Breckinridge. In the same month the San Antonio *Herald* helped lead Democrats who had supported Houston back into the fold when they hauled the General from their masthead and replaced him with Breckinridge. As these Democrats got into the spirit of the campaign, Bell, Breckinridge's only real opponent in Texas, seemed more and more a traditional foe, and the election took on all the trappings of an old-fashioned Whig versus Democrat presidential fracas.[20]

Yet it was not a traditional presidential election, and despite Breckinridge's campaign managers' efforts in Texas to replace concern for the Union with partisanship and pragmatism, all the impulses that had caused the victory of the Opposition party in 1859 remained. Some Democrats, like George Paschal, remained estranged from their party. Sam Houston and his personal followers were also outside the party. Former Whigs and Know-Nothings still disliked Democrats. A shared commitment to the nation and a belief that the action of the Democrats threatened its stability united these three groups. The Democrats were not the only threat to the nation; so were the Republicans and the constant chatter about racial fears and slavery which seemed to accompany presidential elections in the South since the advent of that sectional and, in all Texans' eyes, misguided party. No presidential election had ever seemed so dangerous to the future of the nation, and that danger, together with dislike for the regular Democrats, sparked the rebirth of the old Opposition party in early August.[21]

Opposition leaders had a problem: they wanted to win, not just take the moral high ground. Neither Bell nor Douglas, the two candidates who might have headed their political ticket, suited the broad spectrum of their party. There was no Sam Houston available whose charisma and personal appeal together with the bond of Unionism could weld together the diverse factions of the party. The leadership found a solution to the problem by borrowing an idea from the state of New York and fielding what they termed a "Union Electoral Ticket." Their electors, who were a careful combination of Democrats and Whigs, were pledged to vote for whichever candidate stood the best chance of defeating Lincoln. In Texas these Fusionists, as they were called, basically remained a combination of supporters of Douglas and Bell, but they pledged to vote for Breckinridge if he seemed the best candidate to defeat Lincoln.[22]

Much of the impetus behind the Union electoral ticket came from the unionists of Travis County. Austin, the state capital, had attracted a large number of energetic and talented men to the area, and on 4 August 1860, the day after the Democrats had swept the state elections, a number of these men, worried about the lack of unity among Texas moderates, sent out a letter urging the fusion of all voters opposed to Lincoln and sectionalism. Later a Union Club was formed. Among its members were former Governor E. M. Pease, Representative A. J. Hamilton, and George Paschal. Attending from out of town at the first meeting were state Senator Gustav Schleicher of Bexar County and John H. Robson of Colorado County. These men, together with the rest of those present, drafted a letter which was published in newspapers across the state. Declaring that they were of "various party affiliations," they pointed out that the sectional candidates of the North and the South had a united following, but conservative strength was divided. To rectify this in Texas, they proposed a "Union of Union Men" and called on former Whigs

Ben H. Epperson of Red River County and William Steadman of Rusk County to serve as electors from the eastern portion of the state while former Democrats Paschal and Robson would be the electors from the west. The Union Club went on to form a Correspondence Committee headed by Pease, and made every effort to spread the idea of a Fusion ticket throughout the state.[23]

By the first of October, Union Clubs had sprung up around the state. One of the best-organized and well-attended clubs was the Union Club of San Antonio, which began meeting on 11 September. As had the Opposition party in 1859, it drew support from all three of the major ethnic groups in San Antonio. J. D. Wade was its president, Schleicher was its vice-president, and Pancho Ruiz was an assistant vice-president. James P. Newcomb, editor of the *Alamo Express*, was the secretary of the club and dedicated almost every inch of his newspaper to the election of the Union electors. In Galveston, the Fusion party formed a Constitutional Union Club as early as 18 August. Among its members was prominent lawyer William P. Ballinger.[24] Marshall unionists rallied around the *Harrison Flag* and its editor J. W. Barret. Even though one contributor described the Fusion ticket as being "very much like a squatter sovereignty ticket, half horse, half alligator, and a little touched with snapping turtle," with the help of Lemuel Evans the Union electoral ticket soon had numerous backers in traditionally two-party Harrison County. La Grange and Fayette counties also had a strong Fusionist organization, but its efforts were handicapped by the continued neutral stance of the La Grange *True Issue*. While the editor of the paper was a patriotic unionist, he refused to endorse any candidate in the 1860 election. Rio Grande City, far to the south in Starr County, had another vigorous Union Club and a correspondent of the Austin *Southern Intelligencer* reported that the importance to the economy and security of that region of the federal troops at Ringgold Barracks ensured the victory of the Fusionists. In all of these towns and counties organization was to pay off with a substantial vote for Fusion electors.[25]

Sam Houston and other prominent politicians tried to add to the growing support for the Fusion ticket by speaking at public gatherings around the state. In October Houston spoke at San Antonio, Bastrop, Independence, Navasota, Anderson, Huntsville, and several other smaller places. Speaking almost every other day, he urged his personal followers to support the Fusion ticket and warned all Texans that the United States was not something to be cast aside thoughtlessly.[26]

Joining Houston on the campaign circuit were the Union ticket electors. Presidential electors in antebellum Texas were expected to carry the brunt of electioneering, and Steadman, Paschal, Epperson, and Robson gave numerous speeches and wrote many letters in support of their ticket. They were aided by Lemuel Evans of Harrison County, John A. Wilcox of Bexar County, J. M. Dodson of Rusk County, and A. B. Norton of Travis County, who served as alternate electors for the state at large. Other alternate electors served in the western and eastern congressional districts and lent their names, voices, and pens to the cause. By mid-October, thanks to the efforts of these men on a state and local level and to the Union Clubs, it looked as if the Fusion party might have a slim chance of victory.[27]

Fusion strength, however, waned as fast as it had waxed, and by election time only the most optimistic Fusionists dared predict victory for their ticket. Fusionists faced a well-organized opposition party. They got a late start. They had a novel election strategy, and they lacked an institutionalized following. All these things hurt their chances of victory, and even more damaging were persistent fears about race and slavery and the realization that the fall state elections in key northern states indicated an almost inevitable victory for the Republicans in the presidential election.

Such fears of Republican victory made Texans believe themselves to be under attack. Once so believing, they interpreted what happened around them as proof of their condition. Nothing better highlights this growing tension created by events external to Texas than the so-called Texas Troubles. Here was an incident which might have caused little uproar if it had occurred outside of the context of 1859–1860. Because it happened when it did, Texans believed themselves increasingly vulnerable.[28]

On Sunday, 8 July 1860, a day on which the temperature reached as high as 110 degrees, fires broke out in Dallas, Denton, and Pilot Point. Almost a month of hot, dry weather had dried out the wooden buildings of these North Texas towns, and before their residents knew what had happened, extensive damage was done in each town. Dallas suffered the most destruction, with estimates of property losses ranging as high as $400,000. The previous fall, missionaries of the Methodist Episcopal church had troubled North Texans. Branded as abolitionists, these men of God had been forced to leave the state; at first no one thought to connect the simultaneous fires with an abolitionist conspiracy. Within a few days, however, rumors began to spread of an extensive plot hatched by Negroes and abolitionists. The plan, according to its more fantastic reports, was to create a state of turmoil and destroy provisions and arms by setting the fires and then to murder the white men and older women. The younger women were to be raped. North Texas, like Kansas, was next to be turned into a free state by force of arms.[29]

Soon every fire that broke out that hot, dry summer was blamed on abolitionists and, responding to extraordinary conditions, Texans took the law into their own hands by forming vigilance committees to patrol neighborhoods and stamp out any potential slave insurrections. Before the panic died down, as many as forty to fifty blacks and northerners had been lynched. Northern immigrants were leaving Texas by the wagonful. No stranger, even if he spoke with a southern accent and had the best credentials, was entirely safe as he traveled across the state. Hysteria seized hold of many Texans for a six-week span in the summer of 1860.[30]

Not only were the first fires associated with the Texas Troubles in North Texas; so was the eye of the storm that created the hysteria of the summer of 1860. It was the southern press that took the rumors of incendiarism and abolitionist plots, breathed life into them, and spread them into every state in the south. It was Charles Pryor, editor of the Dallas *Herald*, who supplied the "facts" of the Texas Troubles to other southern newspapers. In July of 1860 Pryor, a champion of John C. Breckinridge for president, wrote other Breckinridge-supporting editors in Austin, Bonham, and Houston frightening accounts of the conspiracy in North Texas. In his letter, published in the *Texas State Gazette*, he declared: "It was determined by certain Abolitionist preachers, who were expelled from the country last year, to devastate, with fire and assassination, the whole of Northern Texas, and when it was reduced to a helpless condition, a general revolt of the slaves, aided by white men of the North in our midst, was to come off on the day of election in August." In other letters Pryor urged Texans in other areas to keep a watchful eye on their own neighborhoods, as he expected more abolitionist plots. Moreover, as the size and scope of the alleged conspiracy grew, Pryor's letters and confirming evidence from other locals were reported in an increasingly large number of newspapers. By the end of the summer, North Texas and the Texas Troubles had become familiar news items to the reading public of the South.[31]

Gradually the Texas Troubles began to have political overtones, with the majority of Breckinridge politicians and newspapers confirming reports of the atrocities and the majority of Bell or Douglas proponents discounting the rumors. The Opposition claimed that the Texas Troubles were used by Breckinridge supporters just as demagogues would use any threat to a community—to provide unity and acceptance of their actions by arousing irrational fears.

Breckinridge men disclaimed any attempt to use the Texas Troubles as a vote-getting device, but there was a ring of truth to the accusation. The Texas Troubles became to the Opposition just another example of the attempt of southern radicals to disrupt the Union.

It was indeed true that the fires and reports of attempted assassinations were exaggerated. At a later date—in a calmer setting—residents of North Texas were able to see that it was hot weather and spontaneous combustion of the newly introduced phosphorus matches that caused the fires. At the same time, they had honestly believed what they had said and written about the Texas Troubles. Instead of consciously conspiring to delude the public, they had reacted to the political and sectional tensions of the times. Nerves were on edge and, as even a few Breckinridge supporters saw, the Texas Troubles caused an extreme reaction among those most willing to think the worst about Northern abolitionists. Breckinridge Democrats were often conditional unionists—unionists only so long as the North respected the rights of the South. Members of the Opposition remained much more adamant in their loyalty to the nation. It was natural for them to look askance at anything that threatened disunion. Given the tensions of the time, it was equally natural that those who had some doubts or who placed restrictions on their Unionism would be moved toward extremes by the Texas Troubles.[32]

Hysteria and violence had faded by the fall of 1860, but the dangers of servile insurrection and northern disruption of southern race relations continued to receive wide coverage in Democratic newspapers through election time. On 8 September the *Texas State Gazette* carried a typical editorial which declared, "We call upon the people to look to their homes and their firesides—to the formidable enemy who is at their door—to the torch of the incendiary—to the poison and dagger of the assassin—and to the demagogues who would sacrifice their existence as a people, and safety of their dwellings, the lives and honors of their families, to the lust of power of the fury of party rage." In such editorials and in similar speeches, Democrats took advantage of and added to a growing public concern for safety in the Union. For Democrats the wolf was at the door of the South, dressed in the garb of the Republican party and the abolitionists. Those southerners who prevented the South from demonstrating the depth of southern commitment to the defense of slavery by uniting behind Breckinridge were almost as odious as the Republicans. Democrats insisted that the deepest of emotions—the need for survival and a commitment to white superiority—demanded that Texans support their candidate. During the summer, Democratic leaders had cleverly used the pull of partisan loyalties and the logic of Breckinridge's candidacy to promote him. Pragmatism and tradition restored the party. In the fall, fear and racism extended the Democrats' sway over the public mind.[33]

Fusionists argued that the fires in Texas and other similar incidents used by the Democrats as proof of abolitionists' malevolent intent were either accidents or events which had been blown out of proportion. Urging a reliance upon reason, not hysteria, they pointed out that Democrats in Texas had branded their opponents abolitionists in every presidential election since 1848. The Fusionists insisted that in this case the fires and the fears and emotions they unleashed were being used for political effect. They were being used to revitalize a morally defunct Democratic party in Texas. Spokesmen like George Paschal hit hard at William Lowndes Yancey, Robert Barnwell Rhett, and other southern fire-eaters, and claimed that these radicals were the guiding spirits behind the Breckinridge candidacy. Insisting that voting for the Fusion ticket was the only course that would save the Union and defeat Lincoln, Fusionists branded a vote for any other party a vote for disunion, sectionalism, and possibly civil war.[34]

As the panic dissipated in October these arguments appeared to be making headway, but then came the news that the Republicans had carried the statewide elections in the key states of Indiana and Pennsylvania. Political analysts of all parties realized that the election of 1860 would be won or lost in the line of states stretching from New York to Illinois. New England seemed safe for the Republicans. The South was sure to vote for Bell or Breckinridge. If Lincoln was to secure a majority of the electoral vote it was obvious that he must defeat Douglas in the populous states between these two regions.[35]

Fusionists based their campaign on defeating Lincoln instead of electing a particular candidate. When the news of the state elections in two of the key states indicated that with all probability Lincoln would win a majority there, the entire basis for the Fusionists' approach to the election evaporated. What reason was there for voting for a party pledged to defeat Lincoln by casting electoral votes for one of three candidates when it was obvious that, no matter what happened in Texas, Lincoln would be elected? It seemed a wiser course to many to follow the advice of the Democrats and demonstrate southern unity by voting overwhelmingly for Breckinridge.[36]

As early as June, militant southern Democrats had insisted that "the rights and honor of the South are paramount to all other considerations." When it became obvious that the North was going to elect a candidate whose following was entirely sectional and whose party threatened the interests of the South, even moderate Democrats began to call for southern unity. Some hoped that a show of unity would save the Union by forcing the North to be cautious, but others seemed motivated by a growing belief that there was a difference between North and South. The nation was no longer bound together by many strands. Instead, in the eyes of a growing number of Texas Democrats, the nation had two parts which could exist together only so long as each respected the divergent rights and interests of the other.[37]

On the eve of the presidential election, Fusionists tried to counter this growing demand for sectional unity by invoking the sanctified memories of Washington, Jefferson, Jackson, Webster, and Clay. These were heroes of a nation, not a section, and Texans were asked to remember these heroes and vote to preserve their nation. The Fusionists urged Texans to rise above party prejudice, sectional interests, and hysterical fears, and vote for the Union Electoral Ticket. They insisted that if New York voted for fusion there was still a chance of victory. They made an emotional plea to each voter "to stand by the flag of his country, the Union and the Constitution." They tried one last time to prove that Bell was not a Know-Nothing and Douglas was not an abolitionist. Their pleas fell on deaf ears. The state's Democrats accrued an unbroken string of victories in the elections.[38]

Election returns from the rest of the nation confirmed Texans' worst fears: a Republican, Abraham Lincoln, was to be the country's next president. After a brief lull, talk of secession began, and the state's Democratic leaders raised a call for a special session of the legislature which could then assemble a secession convention.

Such calls for radical action in defense of slavery and southern rights had been made by southern political leaders before and had been generally ignored. The Democrats' calls for action were not ignored in 1860; the degree of public sentiment in their favor seemed to surprise even secessionist leaders like O. M. Roberts.[39]

Roberts's Democratic party in Texas had always been the party of those most interested in the South and slavery. That party's ideology stressed most clearly the aggressive expansionist character of individual Americans. For Texans expansion meant slavery and the growth of a market economy based on cotton. Any threat to these things threatened the road to wealth, fame, and social standing. Also, the Democrats had always been the defenders of individual rights and local customs and had resisted the homogenizing tendencies of the Whigs and Know-Nothings. Democrats included not just Anglo-Saxon shopkeepers and yeoman farmers, but Germans, Mexicans, planters, and rough frontiersmen. Although they failed to take into account the individual rights of black people, it was still quite in character that they defended the white southerners' peculiar custom of owning slaves. Still, as Roberts, a leader of the annexation movement in 1845, pointed out, even secessionists still had the emotional commitment to the United States that had played such a role in annexation fifteen years earlier. Roberts well remembered the elections of 1859, when Democratic extremism had caused his party's defeat. It had seemed previously that every time Texas's party leaders or public officials threatened the nation, they were rebuked by the average citizen. This did not happen in 1860–1861.[40]

Partisan politics partially explain this failure to rebuke extremism. It was the Democratic party, hoping to gain votes, that spread the word about John Brown, Juan Cortina, the Indian troubles, and anarchy in the House of Representatives. Democrats used the fear of slave rebellion and abolitionist plots to gain votes. The desire of the Democrats to win the election caused even moderate spokesmen of the party to acquiesce in this use of propaganda and to accept Breckinridge as their candidate for president.

Once set before the public, though, both events and partisan goals seemed to have a life and a destiny of their own. Partisan desire to win elections and reward faithful Democrats caused the acceptance of radicals like John Marshall and Louis T. Wigfall in leadership roles in the party. Similar aims caused Democrats to unite behind Breckinridge. Victory demanded the exploitation of events of the past year. Those events, however, were more explosive than most moderates realized. As each event piled upon another, a sense of crisis developed. The worst of all possible things had occurred: the election of a Republican. Moderate Democrats had difficulty arguing that there was no crisis and that the world should go on as it had before. The sense of crisis so artfully used by the Democratic leadership trapped all of them into agreeing to secession, because secession resolved the crisis. Inaction implied that no crisis existed. Besides, the public demanded a solution. The people believed that there was a crisis whose only solution was secession. So O. M. Roberts found himself in the ironic position of having worked to bring Texas into the Union in 1845 and in 1861 chairing the convention that took Texas out of that Union.[41]

Despite the increasing momentum toward secession after Lincoln's election, its opponents, mostly members of the old Opposition party or residents of non–Lower South cultural areas, still argued loudly in the winter of 1860–1861 that the South was not endangered and the nation should continue to exist. They called upon romance, realism, pecuniary gain, and emotion to head off secession. They called for a return to reason. Few would hear.

4

The Other Texas

While the majority of Texans did not listen to the critics of secession in 1861, ever since then both historians and the public have made much of the opposition of certain regions and peoples to secession. Germans and North Texans have long been considered unionists. Frontiersmen's attachment to the Union has received considerable attention. Sam Houston and other prominent unionists have been subjects of numerous books and articles. Among the most commonly used quotations on secession has been James W. Throckmorton's 1866 pronouncement that "in 1860–1861 the South was not ripe for revolution. There were few people who felt that they were going to war because of oppressing wrong, or outrage. There was not one in a thousand who felt that sufficient cause existed demanding of him his life, his all."[1]

Remember, however, that the South's defeat and his own efforts to integrate Texas back into the nation colored Throckmorton's recollection of secession, and that the reality of defeat and the desire to rehabilitate Texas as part of the nation have continued to shade perceptions of secession. Certainly North Texas and some German counties voted against secession on 23 Feburary 1861, but they often did so by narrow margins. Certainly some Germans and North Texans attempted to avoid the draft and aided the Union cause as best they could during the war, but more often they loyally served the Confederacy. Attachment to the Union in Texas was not total or consistent, nor was it uniform in nature. Ironically, the variations in Unionism which gave it such widespread appeal became a major reason unionists could not stop the momentum toward secession. Unionists relied upon multifaceted impulses and complex logic. Secessionists used a simple and direct course of action backed by a growing public consensus. In the heat of the secession crisis simplicity and directness prevailed.[2]

Perhaps no one better illustrates the complexity of Unionism and the reasons it failed to prevent secession than James Throckmorton. Born in Tennessee in 1825, Throckmorton moved to Texas in 1841. In 1844 he returned to the Upper South to study medicine with his uncle in Princeton, Kentucky. After fighting in the Mexican War he settled in Collin County, north of Dallas, and took up the practice of medicine. By 1851 he had tired of medicine and entered politics as a member of the state legislature. For the rest of the antebellum period he served as either a state representative or senator. Throckmorton began his political career as a Whig, and while the influence of Whig ideology never left him, he was not so much a Whig as to be drawn into the Know-Nothing party when his own died. Instead, in the mid-1850s he drifted into the loosely organized Democratic party. By 1858, however, he broke with the regular Democrats and joined the coalition that became the Opposition party of 1859–1860. By 1860 Throckmorton stood second only to Sam Houston among the unionists of Texas. In 1861 he was a Collin County delegate to the Secession Convention and was one of only eight men who voted against secession at that convention. When he cast his vote and explained his reasons for it, some among the crowd of delegates and onlookers hissed. Others then applauded this treatment of Throckmorton. At that point Throckmorton made the famous reply addressed to O. M. Roberts, president of the convention: "Mr. President, when the rabble hiss, well may patriots tremble." When the convention recessed at the end of January 1861, Throckmorton returned to Collin County and helped convince his neighbors to reject secession in the 23 February referendum. Secession passed the state as a whole, however, and the convention reassembled to lead Texas into the Confederacy. Throckmorton attended this second session of the convention and continued to oppose hasty action by the state of Texas. It was at this time that he made another famous statement: "While my judgement dictates to me that we are not justified by the surroundings or the occasion, a majority of the people have declared in favor of secession; the die is cast; the step has been taken and regardless of consequences I expect and intend to share the fortunes of my friends and neighbors." Throckmorton lived up to his words and went on to be a Confederate brigadier general.[3]

Throckmorton's Unionism sprang from Whig ideology, partisan antipathy for the leaders of secession, a rational assessment of the events leading to secession, and membership in a non–Lower South cultural group. Secession flew in the face of the traditional Whig ideology that stressed reverence for the Constitution, government by legal precedent, the sanctity of the nation, and an obligation to the founding fathers to maintain the nation. Besides, secession was a partisan issue, advocated by all of Throckmorton's political enemies and none of his friends. Nor did secession seem wise. It would destabilize society and the economy, causing monetary loss as well as civil war. Throckmorton would not have said these things so loudly and believed them so deeply, however, if he had not lived in and been continually influenced by an Upper South culture. The plantation South never touched Throckmorton. His present interests, future dreams, and past memories lay with Kentucky and Tennessee, not Alabama and South Carolina. He was part of another Texas.[4]

In 1860 immigrants from the South comprised over 80 percent of the Texas population. Southerners, however, were far from homogeneous, and there existed in Texas a clear cultural division which reflected the differences within the South. There were slaveholding plantation southerners in Texas as well as limited-slaveholding southern yeomen and nonslaveholding southern mountain and hill folk. In general, counties dominated by planters drew their population from the Lower South states, while counties dominated by yeomen and mountaineers drew their population from the Upper South. As in the case of Texans from the Lower South, pioneer immigrants from the Upper South settled in areas of Texas in which the landscape resembled their former homes. Once settled they set about duplicating their past lives, and in effect created a favorable cultural environment that, along with the already favorable physical environment, enticed additional settlers from the Upper South to join them in Texas. By 1860 this process had created distinct clusters of Texans from the Upper South that were separated from other Texans by geographic bounds.

There was an Upper South Texas and a Lower South Texas. Certainly Tennesseans and other representatives of the Upper South lived in East Texas and along the lower Brazos, Colorado, and Trinity rivers, but in those regions upper southerners had usually been assimilated into a Lower South culture. Likewise, Alabamians resided in the settled counties of North Texas and western Texas, but yeoman from the Upper South clearly dominated the plains of North Texas and a typical Upper South mixture of mountain and yeoman peoples prevailed in the hills and on the blackland prairies to the north and west of Austin and Travis County.[5]

It was no accident that nineteen of the twenty-nine counties that cast over 40 percent of their ballots against secession on 23 February 1861 lay in the Upper South region of Texas, and that two others were strongly influenced by Upper South culture (see Table 1). Here slaves were scarce, farms were smaller, and farmers grew wheat and corn instead of cotton. The causes of their prosperity in 1860 and their dreams of the future differed from those of the Lower South; so too did their ideology and their politics. Indeed, isolated from the rest of the state by poor transportation facilities, the residents of these

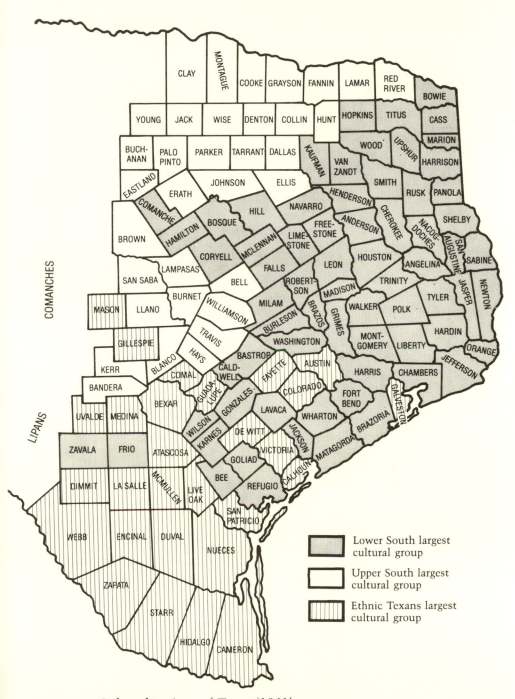

MAP 2. Cultural regions of Texas (1861).

Map by Liz Conrad. (County lines from map no. 13 in *Mitchell's School and Family Geography*, 1858. Cultural regions from Jordan, *The Imprint of the Upper and Lower South*.)

counties were as unassimilated into the culture of the Gulf South as were the Germans of frontier Texas. To these Texans, secession lacked the urgency that it had in the Lower South. As Throckmorton said, they were not "ripe for revolution." Still, some would support secession and, like Throckmorton, the Confederacy. What was impressive about the Upper South counties was the absence of extremism. Until the fall of 1860 the population was almost unanimously devoted to the Union. Even then, secessionists were reluctant to leave their cherished nation. The explanation for this lies in the unique cultural distinctiveness of the Upper South counties and in the political alignments and philosophies of their citizens.[6]

Texans preserved their cultural distinctiveness in these Upper South counties because of the characteristics of the physical location, because of the limited impact of railroads and other technological innovations, and because the upper southern nature of these counties was well established before the onslaught of the rapidly expanding Lower South culture. Among the most important of these Upper South habits were crop selection and limited use of slave labor. Slavery was less important both because settlers from the Upper South were often unused to owning large numbers of slaves and because for them the institution proved less profitable. Farmers grew wheat and corn, not cotton and sugarcane. Many lived on a semisubsistence level by choice and had no use for slavery. Those oriented to the market depended more upon their own labor, hired labor, and horse-drawn machinery than slave labor.

These profit seekers were accustomed to the use of nonslave labor and machinery, but economic reality also underscored their preference. In other areas of Texas, Tennesseans driven by a desire for profit became large slaveholders and cotton planters, but both geography and the limits of technology prevented such a transformation in West and North Texas before the Civil War. The absence of rivers and the gradually diminishing rainfall of western Texas made it costly to ship cotton and increasingly difficult to grow good cotton crops. Railroads would open up portions of North and West Texas for the production of cotton after the war, but prior to their existence cotton proved too bulky to be profitably transported by wagon from North and West Texas. Some residents anxiously looked forward to the spread of railroads and a cotton culture, but for the moment they and their more content fellows were part of a limited slaveholding world.[7]

Physical location was also important because it meant that Upper South counties relied heavily upon the U.S. Army for protection from Indian attack and as a market for their surplus flour and meat.

TABLE 1. Texas Counties that Cast at Least 40 Percent of Their Votes against Secession on 23 February 1861

Dominant Culture and County	Region	For	Against	Percent Against
Upper South				
Bandera	S. Frontier	33	32	49
Blanco	Central	108	170	61
Burnet	Central	157	248	61
Collin	North	405	948	70
Cooke	North	137	221	61
Denton	North	331	256	44
Fannin	North	471	656	58
Grayson	North	463	901	66
Hays	Central	166	115	41
Hunt	North	416	339	45
Jack	North	14	76	84
Kerr	S. Frontier	76	57	43
Lamar	North	553	663	55
Lampasas	Central	85	75	47
Montague	North	50	86	63
Red River	North	347	284	45
Williamson	Central	349	480	58
Wise	North	78	76	49
Lower South				
Angelina	East	139	184	57
Bastrop	Central	335	352	51
Lower South/Upper South				
Titus	East	411	275	40
Van Zandt	East	181	127	41
German				
Fayette	Central	580	626	52
Gillespie	S. Frontier	16	398	96
Mason	S. Frontier	2	75	97
Medina	Central	140	207	60
Mexican				
Uvalde	S. Frontier	16	76	83
German/Mexican				
Bexar	Central	827	709	46

SOURCE: Timmons, "The Referendum in Texas on the Ordinance of Secession"; Jordan, "The Imprint of the Upper and Lower South."

North Texas bordered on Indian Territory. Counties on the western frontier lay adjacent to land controlled by the Comanche until after the Civil War. If the army were removed, both areas would have been open to attack. Moreover, given the transportation problems, even flour was difficult to haul to the coast at a profit. Instead, the army and the Indian agencies purchased most of the surplus. Absence of the army meant dangerous times and reduced profits.[8]

As long as cotton could not be grown profitably, planters avoided northern and western Texas and these regions remained primarily the domain of the small- and medium-sized land-owning farmer. This meant that until after the Civil War there was relatively little assimilation of the Upper South counties into the Gulf South culture. Instead, these Texans retained the values, prejudices, practices, and loyalties of Tennessee, Kentucky, Missouri, Arkansas, and southern Illinois.[9]

This does not mean that these Texans did not share some of the most basic values of Texas and the South. Railroads were demanded as vociferously in Dallas and Austin as they were in Marshall and Houston. Portions of this land of farmers were more given to the tenets of modern capitalism than the rest of the state. Nor did the lack of great numbers of slaves mean that slavery was abhorred. Slavery was often accepted as beneficial for slave, master, and society. Even hill folk considered blacks inferior, and Texans who considered the problem regarded slavery as the best possible solution to the difficulty of controlling racial hatred. In fact, no Texas community believed itself more threatened by abolitionist plots during the Texas Troubles of the summer of 1860 than did the city of Dallas. Upper South Texans, too, lauded democracy and practiced a highly competitive form of politics. No southerners were more deeply devoted to individual and local rights than those from the mountains and hills. In this they closely resembled other Texans.[10]

Texans from the Upper South were different in that they followed the lead of Tennesseans Andrew Jackson, James K. Polk, Andrew Johnson, and Sam Houston, and Kentuckian Henry Clay, all nationalists fervently committed to the Union. Perhaps the citizens of these states realized that their homeland would be a battlefield in any war between North and South. Perhaps their position between these two rival sections gave them a unique perspective. Perhaps they had a more developed nationalist ideology. Perhaps they simply disliked planters and that region of the South dominated by planters. For whatever reason, their Unionism was persistent. It prompted Tennessee to reject secession until after the firing on Fort Sumter and President Lincoln's call up of troops to put down an insurrection in the South. It led to Kentucky's wishful attempt to remain neutral between the two warring factions. Certainly the Upper South portion of Texas had practical reasons for rejecting secession. It, too, was a buffer zone between the rest of Texas and hostile forces to the north and west. Secession meant the loss of the advantages accrued from the presence of the U.S. Army, and secession for the sake of slavery seemed out of place to nonslaveholders. Still, something more than practicality nurtured the Unionism of Kentuckians, Tennesseans, and their cultural offspring in Texas. If any portion of the United States had the capacity to look beyond its own state and region and to view with moderation the arguments of both North and South, it was the border states. One of the many fascinating things about secession in Texas was that within this state, located on the Gulf of Mexico, an almost exact replica of a border state existed.[11]

An important way in which some Upper South counties of Texas mirrored the border states was that they had developed beyond the early frontier stage to a two-party system—a system which, as the 1850s drew to a close, had come to represent the two predominant opinions of Texans from the Upper South on secession and the Union. Both parties had been equally attached to the Union for much of that decade. It was only after the election of Abraham Lincoln in 1860 that Democrats in Upper South counties began to demand secession. They were opposed, just as they had been opposed for political office, by the Opposition party. In East Texas the majority of the Opposition party joined in the call for secession. This was not so in North Texas and western Texas—there the Opposition party provided a kernel of organized support for the Union.[12]

In 1859 the Opposition party won wide support in Upper South counties. Ten of twelve organized counties in North Texas cast the majority of their ballots for Sam Houston. All the Upper South counties surrounding Austin followed suit and voted for their fellow Tennessean. Austin area voters generally supported the whole range of Opposition candidates. North Texans also voted for the entire Opposition slate, with the notable exception of John H. Reagan.[13]

More than any previous political party, the Opposition party clearly drew its strength in Upper South counties from its Unionism. Almost universally the Democratic candidates were identified with radical and extreme southern views, and the Opposition was identified with moderate and conservative views. Reagan, being the major exception, proved the rule. Like other winners he differed with the bulk of Democratic leaders and voiced strong support for the Union. The Clarksville *Standard* reported that in March of 1859 Reagan had engaged in bitter public argument with Guy M. Bryan, former Democratic congressman from the Second District and a leader of the state's party organization. Reagan, "planting himself on the Union platform," declared he "would go before his constituents and advocate the constitution he had sworn to support in spite of combinations and conspiracies to break him down." Convinced of his commitment to the Union and well aware of his popularity, the Opposition party fielded no candidate to oppose Reagan. Instead, Reagan's opponent came from the ranks of those who radically espoused southern rights. The issue between them was clearly that of a moderate unionist versus a radical southerner, and Reagan's tremendous margin of victory indicated that his constituents agreed with his stance. This was particularly true of the Upper South counties of his district, in which he received over 95 percent of the vote. Besides personal popularity, almost all Sam Houston and Reagan had in common was an avowed commitment to the Union, so this cross voting strongly indicated that it was Unionism, not just party affiliation or stances on other issues, that made a candidate win or lose in Upper South counties in 1859.[14]

In 1859 this other Texas stood squarely in favor of the Union. Even the Democratic editors of the area declared their devotion to unionist principles. J. W. Latimer, the editor of the Dallas *Herald*, wrote in January of 1859:

> We want it distinctly understood that we belong to the strictest school of strict construction and States rights—that we believe in the right of secession, and when the proper time comes will be in favor of exercising that right. But in entertaining these views, we have never yielded and trust we never may, a filial love and unfaltering devotion to the Union that our fathers formed when they framed the Constitution . . . while it continues to perform the great functions for which it was "ordained" . . . we shall stand by it.

Editor Charles De Morse of the Clarksville *Standard* was even more forthright in his statements. Blaming Runnels's and the Democrats' defeat on the governor's failure to deny that he was a disunionist, De Morse declared that he would never again support a candidate until he knew where that candidate stood on this vital issue.[15]

Latimer's and De Morse's editorial positions point to an interesting contrast between North Texas and East Texas. In North Texas the opinions of Latimer and De Morse represented the extreme— the faction most committed to defending the rights of the South. In comparison to East Texas editors, both were moderates. Editor J. W. Loughery of the Marshall *Texas Republican* left the Democratic congressional convention because he could not support Reagan. He resented the congressman's attack on southern disunionists and believed the district required a more militant spokesman for southern principles. There were occasional fire-eaters in North Texas, but they lacked both influence and an audience. North Texans in 1859 were unionists of varying hues, but they were almost universally unionists.[16]

Upper South counties surrounding Austin were almost equally in favor of the Union in 1859. Here, though, unlike North Texas, there could be found militant states' rights advocates with influence and an audience. John Marshall's *Texas State Gazette* consistently promoted not only the Democratic party, but also southern rights. The majority of the citizens, however, had demonstrated their loyalty to the Union by breaking partisan ties to the Democratic party and repudiating Marshall's ally, Governor Runnels. Those counties from the Second District also overwhelmingly endorsed Andrew Jackson Hamilton for Congress.[17]

Hamilton based his campaign in 1859 on loyalty to the Constitution and the Union and eloquently called for temperate action to preserve harmony between the states. Hitting hard at Governor Runnels's and Marshall's support for reopening the slave trade, Hamilton declared that step not only threatened the Union by alienating the North, but that it was unconstitutional. Furthermore, it would demean the value and dignity of white labor.[18]

Hamilton and his campaign ally George Paschal struck a vein of gold when they attacked the Democrats as aristocrats whose policies hurt the common man and the nonslaveholder. Historians have argued that appeals to free-soil, free-labor, and free-men were key elements in the North's ability to attract the support of the West in the sectional disputes that led to the Civil War. This appeal was equally potent among Texans in counties which neither enjoyed nor desired direct economic benefit from slavery. Appealing to the "hard fisted yeomanry," Paschal and Hamilton pointed out that self-interest dictated a vote for the Opposition ticket. Outlining the process by which increased numbers of slaves would mean a decrease in the number of jobs and the amount of land available for those unable or disinclined to buy slaves, the two spokesmen for the Opposition declared that the reopening of the slave trade was a conspiracy of the rich and of special-interest groups. Here was a practical and real issue to combine with the more ethereal tenets of Unionism. Southern extremism not only meant a threat to the idea of union, it meant a threat to the upward mobility, dignity, and earning power of the common man. Jacksonian nationalism and desires for economic prosperity and growth were linked together and turned against the radicals. The result in the yeoman-dominated counties surrounding Austin, where this line of reasoning was most attended and seemed to have the greatest appeal, was an overwhelming victory for Hamilton and the Opposition party. They captured over 66 percent of the vote. In Dallas, the perceptive editor of the *Herald* noted that North Texas had also voted against Runnels and other Democrats except for Reagan because these Democratic candidates supported reopening the slave trade. Such extremism and the assault on free labor and national stability which it represented were not popular among Texas yeomen in 1859.[19]

This sentiment for the Union and against secession among Texans from the Upper South withstood the tumultuous events of the fall of 1859—events which caused other Texans to lose hope for the Union. For example, North Texans' initial shock and anger after the violent actions of John Brown soon gave way to moderation. Brown's raid was depicted as an isolated incident. Only certain northerners, not all northerners, were connected with the abolitionist plot. It has long been argued, however, that the excitement over John Brown's raid led to the election of Louis T. Wigfall, the most famous fire-eater in the state. Recently, however, evidence has been assembled which seems to prove that Wigfalls' election to the U.S. Senate was a product of party loyalty, not sectional prejudice. Nowhere was this more true than in North Texas. Charles De Morse, the influential editor of the Clarksville *Standard*, considered Wigfall too radical, and he, together with other leading Democrats, favored John Reagan for the Senate seat. Both the Dallas *Herald* and the *Standard*, however, consistently expressed their editors' and other prominent Democrats' gratitude to Wigfall for his campaign efforts on behalf of all the Democratic candidates. He was presented as a party man. When Wigfall began moderating his views on disunion the *Herald* went so far as to endorse him. Once Wigfall was elected, De Morse and other moderate Democrats were willing to accept him as long as he kept his states' rights views in check.[20]

Once again the Austin area was more complex than North Texas. Because Austin was the state capital the region had attracted a wide assortment of politicians, editors, and lawyers. These leaders and articulators of public opinion expressed every conceivable attitude toward the events of the fall of 1859. Marshall, of the *State Gazette*, accentuated the evilness of John Brown and his backers and supported Wigfall for the Senate. Even Marshall, though, did not go so far as to demand secession because of Harpers Ferry, and he aided Wigfall in his attempt to move toward the political center and away from southern extremism. George Paschal, editor of the Austin *Southern Intelligencer*, opposed Wigfall and took a more moderate view of Brown's ties to the North. Brown was wicked in his eyes, but that did not implicate all northerners. A. B. Norton, a member of the state legislature and soon to be editor of the *Southern Intelligencer*, led the fight against Wigfall, and cautioned that southern extremists were using Brown's raid to further their cause. State legislators from the Travis County area followed Norton's example and almost unanimously voted against Wigfall, thus expressing their dislike for both his states' rights philosophy and his affiliation with the regular Democratic party. Unionism was intact and calm restored among Texans from a yeoman culture in December of 1859. The furor over John Brown's raid ebbed. Wigfall was acceptable if he restrained his states' rights inclinations. Only the persistent threat to the Texas border from Indian and Mexican attack disturbed the serenity of that pre-Christmas season.[21]

Once Wigfall and the other members of the Texas delegation arrived in Washington, D.C., the agitation that marked the fall of 1859 resumed. In fact, the issue of defending Texas borders from the recently increased attacks by Indians and Mexicans now became intertwined with party strife between the Republicans and the Democrats. Texans regarded these attacks as external threats and insisted that the federal government provide protection, or at least pay for the cost of Texas troops. Unfortunately, while the House quarreled over the speakership, little could be done for Texas. Once the House was organized under the control of the Republicans, Texas claims were repeatedly ignored by House leadership and fared little better in the Senate. John Brown's raid could be regarded as only an isolated incident, but the lesson of federal failure to meet the threats of trouble along the Rio Grande and of Indian raids hit home immediately. Texans in Upper South regions of the state still saw the army and the federal government as vital to their interests, but the winter of 1859–1860 marked a turning point. A seed of doubt had been planted. Few lost their romantic attachment to the nation, but some began to speculate about the fate of frontier Texas if the Republicans controlled all branches of the federal government.[22]

News of presidential aspirants and upcoming political conventions coincided with reports from the U.S. Congress in the winter and early spring of 1860. Sam Houston was the candidate generally favored in Upper South counties. Houston, it was claimed, was the only candidate with the strength of purpose needed to save the Union. Like his mentor Andrew Jackson, he mixed democratic ideals with a strong brand of nationalism. He was approaching seventy, and at times his political philosophy seemed dated, but he still was touted as the best man for the job. When he failed to receive the nomination of any national party, moderate Texans were left with a difficult choice for the presidency.[23]

Even before Houston was denied the nomination, Democrats in Upper South Texas perceived that Houston was not a realistic candidate for their party. They focused their attention on the Charleston convention where the party had assembled to select a candidate. North Texans in particular remained national Democrats, not sectional Democrats, and the optimistic editor of the Dallas *Herald* predicted that the Charleston convention would be "the grand beacon light of safety for the nation." North Texas Democrats called for a united party and reminded their members that it was one of the few remaining national institutions. Although John C. Breckinridge was the candidate most often mentioned, editor De Morse and others were willing to support Stephen A. Douglas if he were the convention's nominee. Unity, for them, was more important than ideology.[24]

When news reached Texas of the breakup of the Charleston convention and the walkout of the southern delegates, North Texans did not go so far as to condemn the Texas delegation, but the Democrats of Hunt and Fannin counties did meet and issue a call for the Texas delegation to attend the Baltimore convention and support the party nominee. De Morse, who had been arguing against both the constitutionality and feasibility of secession all spring, again reiterated that he would support Douglas if he were the nominee. The Dallas *Herald* accused the northern Democrats of being obstinate but echoed the *Standard*'s hope that the party would be reunited.

In the Austin area Marshall and his allies celebrated the breakup of the Charleston convention and applauded the honesty of the southern delegates. The *State Gazette* attacked E. M. Pease and other former Democrats who had joined the Opposition as unprincipled and belittled their efforts to reunite the Democratic party. Here was an important difference between North Texas and Central Texas. In the North the Democratic party remained in the hands of unionists like Charles De Morse and John Reagan. In the rest of the state the party was staunchly allied with the states' rights Democrats of the Lower South. Unionists in the Austin area were forced to find another political organization to express their beliefs.[25]

When the Democrats failed to unite on any one candidate at the Baltimore convention, the majority of Texas Democrats lined up behind Breckinridge, but the choice was not so simple for the Opposition party. This was especially true in the Upper South areas. In East Texas John Bell, as a former Whig and a long-standing opponent of the Democrats, won the easy support of a party whose antipathy to all things Democratic was equally well established. The Opposition party in the Upper South counties, however, had a different character. Particularly in the Austin area, the party consisted primarily of former Democrats who now supported Douglas. In North Texas Douglas had some support, but it appeared that the Democrats in the party were about to move back into the fold and support Breckinridge. The failure to find a suitable candidate was a severe problem to the Opposition party in Upper South counties and threatened to destroy the fragile coalition upon which that party rested.[26]

Before any solution to the problems of the Opposition party could be reached, North Texas was swept by the series of suspected cases of arson called the Texas Troubles. For a time politics receded in importance as Texans chased abolitionists, organized vigilante groups, and ferreted out conspirators. In North Texas, and indeed in the rest of the South, the Texas Troubles were to reconfirm and drive home the lessons of John Brown's raid. Southern society was not safe as long as northern abolitionists were free to move south to spread incendiary doctrines and incite slave insurrections. Moderates began to reconsider their attachment to the Union in the light of flames from North Texas.[27]

As a consequence of the publicity given to these suspected cases of arson and assassination, the hitherto solid facade of support for the Union in North Texas began to evaporate. In every election, on every issue, the Upper South counties of North Texas had supported the Union. Beneath the surface, however, there had always been two types of unionists. One type consisted primarily of former Whigs and dissenting Democrats who were willing to make almost any sacrifice to maintain the nation—Unionism for them was a matter of faith as well as one of physical well-being. The second group was composed mainly of consistent backers of the Democratic party, also unionists, but placing a condition on their Unionism. They shared a reverence for the nation, but they were equally moved by a determination to maintain their rights and the rights of all southerners. With the Texas Troubles, the rift between these two types of unionists surfaced and did not again submerge until after secession.[28]

For the Austin area counties of Upper South origin, the Texas Troubles had a different meaning. Here Unionism and dis-Unionism of all shades and opinions had long been present. The Texas Troubles reinforced the John Brown syndrome. They suggested that John Brown's raid was not an isolated incident and gave credence to the argument that southerners were not safe in a union with northern abolitionists. Here not only were conditional unionists moved to doubt the value of the Union, but disunionists were given a potent argument for secession.[29]

As the hysteria surrounding the Texas Troubles began to subside, the anti-Breckinridge forces in Texas made a final effort to defeat extremism. At a meeting in Austin in early August, leading supporters of Bell and Douglas promised to vote for whichever candidate, including Breckinridge, stood the best chance of beating Lincoln. The birth of the Fusion party at that particular time and in that particular place signaled two things. First, in the wake of the Texas Troubles the presidential campaign in Texas was undergoing a subtle shift. Prior to August proponents of Douglas, Bell, and Breckinridge had attacked each other vociferously with little apparent thought of the Republican candidate in the North. By August, however, the campaign had shifted focus from intrastate political rivalry to a confrontation between conservative unionists and those less committed to the preservation of the nation. Second, Fusionist appeals based on the preservation of the Union were to have their greatest impact in Upper South counties like those surrounding Austin.[30]

James Newcomb, editor of the San Antonio *Alamo Express*, who took many of his cues from Austin, boldly announced this shift in focus from party politics to preservation of the Union. In the first issue of his paper on 18 August 1860, he declared: "Politically, we are in favor of an opposition to secession and disunion whether headed by Lincoln or Breckinridge. We are for the 'Constitution, the Union and the enforcement of the laws,' a platform broad enough to hold every American citizen within the borders of our great Republic." Although Newcomb's first choice for president was John Bell, he went on to write that he would be more than willing to support fusion. The Union mattered more than politics. The letters from the Union Club in Travis County, the public statements of its representatives, and the speeches of its campaign orators all echoed these sentiments—Union above party.[31]

There was an important difference between those clubs in western cities and those in the east. In traditional two-party counties in eastern Texas, such as Harrison and Galveston counties, the Union Clubs drew almost all their membership from former Whigs and Know-Nothings. In the western regions of Texas and in the Upper South portion of the state, party was supplanted by principle. This was never completely true in the Lower South portion of the state.[32]

North Texas, the other major Upper South region in the state, was an interesting compromise between the two extremes. Here the Democratic party had never been identified with disunion, and party leaders like Charles De Morse prevented Breckinridge from being labeled a secessionist. Nonetheless, Union Clubs were formed in most North Texas counties, and these clubs did manage to attract a number of former Democrats. The issue was not as clear cut here; the election was not perceived entirely as union versus disunion. Still, party lines gave way in many cases to the principle of Unionism.[33]

Election day came with Fusionists making last-minute appeals for the safety and sanctity of the Union. Statewide, these appeals resulted in their ticket receiving little more than 25 percent of the vote. In counties around Austin, however, the ticket received over 37 percent of the vote. North Texas counties, with the notable exception of Dallas and Denton counties (the places where the Texas Troubles originated) also exceeded the statewide average vote for the Fusion ticket. Moreover, compared with previous presidential elections the vote for the non-Democrat increased in Upper South counties. Excluding the frontier, only in those counties did the unionist appeals of the Fusion party have any success. There, a sizable minority of determined unionists were willing to accept a hybrid as strange as the Union electoral ticket rather than risk the disruption of their nation.[34]

When news of Lincoln's election victory arrived in North Texas there was no immediate call for secession except in Dallas, where the Texas Troubles had convinced Charles Pryor, editor of the Dallas *Herald*, of the wickedness of the North. In Red River and Lamar counties on the eastern border of North Texas, Charles De Morse led a faction which gradually came to accept secession, while Ben Epperson led the opposition. Epperson, although born in Mississippi, was educated at Princeton. A former Whig, interested in commercial expansion and government aid to railroads, Epperson had been one of the Fusion party's electors. Like many other former Whigs, Epperson expressed filial devotion to the founding fathers and an intense reverence for the nation. At times during the 1860 campaign, Epperson had been inspired to heights of oratory which had even impressed his opponents, but after the election he was unable to prevent the two counties with which he was most closely associated from condemning northern aggression and moving steadily toward secession.[35]

De Morse was one of the reasons for this failure. A lawyer and prominent member of the Democratic party as well as a journalist, De Morse's newspaper, the Clarksville *Standard*, was one of the oldest, most influential, and well-respected journals in the state. By habit a moderate, De Morse attempted to be impartial and truthful in his reporting, and only in his editorials did he engage in serious political discussion. His *Standard* was indeed the standard by which other Texas newspapers were measured. As late as 20 October 1860, even though he feared Lincoln would be elected, the editor reiterated his love for the Union and his dedication to its preservation. The Union had long been for De Morse the perfect guarantor of public freedom. By 22 December, however, he had joined the call for a convention to determine whether Texas should secede. As a Jacksonian Democrat, De Morse had always put his faith in the sovereign people. He was a nationalist, but he believed equally strongly in individual rights and local autonomy. If the people believed that a convention was needed to discuss the security of their rights within the Union, De Morse argued, then that convention should take place. De Morse was not ready to give up on the Union and hoped that a northern guarantee of the rights of southerners would convince the southern people that secession was unnecessary. Until that time the issue deserved to be discussed in a convention.[36]

In Clarksville resided diminutive models of Henry Clay and Andrew Jackson in a more modern setting. For the Jacksonian Democrat the advance of time was crucial. Sectional tensions had brought to the fore inherent contradictions between nationalism and individualistic democracy. Individual rights, popular rule, and faith in an ongoing nation destined for greatness no longer held together easily and simply. For the disciple of Clay the Union meant much the same thing it always had—devotion to the founding fathers, reverence for the Constitution and the nation, a concern for a stable society, and a desire for steady economic growth. Epperson and De Morse symbolized the dualism of antebellum Upper South politics. In neither man's ideology was slavery an overriding issue. Each accepted slavery, yet neither was moved to defend it with radical actions or words. Slavery was one of many rights to be defended, but for the Massachusetts-born De Morse, the ability of the South to pursue its own course free from northern interference was most important. For Epperson, slavery had to be subordinated to the Union.[37]

Through December of 1860 Epperson and De Morse argued about the need to call a convention to consider the secession question. In other Upper South areas, unionists made the perhaps fatal decision to ignore the debate and hope that with time strong Unionism would return. It did not return that December, and early in January most counties in Texas sent delegations pledged to speed secession to the Secession Convention. Only the delegates from the Upper South counties, where the unionists competed for position, elected uncompromising unionists. Of all the delegates, only those from

Collin, Williamson, Lamar, Titus and Wood counties, all strongly influenced by an Upper South culture, refused to endorse secession.[38]

It is significant, however, that the debate was not finished in the Upper South counties. Opposition to secession remained legitimate until after the 23 February popular referendum. It did so because Unionism was such a vital part of their culture. Moderate Democrats like De Morse might have submerged their Unionism but men like Epperson and Throckmorton had not. The fact that they continued to speak out meant that others who were not as articulate and aggressive had an alternative to secession. They could follow the path of their respected leaders. As always, Unionism was more persistent in the other Texas.

5

Orthodoxy and Ethnicity

Texas society in 1860 was characterized by pluralism. Not only yeomen and mountaineers from the Upper South but also German and Mexican Texans prevented the state from being an homogeneous extension of the Lower South. Political and ideological diversity added to this cultural pluralism. In such a society, diverse attitudes toward the Union persisted even in the face of the drive for orthodox behavior that has typically accompanied a crisis in American life. Yet for both the Germans and the Mexicans their very lack of orthodoxy in a society dominated by white southerners compelled them to act like other Texans. To do otherwise was to risk a repeat of the censure that had often been a part of those groups' assimilation into Texas society. To do otherwise was to impossibly reverse a process that caused all Texans, including Germans and Mexicans, increasingly to behave according to a Lower South model.

Yet Germans and Mexicans retained an ethnic identity in 1860. As in the case of Texans from the Upper South, either their desire for profit or their residence in areas in which the Lower South role model dominated sometimes made Germans and Mexicans act like planters, but, particularly among Mexicans, the appeals of a Lower South culture were limited. The necessity to behave in public like other white southerners was not so limited, and both ethnic groups faced overt and covert discrimination.

In the 1850s, when ethnic Texans moved outside of their homes and isolated communities they were forced to take on the trappings of orthodoxy. Other Texans accepted a degree of individualism. Germans continued to smoke their long-stemmed pipes. Mexicans continued to smoke rolled cigarritos. Opposing the basic values of the society in which they found themselves a minor part, however, was not accepted. Seeming to oppose slavery, for example, was not tolerated.

This process of assimilation, which began as early as 1848, had a cumulative effect. Conforming to orthodoxy meant that gradually, the more the minorities moved in the political, economic, and social world of other Texans, the more Texan and the less German or Mexican they became. Obviously if they still remained isolated from that world in 1861, they reacted to secession in a uniquely ethnic way. The number of Germans and Mexicans, however, who had remained totally unassimilated into a Texas increasingly comprised of cotton growers, slaveowners, and secessionists was much smaller than the myths of the Civil War period have suggested.[1] On the other hand, few members of either ethnic group were completely assimilated or assimilated to the same degree. The net result was that Germans and Mexicans, balancing orthodoxy with ethnicity, became as fragmented as Texans from the Upper South. They accepted secession unenthusiastically after the election of Abraham Lincoln, or they accepted secession only after the referendum of 23 February 1861, or they never accepted secession at all. Neither group acted as a cohesive impediment to the secession movement. Germans and Mexicans acted as they did for special ethnic reasons. In fact, because orthodoxy was demanded of Germans and Mexicans long before secession, their history offers an instructive precedent to the secession crisis, when different forms of intimidation and discrimination would force other recalcitrant Texans to go along with the herd and accept secession.

Texas was the only state in the Gulf South to attract large numbers of German immigrants in the antebellum period. Initial German pioneers came to Texas before annexation. Then, through letters home, immigration company efforts, and travel books about Texas, the region became quite well known in Germany, and in the late 1840s German immigrants began to cluster around earlier German settlements. Steady immigration and clustering continued through the 1850s, and by the end of the decade those who were German-born and their children numbered around 30,000, about 7.5 percent of the free white population.[2]

These numbers are a deceptively low indication of German importance, however, because they do not reveal the concentrated nature and strategic location of the German population. By 1860 two strings of counties, running from Galveston and Matagorda counties to Medina and Gillespie counties, contained almost all of the Germans in Texas. Within these counties were the state's three largest cities, Galveston, Houston, and San Antonio, each of which was one-third German. Concentrated numbers gave Germans political control of some counties and made them vital blocs in others. Their location in the largest cities also gave them influence in these centers of journalism, the arts, trade, commerce, and manufacturing in

Texas. In 1860 the state remained overwhelmingly rural, agrarian, and southern, but where Texans touched a more modern world, they did so in cities heavily influenced by Germans.

These same Germans, however, were changed by their contact with Texans from all regions of the South and, from their arrival in Texas, Germans began a process of assimilation into Texas society. German farmers rapidly adopted the cultivation of southern crops. Germans, too, began to settle in the dispersed fashion common in the South. Still, assimilation was only partial. Within their rural and urban enclaves the immigrants remained relatively unchanged. Germans married other Germans and continued to speak their native tongue. In fact, whenever the state government printed an important public document it was usually printed in both English and German. Germans formed their own Catholic, Lutheran, and Methodist churches; they had German schools and German newspapers. German farmers retained the European habits of locational stability, more intensive farming methods, and greater production per unit of land. In one important area, however, Germans became rapidly assimilated. At least by 1856, some ten years after the founding of major German settlements, the majority of Germans had adopted the primary social and political values of southern whites. With only a few modifications, Germans came to accept a value system based upon liberal capitalism, individual democracy, and slavery.[3]

Germans adapted quickly to Texas-style capitalism, and German-born entrepreneurs and commercial farmers soon became common. In Galveston, talented immigrants like Henry Rosenberg, Ferdinand Flake, and Adolph Flake were among the island's mercantile and political elite by 1860. In San Antonio, William A. Menger and Carl H. Guenther became leaders of the brewing and milling industries. German farmers quickly abandoned semisubsistence farming and began producing goods for market. In fact, by 1852 the leaders of Comal County were calling for a railroad to New Braunfels so that marketing of goods would be easier. Urban craftsmen and workers were also quick to see a need for their products and labor. Both skilled craftsmen and common laborers were in great demand. Moreover, as nineteenth-century Western Europeans, Germans shared common attitudes with Americans toward work and leisure. Newspapers of the day were filled with comments on the German's thriftiness, his ability to work hard, his willingness to sacrifice his present happiness for his future prosperity, and his desire to accumulate worldly goods. Germans did modify the American pattern: they were somewhat more deferential and less concerned with rising in social station, and they were more communal. To a remarkable degree, however, Germans conformed to both the spirit and the form of American capitalism.[4]

German Texans were equally quick to adopt the political values of the dominant culture group. Democratic principles enjoyed widespread popularity among German intellectuals, and in many other ways they shared a common political culture with Americans. Still, especially for German peasant farmers, operating within a working democracy involved many changes. The most important of these was transferring emotional commitment to the United States from their old homeland. In this, most had few difficulties, and at times their devotion to the Union exceeded that of the native-born. George Schneider powerfully summed up his and many other Germans' devotion to the Union when in 1859 he wrote: "We have long sought for the country which guarantees us that full share of political and religious liberty denied to us at home. We found that blessed country in this great Union, and this imposing Confederacy of several states, and we will cling to it forever. Do not talk to us of dissolution of the Union. We do not believe in a Northern and Southern Confederacy, but we do know, that if this Union is dissolved the great bulwark of liberty will be destroyed."[5]

Another obvious change was a willingness both to participate in elections and to abide by their results. By 1856 the proportion of Germans voting equaled that of native-born Americans. In Galveston, where Germans could vote in city elections without being naturalized citizens, Germans voted in large numbers. Even when those elections did not go as they wished, Texas Germans usually accepted their results. In 1861 Ferdinand Flake, Gustav Schleicher, and many Germans who shared their doubts about secession supported the action of their state after the popular referendum on secession.[6]

There were, of course, German modifications to Texas values. Germans operated in groups, societies, and organizations, while other Americans acted as individuals. They had a habit of deference lacking in other Americans. The similarities between German and American-born Texans, however, were more important than the differences. To a degree which has never been clearly recognized, Germans had become Texans by 1861.[7]

Nothing exemplifies this behavioral assimilation more starkly than the attitude of Texas Germans toward slavery. Some Germans opposed slavery, others gave it their tacit approval. Most were, as Frederick Law Olmsted pointed out, indifferent to the institution. By 1859, however, German leaders were going to extreme lengths to make it clear that neither they nor their fellow Germans opposed

slavery. Newspaper editors Ferdinand Flake's and Ferdinand Lindheimer's opinions on slavery were the most visible to other Texans.
Flake, perhaps, had some doubts about the morality of slavery, but
he was one of the few Germans who actually owned a slave. Lindheimer, who was always quite concerned about the Germans' image, tried to explain the Germans attitude toward slavery by publishing an article which read in part: "The majority of the Germans
are not against the institution of slave labor and will support this
institution in every political struggle. The Republicans have, of
course, maintained that the Germans own no slaves, because it is
not morally right. This is not true." The article went on to say that it
was the high cost of slaves, the relative poverty of the Germans, and
the small scale of their farms which made slaveholding uncommon
among Texas Germans. Furthermore, Germans like Lindheimer and
Flake often defended the South and slavery in the same states' rights
terms as their non-German fellow editors. Slavery was the truest test
of orthodoxy in the South. Some Germans, like the 48ers Adolph
Douai and August Semering, did oppose slavery. Most Germans,
however, either were indifferent to slavery or defended southerners'
rights to own slaves.[8]

Such orthodoxy is well illustrated by the comments of other influential editors on the Germans. John Marshall, editor of the *Texas
State Gazette* and the chairman of the state Democratic party, described the Germans as a race with a great desire for liberty. He admitted that there were some language problems, but he insisted that
"their superior adaptation to our institutions now gives to them an
ascendancy over all other citizens of foreign birth, speaking a foreign
language." When surveying the wreckage after Sam Houston defeated the Democracy in the gubernatorial race of 1859, Charles De
Morse of the Clarksville *Standard* took solace in the fact that the
Germans had held firm. They at least had stood by the party. Caleb
Cushing, editor of the Houston *Telegraph*, maintained that although
some Germans criticized slavery, Germans were "peaceful and law
abiding citizens." Both Hamilton Stuart of the Galveston *Civilian*
and Willard Richardson of the Galveston *News* welcomed the Germans and lauded their skill, industry, and sense of order. Germans
were no threat to society.[9]

Mexican Texans, however, were not so easily accepted. Mexicans lacked a common Western European background and homogeneity of values. Instead, Mexicans and Texans of Western European
origin had a long history of animosity. There were some Mexican
families who were exceptions to this rule and had much in common
with other Texans. Their significance was much greater than their

number because they were usually wealthy and politically powerful. Still, most Mexicans not only lived within a distinct cultural environment, they had an almost totally separate value system.

Mexican settlement of Texas existed prior to the onslaught of Anglo-Americans in the 1820s and was confined to the area around San Antonio, a small village in East Texas, and along the Rio Grande. By 1850, however, Texas Mexicans found themselves increasingly surrounded by Americans or, at least in San Antonio, by Germans. By 1850 the total number of Spanish-surnamed individuals in Texas had risen from the level in 1820 of less than 4,000 to 11,212, but this was only about 7 percent of the total free population. In San Antonio, the center of Mexican Texas, there were 1,220 Mexicans in 1860, but there were 1,477 Germans. In fact, as early as 1850 the total number of Germans in the state surpassed the number of Mexicans. Despite this decline in relative importance, the Mexican concentration south of San Antonio made them highly influential in local politics. As in the case of the Germans, the highly decentralized nature of government in antebellum Texas made the Mexicans more influential than a simple numerical count might indicate.[10]

Not unexpectedly, the deluge of American and European settlers on the Mexicans brought about some merging of the three groups. Even before independence, men like Lorenzo de Zavala, Juan Seguín, and José Antonio Navarro came to have more in common with their fellow Texans than the people of Mexico. During the Texas Revolution they fought for Texas and became prominent leaders of the Republic. The protracted military struggle between Texas and Mexico which lasted through the Mexican War, however, cast all Mexicans in a bad light. The distrust bred by constant border troubles, together with the rapacity with which Americans seized land formerly controlled by Mexican families, caused many of the most prominent Mexican Texans, among them Juan Seguín, to leave the state. Along the Rio Grande, designated part of Texas after the war with Mexico, Americans steadily encroached upon land long owned by Mexicans. The old landed families either allied themselves with Americans or were gradually forced across the river. In the period from 1836 to 1860, then, the Mexican upper class either became firmly integrated into Anglo-Texan society or emigrated to Mexico.[11]

This revolution at the top little affected the Mexican caste system. Instead of being basically one large middle class, as were the Germans and Americans, the Mexican was part of either an upper or a lower class. In most parts of Texas it was the poor lower class which was the most visible and certainly the largest. In 1828 a Mexican official reported that the Mexicans in Nacogdoches comprised "what in all countries is called the lowest class—the very poor and the very ignorant." He further observed that they were "the most ignorant of negroes and Indians," thus pointing to the racial basis of the Mexican class system. Large landowners whose families were directly descended from European immigrants and who for over one hundred years had intermarried with others of European lineage were at the pinnacle of the class structure. Merchants, traders, and priests of mixed European and Indian descent sometimes occupied a position between these two groups; just as often they merged into either the upper or lower class. At the bottom were those of mixed descent or of nearly pure Indian blood. The poorer class worked as ranchhands, craftsmen, cartsmen, or as other types of laborers. Oftentimes this class was bound to the landowner by peonage. It was on the whole a highly stratified society.[12]

Like the Germans, the majority of Mexicans in Texas lived according to their own customs. They married among themselves. Their important friendships and group associations were with other Mexican Texans. Since many Mexicans were illiterate, the Spanish-language press and schools were not as important as those of the Germans. The communal life of the Mexican, however, was as pronounced as that of the German. Even itinerant traders and teamsters usually kept San Antonio or a similar community as their home base. Farmers continued to live in town and to walk to their irrigated fields each morning, farming small plots of land and producing crops for their own consumption instead of for market. The Catholic church, with its traditional rituals and festive holidays, added to this sense of community. Thus, not only were the Mexicans separated from white southerners by class differences, but also by cultural differences. Southerners were Protestant, pietist, English-speaking, and highly individualistic. Mexicans were Catholic, ritualistic, Spanish-speaking, and communal.[13]

After the Texas Revolution more Mexicans began to reflect common Texas values, but the differences between the two groups continued to be great. True or not, Mexicans never became noted by other Texans for their diligence, thrift, and sobriety. The work ethic which united the middle class of the Germans and the Americans only estranged these two groups from the majority of Mexicans. Most visitors to San Antonio were struck by the difference between Mexican Texans and other citizens of the state. A German immigrant who fought in the Texas Revoluiton noted that when he visited a Mexican family, "no matter whether we came late in the morning or early in the afternoon, we would usually find all the inmates of the house sitting on the rug which covered the floor of the room." Frederick Law Olmsted, in the mid-1850s, described the Mexicans as lacking in ambition and recounted that "a free-and-easy, loloppy sort of life generally seemed to have been adopted as possessing, on the whole, the greatest advantages for a reasonable being." Olmsted found some of the women charming and alluring, but he was more ambivalent about the men. He reported that "the men lounged in roundabouts and cigarritos as was to be expected, and in fact, the whole picture lacked nothing that is Mexican." Later, though, he noted that "nevertheless, with good stimulus, the men make admirable laborers." This image of the Mexican as lazy, happy, carefree, and given to work only when well stimulated was echoed later in the decade by the *Texas State Gazette*. It was reported in the pages of this newspaper that the Mexican "lies down with the declining sun to smoke a cigarrito and he joins the mirthful throng of the fandango, or he retires to the more exciting pleasures of the monte table."[14]

In the minds of many non-Tejanos, however, what really set Mexicans apart was that they seemed to oppose slavery. Many counties organized vigilante groups to prevent them from harboring runaway slaves. Other counties forced Mexican Texans to carry passports, showing that they were law-abiding citizens of the state. Olmsted reported in the 1850s that the Mexicans "regard slavery with abhorrence," and that "they are regarded by slaveholders with great contempt and suspicion, for their intimacy with slaves and their competition with plantation labor." It was true that in the 1820s revolutionary idealists had opposed the introduction of slavery into Texas and until the Texas Revolution had worked toward its elimination. Mexican leaders educated in the tradition of the French Revolution were, however, quite different from the people who made up the bulk of the Texas Mexican population. In fact, upper-class leaders who did remain in the state after 1836 often owned a few slaves, or at least supported slavery. Slavery, though, was almost impossible to practice near the border because the slaves would escape across the river. It seems, too, that Mexicans were much more willing to accept Negroes as equals than were other Texans. It would be difficult, however, to characterize Tejanos as being profoundly opposed to slavery. Slavery had no real importance in their lives, and like the Germans, most Mexicans were more concerned with their own existence than they were with the abolition of slavery.[15]

Mexicans' sociability with black slaves, together with their brown skin and their different habits, led many Texans to regard the Tejano as a racially inferior being. They regarded the brown man much as they regarded the black and red man. This color prejudice was further abetted by the mixture of Negro, Indian, and Spanish blood in many Mexicans. Texans often referred to Texas Mexicans as a mongrel Spanish-Indian and Negro race. Even German observers like Ferdinand Roemer and Prince Carl von Solms-Braunfels viewed Mexicans as a mongrel race in which the bad characteristics of their mixed parentage tended to predominate. Color questions also plagued lawmakers. In the Constitutional Convention of 1845 delegates decided that the word "white" should not be used to define qualification for suffrage because that might exclude the Mexican from voting. This incident highlights two things: first, some Texans of North American lineage did indeed have a conception of Mexicans as nonwhite; second, they nonetheless went out of their way to guarantee Mexicans the right to vote.[16]

Like Germans, Mexicans voted in large numbers, and it was in the areas of voter participation and political values that Mexicans were most like other Texans. Anglo-American democracy was not a part of the Mexican's cultural heritage. Under Spain and Mexico the government had usually been highly centralized and local matters had been controlled by the upper class. Because of this lack of experience and their high rate of illiteracy, Mexican voters were often manipulated during antebellum times. Both Mexican leaders and American-born politicians used Mexican voters to rule local politics. Still, during the years leading to secession, Mexicans made efforts to vote independently and expressed pride in the free institutions of democratic government. *El Bejareno*, a Spanish-language newspaper in San Antonio, was a leading force behind the political assimilation of the Mexican. Its editors hoped that through education and increased knowledge all Mexicans would soon become "worthy of belonging in a free country." Another Spanish-language newspaper in San Antonio, *El Ranchero*, led the fight against the Know-Nothings in that city. Urging Mexicans to "open their eyes," J. A. Quintero, the editor of *El Ranchero*, helped form a coalition of Mexicans, Germans, and Democrats which soundly defeated the Know-Nothings at the polls. This incident served notice to all that the Mexican voter was a force to be reckoned with in state politics.[17]

Despite this increase in political awareness, Mexicans never exhibited the emotional attachment to the Union common to Americans and Germans, and this was to have a most telling effect upon their attitude toward secession. This dearth of Unionism or even nationalism was a complex phenomenon whose most obvious roots lay in the antipathy for the U.S. government which many Mexicans still held as a result of the Mexican War, in the locational stability and isolation of the Mexican population, in the absence of familial or philosophical ties to the rest of the nation, and in the traditional nature of the Mexican communities. Many Mexicans who resided in the disputed region between the Nueces River and the Rio Grande, among them Juan Cortina, had fought for Mexico during the Mexican War. Others, like Juan Seguín, resented the annexation of Texas and the expansion of the United States. Still others had been ill treated by U.S. soldiers. All of this left many Mexicans bitter. After the war, however, most Mexicans elected to remain in their traditional homeland, and thus continued the striking characteristic of locational stability. In 1860 many Mexican Texans still lived within a few miles of where their parents and grandparents lived. They did not have to develop an attachment to the region in which they lived; they were born with it. Furthermore, since they usually lived out their lives in one area, and that an isolated area, they had very little direct contact with the rest of the United States. Locational stability and isolation made it difficult for the Texas Mexican to assign any significance to the nation.

This lack of commitment to the Union was reinforced by the absence of familial or philosophical ties to the rest of the United States. Mexican families were concentrated in one area, not scattered across the United States, as was often the case with Anglo-Americans. There was no son, father, brother, mother, sister, or daughter to write of events in another state or region. Nor was there a philosophical adherence to the idea of national unity. Mexicans had neither the German idealists' conception of creating a great nation, nor the American expansionists' concept of extending and building a great domain, nor the classical conservatives' notion of defending and preserving the nation. Instead, the focus of the Mexican people was on their community. These communities were not integrated into the national economy by communication or transportation innovations, nor were they directly influenced by market forces. Their economy, based upon ranching, semisubsistence agriculture, and commerce, connected with the national economy only on the borders of Mexican Texas, and then in a manner almost imperceivable to most Mexicans. Within these communities life followed a traditional pattern; events were significant only within a local context. Isolated by distance, language, and custom, lacking ties to the rest of the United States, indeed often harboring resentment toward that government, and following a pattern of life largely independent of the outside world, Mexicans attached slight importance to a Union which had so little value in their daily lives.[18]

Mexican communities were different from the other scattered communities of nineteenth-century America. They were isolated not only by the lack of transportation and communication innovations, but by distance, language, and custom. They were more traditional—that is, their members were not highly individualistic or capitalistic. Furthermore, these communities were dominated by an aristocracy whose position rested upon a fixed racial caste system. It was the gentry and their American replacements at the pinnacle of this caste system that took the lead in politics.[19] Ultimately, it was this upper class that played the decisive role in determining the attitude of all Mexicans toward secession.

The most prominent Mexicans in antebellum Texas were all descendants of old and distinguished families of European lineage. José Antonio Navarro, Santos Benavides, and Juan Cortina were all members of these upper-class families. Navarro was the most distinguished Texas Mexican of his day. Active in the revolution against Spain and a close friend of Stephen F. Austin, he had long defended the rights of Texans before the Mexican government. Later he was one of the signers of the Texas Declaration of Independence and was the only Mexican who took part in the Constitutional Convention of 1845. Throughout antebellum statehood he served as a state senator or representative. At the same time he devoted himself to his extensive ranching and commercial interests as well as to practicing law. In 1861 he supported his third revolution, and four of his sons fought in the Confederate army. Santos Benavides, born in 1827, was descended from the founding families of Laredo. In 1842 he was appointed a city official of Laredo by the Mexican government. After the Mexican War firmly established the Laredo area as part of Texas, Benavides served as mayor of Laredo and chief justice of Webb County. While advancing politically, Benavides also advanced economically and by 1861 was one of the wealthiest merchants and ranchers in Texas. When war broke out, as Rip Ford put it, "The Benavides family did the Confederacy a great favor by declaring for her." Juan Cortina, scion of one of the leading families in the lower Rio Grande Valley, was a prominent political leader in the Brownsville area during the 1850s. In 1859, however, angered by American encroachment on his family's land and prerogatives, he seized the city of Brownsville. After being driven out of Texas, Cortina and his followers espoused the Union cause in 1861 and contested Benavides's control of the Rio Grande Valley.[20]

These three men set the pattern for other members of the gentry. All considered themselves Texans. Like the lower-class Mexicans, they had a deep commitment to the land in which they were born. Navarro and Benavides were accepted and respected by Texans of all origins. Moreover, they shared common values with Anglo-

Texans. Navarro had defended the Texas colonists' rights to hold slaves while Texas was still a part of Mexico. Benavides had consistently aided planters in the recovery of runaway slaves. Both men were wealthy and industrious capitalists. Both men could be classified as part of the ruling order. It was to be expected, then, that in 1861 they would support their state. This support was made all the easier because they, like other Mexicans, had few reasons to value the Union. Cortina, on the other hand, had failed to become a permanent member of the establishment. Brownsville in 1861 was dominated by his antagonists Adolphus Glavecke and Charles Stillwell. When the Civil War came he supported the Union cause not out of love for the Union but out of expediency. It offered him an opportunity to strike at his enemies in Texas. Among members of the upper class the level of assimilation, the acceptance or rejection of their position in society by other Texans, the depth of their feeling for Texas, and their prewar animosities and friendships were to be the important determinants of their position on secession.[21]

No single event did more to establish the prewar animosities and friendships among Mexicans, Germans, and Americans than the Know-Nothing movement of the mid-1850s, and nothing gave the ethnic minorities of Texas as unique an attitude toward secession as this political upheaval. Nativist planks of the Know-Nothing platform—the moves to extend the naturalization period, limit the suffrage of the foreigners, and regulate morality—struck directly at the Mexicans and Germans. As a result of the Know-Nothing movement, not only did Germans and Mexicans regard all former Know-Nothings with lingering hostility, but they developed long-lasting ties to the Democratic party that defended their rights. Under attack, these foreign-language groups became more cohesive and politicized. Perhaps most important, Germans and Mexicans learned the value of conformity on the basic issue of slavery.[22]

It was the German and Mexican presses that led their ethnic groups in the fight against the Know-Nothings. In the San Antonio and Austin area, the *Neu Braunfelser Zeitung, El Bejareno*, and *El Ranchero* were the most prominent foreign-language papers. The Galveston *Zeitung* was important near the Gulf Coast. A major goal of all these papers was group unity. They argued that Mexicans and Germans should vote en masse against the Know-Nothings. The editors of *El Bejareno* urged Mexicans not to be deluded by the words of the Know-Nothings, for that would be "an act of treason against you, your families, your religion, your land." When J. A. Quintero, the editor of *El Ranchero*, was assaulted in 1856 by a group of Know-Nothings, his paper proclaimed to his Mexican readers that the indignities he suffered "because he defended your rights and has the same origin prove to all what we will suffer if we lose this election." Editor Lindheimer worked equally hard to unite the Germans in opposition to the Know-Nothings and to defend Germans against the accusations that they were all abolitionists.[23]

Ironically, much of the Know-Nothing furor in Texas sprang from the actions of a German editor. Know-Nothingism was imported into Texas from other states in the Union, but it gained its initial strength in the state by capitalizing on the abolitionist proclivities of Adoph Douai, editor of the San Antonio *Zeitung*. Douai's career as an abolitionist in Texas started innocently enough with a convention of German singing societies in San Antonio in 1854. Following the lead of the *Freier Mann Verein*, organized by fellow Germans in northern states, these Germans adopted a platform which they hoped could be enacted in Texas. Among their reforms was a mildly worded plank which favored the gradual removal of slavery from Texas. Alarmed by this feature of the platform, Know-Nothings, as well as many Democrats, raised an immediate hue and cry against all Germans. Lindheimer and other conservative Germans quickly came out in opposition to the San Antonio convention and argued that the members of the convention were an unrepresentative minority of the state's German population. The situation probably would have quickly blown over if Douai had not taken an ever more strident stand against slavery in his newspaper. German readers and advertisers, however, withdrew their backing from the San Antonio *Zeitung*, and despite economic support from Frederick Law Olmsted, Douai was forced to sell his paper. Soon thereafter he left Texas for New York. The storm he did so much to foment remained, and from that time onward Lindheimer and others went to great lengths to prove that Germans were sound on the slavery issue.[24]

Douai's counterpart on the extreme right was M. Buechner, editor of the Galveston *Zeitung*. He and some Germans who regularly wrote for his editorial page advocated the organization of Germans in each community into paramilitary societies which would defend German rights and preserve German culture. Most Germans, though, found the Prussian editor's measures too extreme for their tastes. Instead, Germans and Mexicans were content to use more peaceful and orthodox means to defeat the Know-Nothings.[25]

Ballots became the primary tool of the non-English-speaking citizens. The Democratic party, reacting to the competition of the Know-Nothings, became an effective defender of Texas Mexicans and Germans. Once assured that neither group really threatened the stability of the state, Democratic editors became ardent champions of the ethnic minorities. Encouraged by this show of support, Germans in La Grange formed a "Social Democratic Society" which hoped "to unite the German population as a body, encourage and assist the more ignorant and indifferent of their countrymen to become citizens of the United States, and use all means, as a political body, to defend and uphold Democratic principles." Led by their newspapers, Mexicans and Germans in San Antonio also formed Democratic clubs. Across the state Germans and Mexicans followed suit, and in the elections of 1855 and 1856 they played an important role in the defeat of the Know-Nothings.[26]

In some cases Germans and Mexicans went beyond electoral sanctions and imposed economic sanctions on Know-Nothings. When the La Grange *Paper* was purchased and converted into the Know-Nothing *True Issue*, German subscribers and advertisers immediately withdrew their support and vowed to start a rival sheet to drive the *True Issue* out of business.[27]

Know-Nothings were equally adept at economic boycotts and other forms of intimidation. In Galveston, the competition of German craftsmen induced many native-born workers to support the Know-Nothings and led to an effort on their part to prevent the hiring of German workers. Mexican cartsmen who hauled goods from the coast to San Antonio were also singled out because of their economic threat to Anglo-Texans. The so-called "Cart War" was the most violent episode of the nativist movement. Several cartsmen were murdered. Others had their carts destroyed, or their lives and property threatened. Such incidents as the "Cart War" and the trouble at Galveston reinforced the Germans' and Mexicans' ties to the Democratic party because that party and its leaders, like Governor E. M. Pease, did the most to put an end to persecution of Germans and Mexicans. These incidents reinforced, too, the bitter resentment Germans and Mexicans felt toward the Know-Nothings. Even after the Know-Nothing party was effectively dead the taint of Know-Nothingism marked certain prominent Texas politicians in the eyes of Germans and Mexicans. Long after the elections of 1855 and 1856 Germans and Mexicans voted for the Democratic party out of loyalty to the party that had defended their personal freedom. Their slogan, like that of J. A. Quintero, editor of *El Ranchero*, became "The Democracy now, the Democracy later, the Democracy always!"[28]

After 1857 the relatively high degree of political unity spawned in reaction to Know-Nothingism began to diminish. Ethnic voters continued to be loyal to the Democratic party, but the party itself had split into two factions. As these factions contended for elected positions from 1858 to 1861, German and Mexican voters were attracted to both sides. By 1861 firm political divisions existed within the German and Mexican communities. German vociferously opposed German; Mexican contended with Mexican. In so doing they formed political ties that cut across ethnic, racial, or religious bounds, and they developed among themselves well-defined political groups which almost by habit opposed each other and supported other Texans. These ties that cut across ethnic bounds would make acceptance of secession easier.

In the 1859 gubernatorial race three distinct groups began to emerge among the Germans. In that year Sam Houston disavowed the Know-Nothing party, and one group of Germans, led by Ferdinand Flake and Gustav Schleicher, backed Houston because of his strong stand in opposition to reopening the slave trade and in support of the Union. In the middle were Germans who were angered by incumbent Hardin Runnels's failure to protect the frontier from Indian attack and his radical southern views, but who still had a difficult time choosing between the two candidates. Other Germans, like Ferdinand Lindheimer, could not forgive Houston for his Know-Nothingism and were reluctant to abandon the Democratic party.[29]

Election results, in general, indicated that Germans agreed that Runnels deserved their support because he had staunchly opposed Know-Nothingism and was the nominee of the Democratic party. For frontier Germans, however, neither candidate proved attractive. The voting in these counties was much lower in 1859 than in past and future elections, and each candidate received almost an equal share of the vote. In more settled and populous German regions, though, voters continued to favor Runnels.

Houston's strength in German counties was greater, however, than might have been expected. Only in Comal County, the home of Lindheimer and the *Neu Braunfelser Zeitung*, was he overwhelmingly defeated. In fact, in comparison with Edward Clark, his running mate for lieutenant governor, Houston did quite well in German counties. Clark had been a prominent and highly visible Know-Nothing, and he did not go to such great pains as Houston to disavow any lingering Know-Nothingism. His opponent, Francis R. Lubbock, on the other hand, was a great friend of the Germans. They responded by voting for him in overwhelming numbers in 1859. In Gillespie County Lubbock won by a margin of 174 to 44 votes. In Comal County he received 359 votes to Clark's 28. In every German county Houston's vote was greater than Clark's, and Lubbock's vote was greater than Runnels's. As Lubbock wrote later, many of the citizens of these counties "knew of my active canvass against the Know-Nothings, and they appeared to appreciate the stand I had taken against that secret society." If a candidate could be clearly identified as a Know-Nothing, it still made a difference in 1859. Houston, however, had been fairly successful in muffling his brief association with the Know-Nothings and was able to attract a sizable minority of the German vote.[30]

When Know-Nothingism began to fade from the political picture, Mexican voters also lost their unanimity. In 1858 José A. Navarro was a distinguished member of the Democratic party's state convention. In 1859 his son, Angel Navarro, strayed from the Democratic fold and ran for state representative on the Union Democratic ticket with his father's old friend Sam Houston. Also on the ticket were Gustav Schleicher, who sought a position in the state senate, and Samuel A. Maverick, Jacob Waelder, and L. B. Camp, each seeking one of the state representative positions in Bexar County. The journalistic mouthpiece for this group was the San Antonio *Herald*, a former Know-Nothing paper which attempted to reverse its field and become the representative of all unionists—Germans, Mexicans, and Americans alike. Its editor even accused the Democracy of being composed of "closet nativists" when it excluded Mexican delegates from its convention. With the support of the *Herald*, the blunders of the Democrats, and the well-known names of Houston, Maverick, Navarro, and Schleicher, the "Union Democrats" appealed to the widest possible cross section of the voters of Bexar County, and their candidates led county-wide voting in each race.[31]

Sam Houston's brief affiliation with the Know-Nothings seems to have done him little harm in the eyes of the Mexican voters. He had many good friends in San Antonio, among them the Rodríguez, Navarro, and Menchaca families, and their support of the Opposition undoubtedly did much to ensure the defeat in Bexar County of Hardin Runnels and the other nominees of the Democratic party. In the other Mexican counties he carried, Houston repeatedly outpolled Clark, testifying to Houston's personal appeal and the distaste that Mexican voters still retained for the Know-Nothings. In the Lower Rio Grande Valley, however, the Democratic machine had been churning out victories since 1854, and the gubernatorial race of 1859 was no exception to this trend. In an area where there was already a long history of voter control and manipulation, Houston was beaten by sizable majorities. In Zapata and Hidalgo counties the machine organization was particularly thorough, defeating both Houston and Clark by exactly the same counts of 42 to 130 in Zapata County and 3 to 227 in Hidalgo County. These were the only two counties in Texas in which the tallies in both the governor's and lieutenant governor's race were identical. In Mexican counties lacking any articulate expression of opinion, it is difficult to determine whether voters supported Houston because of his personal magnetism or because of his support of the Union and opposition to the slave trade. Given the lack of strong support for the Union by the Mexicans in other elections, however, it seems safe to assume that it was the attraction of Houston's personality and his friendship with prominent Mexicans that won him most of the votes he received from the Mexican citizens of Texas.[32]

With the close of the state elections in August of 1859, ethnic Texans, like most Texans, undoubtedly looked forward to a respite from politics. Such was not to be the case; in retrospect, 1859 was only the beginning of an extended period of political turmoil. In the fall of that year all Texans were shocked by John Brown's raid at Harpers Ferry. Even the unionist Ferdinand Flake admitted that "the conspiracy against the life and property of the white residents of the South was spread throughout the North."[33] At about the same time Texans were shocked by a raid much closer to home, a raid that cast all Mexicans in a bad light and contributed to their estrangement from the rest of society.

In September of 1859, claiming to be a Texas citizen defending the rights of Mexican Texans, Juan N. Cortina and his followers seized the border city of Brownsville. Born in 1824 into one of the leading families of the Lower Rio Grande Valley, Cortina emerged in the 1850s as a popular leader of Mexicans on both sides of the river. Capable of delivering large blocs of votes, Cortina secured the election of many of his friends and family to office. By 1859, however, he was losing ground to the political faction headed by Adolphus Glavecke and was becoming increasingly irritated with American treatment of Mexicans, in particular the Americans' use of the law to expropriate the Mexicans' land. After a shooting incident with the Brownsville marshal in July, Cortina and his men seized the city of Brownsville on 28 September. He soon left the city and returned to his ranch, where he repelled attacks by unorganized Brownsville citizens and Texas Rangers. Eventually, Texas forces under Rip Ford and the U.S. Army under Major S. P. Heintzelman forced Cortina to retreat into Mexico. Colonel Robert E. Lee, just back from Virginia, where he had led the forces that captured John Brown, then took command in the Valley and effectively ended the "Cortina Wars."[34]

Up until Cortina's raid on Brownsville, relations between Germans and Mexicans had been cordial. They had fought the Know-Nothings together, and Germans had generally tried to defend Mexican Texans' rights. Cortina's raid strained but did not sever these bonds. Editor Lindheimer, the spokesman for stability and conservatism among the Germans, was careful to distinguish between "hostile Mexicans" on the border and other Mexican Texans. He tried to wait until all the evidence was in before passing judgment on Cortina, and he suggested that events had been magnified out of proportion. The editor was particularly disturbed by a letter written to the New York *Democrat* by a German who sounded suspiciously like Adolph Douai, the former editor of the San Antonio *Zeitung*. Lindheimer denied that the Cortina incident had been prompted by the Mexicans' opposition to slavery and accused the letter's author of trying to divert German immigrants from Texas and of having "hostile intentions" toward the state. As in the case of John Brown, Germans consistently held to a moderate point of view and discouraged extremism.

Mexican Texans' reaction to Cortina was mixed, but most in the Rio Grande Valley seemed to believe that Cortina was indeed fighting in defense of Mexican rights as United States citizens. Major Heintzelman, who commanded U.S. forces in the Valley, reported that in Matamoros, across the border from Brownsville, Cortina "was received as the champion of his race—as the man who would right the wrongs the Mexicans had received." Cortina and his followers consistently maintained that all they wanted was "legal protection of the Mexicans in Texas," and they appealed to newly elected Governor Sam Houston for this protection.[35]

Not all Mexicans, however, supported the "Robin Hood of the Rio Grande." Mexican troops from neighboring Matamoros dispatched by Mexican officials of that city together with Texas Mexican volunteers fought against Cortina. Mexican friends of Cortina's enemy Adophus Glavecke condemned Cortina's actions. Perhaps most important, prominent landowners like Francisco Yturria publicly denounced Cortina. Yet as long as Cortina portrayed himself as the defender of Mexican rights and privileges, he retained the support of the majority of his people.[36]

Soon after peace was restored to the Rio Grande Valley, the presidential campaign of 1860 got under way. As in 1859, the German community failed to unite behind any one candidate, but, unlike 1859, Mexicans lent their support to a single candidate—John C. Breckinridge, the nominee backed by the Texas Democratic party.

Once again the leaders of the two opposing factions within the German community were the journalists Lindheimer and Flake. Gustav Schleicher, who had begun a long career in politics before the war, also played a prominent role. These three men and most Germans were confirmed unionists in January of 1860. Lindheimer spoke for all Germans when he declared an abhorrence for the idea of dividing the Union and urged caution and moderation. At that point even a confirmed Democrat like Lindheimer was willing to give whoever was elected president a chance to prove what he would do in office. Beyond this common belief in the value of the Union, however, there were a number of serious disagreements between factions within the German community.

Defining the true nature of the Democracy was at the base of many of these disagreements. For Lindheimer, party discipline, party unity, and support of the convention's nominee were important. Flake and Schleicher were not so sure that being a Democrat involved supporting the state Democratic convention or the national Democratic convention's nominee. Schleicher had been elected to office in 1859 as a Union Democrat and his name had appeared on the same ticket with Sam Houston and A. J. Hamilton. Flake had been among the most prominent of Houston's supporters. Yet each man considered himself a Democrat. All three editors supported the party's defense of personal liberty and the other tenets of the Democratic party as stated in the 1856 Cincinnati platform. What divided them was their commitment to the convention system, their commitment to the Union, and the clash of personalities with other Texas Democrats.[37]

Much to the disappointment of Germans who followed politics, the Democratic conventioneers in 1860 at Charleston were not able to find the common ground of the Cincinnati convention. Germans observed with dismay as southern Democrats, with the Texas delegation prominent among them, walked out of the convention. Most Germans hoped with Lindheimer that when the Democrats again tried to hold a convention in May of 1860 that an "eleventh hour" compromise could be worked out.[38]

When such a compromise did not occur, Lindheimer quickly pledged support of John C. Breckinridge, and Flake promoted Stephen A. Douglas. Schleicher, however, became a major leader in the effort to form a Fusion ticket of John Bell and Douglas supporters. These three editors clearly reflected the division within the German community. Those equally committed to the Union and the National Democratic party joined Flake in support of Douglas. Those who placed the Texas Democratic party and southern rights ahead of the Union joined Lindheimer in support of Breckinridge. A third group, eager to compromise in order to save the Union, followed the example of Schleicher and backed the Fusion ticket.[39]

While the Germans were divided on which presidential candidate to support and while the intensity of their support for the Union varied, all Germans displayed a sincere commitment to the

Union throughout the presidential election of 1860. A Breckinridge supporter was not necessarily a disunionist, as Lindheimer proved. He voiced support for the Union during the entire campaign and as late as October 1860 retained some optimism about the future of the Union. As he said, "We have Union men and Disunion men in both parties, it is, meanwhile, certainly not so far advanced that Disunionists can count on success and the destruction of the Union." Earlier in the campaign he had made it clear that slavery was not worth the disruption of the Union. As he saw it, if slavery was an evil, "then it is in any case a very old evil that can only be cured little by little, like a chronic illness, and not merely by a sudden crisis as with an acute disease." Always conservative, Lindheimer urged both sides to examine the value of the Union before destroying it for some other cause.[40]

Schleicher, like Lindheimer, was an advocate of moderation, and believed that most Germans who had witnessed the plight of various German states placed a high value on the American political system. He summed up his views when he wrote: "Even the active revolutionary from Europe, becomes in America, conservative; and will think twice ere he lends his aid to the subversion of a political fabric which has so signally proved its practical value."[41]

Flake was the most confirmed unionist and nationalist of the three German editors, and still he defended southern rights; he had a southern point of view. He argued in favor of the Fugitive Slave Law, condemned John Brown's raid, and abhorred the Republican party. Yet he insisted that Germans "view themselves not as citizens of Texas, Louisiana or any separate state, but as citizens of the entire Union." He tried to balance his nationalism with his southern point of view and insisted that Germans should be "neither southern nor northern." The tragedy of Flake's situation was that such neutrality would soon be impossible.[42]

In the midst of the election, all three editors were diverted from politics by the Texas Troubles which, as in the case of other southerners, contributed to the radicalization of German attitudes toward secession and the Union. From May until August, when the excitement over the conflagrations was greatest, Flake tried to downplay the sensationalism that placed an abolitionist behind every tree. He admitted that abolitionists were responsible for some of the fires but urged caution and moderation. Lindheimer at first shared Flake's temperate stand, but by August he believed abolitionists were at work in his own county. Once again the German editors, the weathervanes of German public opinion, reacted in a fashion similar to other Texas editors, and agreed that abolitionists caused the fires. Yet even then they remained more moderate than most Texas editors. By August, however, Lindheimer's moderation had begun to evaporate. He, like many other southerners, began to question the value of a union with aggressive opponents of the southern way of life.[43]

On the opposite end of the political spectrum from Lindheimer, frontier German unionists and opponents of slavery were also moving toward a more radical position. Frontier Germans were relatively isolated from the influence of other Texans. Gillespie County, for example, had been a German outpost on the frontier since the 1840s, and in 1861 it still retained many of its original characteristics. Not until the late 1850s did a significant number of non-Germans settle in the area. Even then southern influence was small; slavery was almost unknown. The army stationed at nearby Fort Mason and Fort Martin Scott dominated the semisubsistence agrarian economy of the region. It supplied a market for agricultural products and a source of jobs. The army, too, provided protection from Indian attack. The frontier also was the home of a group of highly articulate Germans who opposed slavery and were staunch nationalists. Hermann Speiss, for example, wrote this to his sister in Germany at the close of the 1860 presidential election: "The issue of the whole election, in essence, is *for* or *against* slavery. Lincoln is the candidate of freedom—of the north, so-to-say. Here in the whole of Texas not one could vote for him, such is the terrorism. Naturally the whole riff-raff of Germans in Texas, led by a few corrupt office hunters, is on the side of the meanness. Your brother was with no more than six or eight outstanding Germans in the extreme opposition, of course." As the secession crisis grew in intensity these few men to which Speiss referred, together with a larger number of Douglas supporters who also disliked slavery, were more reluctant than ever to leave the Union and perhaps fight a war in order to preserve the South's peculiar institution. For these three sets of reasons—the isolation and concomitant low degree of assimilation into Texas society of frontier Germans, the significance of the U.S. Army in the region, and the force of articulate and influential unionists—frontier German counties began to take a stronger stand in favor of the Union.[44]

Unionism led some Germans on the frontier to favor the Fusion ticket, but even on the frontier this ticket never attracted overwhelming support among the Germans. Fusion suffered from the diverse background of its supporters. While they might have been staunch unionists, many were former Know-Nothings. Others were Sam Houston men who followed his lead into the ranks of the Fusionists. Still others were Douglas Democrats who sacrificed an independent ticket for an opportunity to defeat Lincoln. Flake made an unenthusiastic attempt to support the Fusion party in the fall of 1860, but by 6 November he was despondent about the election's outcome. As he put it: "Everyone knows that Breckinridge will have the majority of the vote. Douglas people are indifferent because they cannot gain support for their opinions at the ballot box. A great number of these same people prefer absolutely not to vote—Houston is not palatable to them. Then the universal fear, that Lincoln will be the choice of the people is not encouraging for Southern men of all parties."[45]

Flake's predictions were right. The state voted overwhelmingly for Breckinridge, and in German counties in particular the choice between radical southern Democrats and the Fusion ticket led many simply not to vote. Lindheimer was angered by the poor voter turnout and condemned the Germans for their political apathy. He compared them unfavorably with the Americans who never let their votes go uncounted. Flake, however, spoke for many Germans when he announced that he had declined to vote because in the end he could stomach neither candidate. It was not apathy, it was the "unnatural alliance with the Bell people" and the radicalism of the Breckinridge Democrats that kept Germans at home on election day.[46]

Like the Germans, the Mexicans' approach to the 1860 presidential election was a mixture of apathy and enthusiasm. In San Antonio, the Fusion ticket got a late start, but it did attract substantial Mexican support. A political club which supported the Union and the Fusion ticket was organized on 11 September 1860. Among its members were Angel Navarro, Nepo Flores, Juan N. Seguín, Antonio Menchaca, A. M. Ruis, and R. Quintana. Francisco Ruis, commonly called Pancho, was one of the club's officers. This Union Club was in effect the old Union Democratic organization which had been so successful in 1859. The San Antonio *Herald*, however, refused to support the Fusion party. The editors had at first endorsed Sam Houston for president, but after Houston was denied the nomination by the Constitutional Union party, they supported Breckinridge. Houston, in fact, was the key to the political actions of Mexicans in San Antonio. All the Mexican members of the Union Club came from old families with close ties to General Houston. All worked hardest for the Fusion ticket when Houston came down to speak on its behalf. Without Houston's presence on the ballot or on the speaker's podium, Mexican support for the Fusion ticket lagged. Editor James P. Newcomb of the *Alamo Express* tried to combat both this lack of personal interest in the election and the growing radicalism of the *Herald*. Newcomb declared that the presidential election was a referendum on secession and urged "every good citizen to stand by the flag of his country, the Union and the Constitution." Such strident calls for action failed to move the voters, and most San Antonians either stayed at home or voted for Breckinridge on election day.[47]

In South Texas, Mexican Texans showed even less enthusiasm for the election than in San Antonio. In Nueces County, the region's major newspaper, the Corpus Christi *Ranchero*, echoed the *Herald* in support of Breckinridge. Although it ridiculed the Knights of the Golden Circle and called for the South to solve its problems within the Union, the *Ranchero* also argued that the South should unite behind Breckinridge to prove to the North the unanimity of southern resistance to northern aggression. Here, as in Hidalgo and Cameron counties, the Fusion party never developed an effective organization. Lacking competition to stir the political fires, the three-county area continued to focus on Cortina and the possibility of his recrossing the Rio Grande. Only Starr County, of all the counties near the border, developed a Union Club similar to that in San Antonio. In every other county in South Texas the pattern of Nueces and Cameron counties was repeated. Lacking competition or the perception of a personal stake in the election, South Texans approached the election with a noticeable lack of enthusiasm.

The ineffectiveness of the organized opposition to Breckinridge and the dearth of interest in the campaign in Mexican counties were reflected in the almost complete triumph of the Democratic party in those counties and the consistently low voter turnout. Bexar County's voters cast 986 votes for Breckinridge and only 293 votes for the Fusion ticket; in the Rio Grande Valley Breckinridge won by an even greater margin. Starr County, thanks to the work of its Union Club, was an exception to the rule and gave the Fusion ticket 106 votes to only 40 for Breckinridge. Here, though, voter turnout was only 56 percent of what it had been in 1859. Voter turnout in other Mexican counties did not drop so drastically, but in almost every case it was substantially lower than in 1859. Thus, in county after county the Democracy won by large margins, and many voters stayed at home.[48]

Germans stayed home because they did not like either candidate or because they thought that Breckinridge would win regardless of what they did. Mexicans did not vote because of their isolation from the rest of the United States, the distraction of local affairs, the lack of competition between parties in their counties, and the absence of either a strong motivating issue such as nativism or a compelling personality like Sam Houston. This absence of motivation exemplifies one of the most striking differences between Germans and Mexicans. Those Germans who did become involved in politics in 1860 usually did so either to preserve or perfect the Union. Many who opposed Breckinridge did so because they perceived him as a threat to the nation. Those who supported Breckinridge believed northern aggressors threatened the stability of the nation, and that only through northern acquiescence to southern demands could the nation and the relationship between North and South be improved. This concern with the idea of union was almost totally absent among Mexicans.[49]

With the news of Lincoln's election in November 1860, there came a pause for reflection on the future. A disinterested observer would have realized that for the Germans and Mexicans of Texas in particular, secession could not be divorced from the preceding weeks, months, and years. Many Mexicans and Germans were uninformed and apathetic, isolated by language, custom, culture, distance, and in the case of some Mexicans, caste. Secession was but another dimly perceived event for these members of the body politic. They would follow the lead of prominent individuals or act according to their particular local situation. For a variety of reasons, however, the politicized among them were to assume conflicting positions on secession. To be politicized was to be at least in some way assimilated—to be familiar with American politics and to know the implications of Lincoln's election. While existing within their own cultures Germans and Mexicans to varying degrees shared the values of Texans, southerners, or citizens of the United States. The extent of assimilation into a larger culture was the critical determinant of the Mexicans' and Germans' attitudes toward secession. Still, as for all Texans, local conditions and cultural considerations were also to play important roles. Dependence on U.S. troops and isolation from the rest of Texas encouraged an ethnocentrism which helped form unique conceptions of the value and purpose of secession and the Union. Ethnic animosities and political friendships also made their attitudes unique. By November of 1860, German had opposed German in political campaign after campaign. Mexican had fought Mexican with guns instead of ballots. Both had united against the nativist movement. It was difficult for the allies and foes of these wars not to remain allies and foes during the secession crisis. A foe could become a friend, however, if personal philosophies meshed on current issues—if there was a shared conception of the value of the Union or the threat of northern aggression.

By the end of November and the beginning of the drive to take Texas out of the Union, these factors had produced three distinct opinion groups among the Germans and two such groups among

Texas Mexicans. One group, represented by men like talented editor and naturalist Ferdinand Lindheimer, held a value system highly similar to that of a southern white, was integrated into the established political or economic system of Texas, retained a prejudice against former Know-Nothings and supporters of Sam Houston, was highly loyal to the state's Democratic party, and had a personal philosophy which was more localistic than nationalistic. While reluctant to see the Union destroyed, this group was willing to accept secession.

On the other end of the spectrum were highly cultured and articulate Edward Degener and Ernst Kapp. Isolated on the frontier of Texas, filled with the nationalistic spirit of the 1848 revolution, aware of the importance of the U.S. Army to the well-being of their region, and with a long history of opposition to slavery, men of this type proved to be the most militant and consistent unionists.

Between these two factions stood politician and editor Gustav Schleicher and businessman and editor Ferdinand Flake. Both shared Texas values, considered themselves southerners, detested Know-Nothings, had supported Sam Houston, operated outside of the state's Democratic party, and were deeply committed to the Union. Men of this type were to campaign actively against secession until it became obvious that Texas would secede, at which time most elected to go with their state.

Certain Mexicans, the most prominent of whom were José Antonio Navarro and Santos Benavides, shared southern values, were an accepted part of the economic and political life of Texas, distrusted Know-Nothings but had a high degree of personal loyalty to Sam Houston, usually supported the Democratic party, and conceived of Texas, not the United States, as being their homeland. Despite the personal appeals of Houston this group was to support secession.

Other Mexicans, typified by Juan Cortina, considered themselves Texan by right of birth, but shared few southern values. They operated outside the political and economic system and resented the incursions of Americans in their homeland. Secession and the Civil War were to offer them a convenient way of striking back at the American-born intruders.

Germans and Mexicans were followers, not leaders, in the secession movement. Lacking both long-standing cultural ties to the South and an interest in slavery, they were never among the fire-eating secessionists. That did not mean they uniformly opposed secession. By November 1860, many of the ethnic citizens of Texas were ready to accept secession. Others stood unalterably opposed to the division of the Union. Their position was fixed: a product of their own personal philosophy, the history of their ethnic communities, their own peculiar local circumstances, and their level of assimilation. In the next few months the pressures of conformity and loyalty to Texas would move many who were hesitant and undecided into the secessionist camp. By January 1861, divisions within the ethnic communities paralleled those of American-born Texans, particularly Upper South Texans. Germans and Mexicans appeared orthodox. While not acting for the same reasons as other Texans, they looked like Texans. Like other groups in Texas which could have counterbalanced disunion, they were too fragmented at the start of the secession movement to slow its growth. As other divided cultural, economic, and political groups were to learn that January, acting in an orthodox Lower South fashion was not only the easiest course of action, it was the safest.

6

The Frontier

When planters and slaves entered the eastern half of Texas, they came into a familiar environment, an environment conducive to the traditional patterns of their culture. When the yeoman and hill folk entered northern and central Texas, they too entered an environment well suited to their culture. Germans and Mexicans in urban areas and in the southern and central regions of the state conformed to the basic tenets of the dominant cultures of their new regions, but nonetheless retained much of their past heritage. In all three cases, ideas, modes of thought, habits, and values from the past influenced these groups' approaches to secession. For the frontiersman who might have originated from any of these groups, however, place was more important than past. The frontiersman's new and unique environment made his reaction to secession and his attitude toward the Union special.

In the late 1850s, the Union had a dual appeal. It was a thing of value in itself, and it was a means to an end. In the abstract, it was a cherished possession of mind and spirit—an idea, a hope, a dream, a myth—brought by Texans from their former homes. At the same time, the Union protected and preserved life, liberty, and property. These two conceptions of the value of the Union did not exist in perfect equipoise. At different times and in different places one was the superior, the other the inferior cause for attachment to the Union. At times one force pulled away from the Union, while the other pulled toward it. On the Texas frontier the balance was clear: survival and protection of property took precedence over ideology. The Union, as symbolized by the U.S. Army, was important for the protection it gave to citizens and the stimulus it gave to the local economy. Depending upon how well it fulfilled its functions the army could arouse positive or negative reactions among frontier residents. Ideology, cultural background, and party ties added to the complex impulses which molded frontier opinions. Still, in no other portion of the state were environment and pragmatic considerations of such overriding importance in determining attitudes toward secession and the Union.[1]

Throughout the 1850s the Texas frontier moved rapidly westward, with each new line of settlements and forts serving as a protective buffer for the interior regions. In 1860 the frontier was a two- or three-deep tier of counties ranging from Clay and Montague in the north to Webb County in the south. Behind this buffer, in the course of a decade a secondary tier of counties had evolved from a frontier to a more stable environment. Frontier influences still touched these interior counties—Comanche raiders occasionally penetrated to the secondary tier and its citizens were connected to the frontier counties by friendship and kinship ties—and yet their interests were not entirely those of the frontier. It was only in the exterior tier of counties that the impact of the frontier on Unionism could be considered direct and all-encompassing.[2]

Typically, the frontiersman came from the Upper South with stopovers in Arkansas or in the interior of Texas. Mason, Gillespie, and Medina counties, in the middle portion of the frontier, however, were overwhelmingly German. Farther south, Uvalde County was peopled primarily by Mexican Texans. While these three groups had distinct cultures, they were unified by the challenge of their unique environment.[3]

Walter Prescott Webb made famous the differences between a plains and a forest environment. Pointing to a line running through the middle of Texas and up to the Dakotas, he proclaimed that once the frontiersmen moved westward into the plains environment, "In the new region—level, timberless, and semi-arid—they were thrown by Mother Necessity into the clutch of new circumstances." The frontier counties of Texas in 1860 stood astride Webb's divide. Settlers who ventured into this transitional zone felt the effects of the plains environment, and it separated them from other Texans and from other southerners.[4]

Located between the 98th and 100th parallels, the frontier counties were, as one cultural geographer has described them, "on the rim of the desert." There were a few more trees and hills, and there was a bit more rain than on the Great Plains proper. Still, annual rainfall fluctuated widely from year to year and averaged only slightly more than twenty inches. This made it difficult to grow cotton and required that corn and wheat be grown by methods that conserved moisture. Lack of water also meant that there were no large rivers to transport goods to market. All of Texas was handicapped by poor river transportation, but in the east, at least during the rainy season, the rivers rose sufficiently to allow passage over sandbars and snags. Because trees were sparse in the semiarid plains environment, there was no steady supply of building material and fuel. Instead of forested river bottoms considered ideal for cotton, there was only thick grass with roots that resisted plows.

Huge herds of buffalo and antelope subsisted on the plains grass, and nomadic Indian tribes in turn depended on the buffalo and the antelope. The Plains tribes differed from the more sedentary Indians to the east. They had no stable villages which could be attacked and destroyed, and no crops or houses to be burned. Plains Indians roved with their herds of horses across great territory. They fought as light cavalry, avoided pitched battles, and had mastered what in a later day would be termed guerrilla warfare.[5]

In the Comanches, Kiowas, and Lipan-Apaches, Texans on the frontier encountered a barrier that they would not penetrate until the 1870s. The image of the Comanche which comes down to us to-day—a fierce warrior armed with a short stout bow, mounted on a swift wiry pony, and engaging in hit-and-run raids on frontier settlements—was all too real in the 1850s. The army tried to fight the Plains Indians as it had fought other tribes to the east. It often used infantry armed with rifles which could fire one shot to the Indian's three or four arrows. It depended upon artillery to destroy Indian villages, yet except in winter, there were no big villages, only small nomadic bands. The army often used wagons to pursue mounted tribesmen: there would never be a day when soldiers in wagons could catch men on horseback and, meanwhile, the Comanches continued raiding. Texans realized that defeating the Plains Indians would require men who could move as fast as the Indians, who knew the land, and who, armed with the newly introduced six-gun, could fire as fast as the Indians could shoot their arrows. Until the army or some other organized, readily available force could fight the Indian on his own terms, life would be hazardous on the border.[6]

In other important ways environment separated frontier Texans from their fellows. Semisubsistence farming and stock raising typically dominated all frontier economies. This was true in Texas, but there was an important difference. Earlier frontiers had not been totally isolated from the rest of the economic world. Particularly in the South and in the Mississippi basin, rivers had provided an outlet for surplus stock and crops and an inlet for manufactured goods and a few luxury items. This was not true of riverless frontier Texas. Livestock could be driven to market, but crops could only be transported by wagon at tremendous cost. Although some counties did pass rapidly from frontier status into a more mature economic and social state in the 1850s, where the westward line of advance reached a point at which transportation costs were excessively high, counties remained isolated and in the frontier stage of development for relatively long periods of time. Gillespie County, for example, although founded in the 1840s, remained basically a frontier county until after the Civil War, when the construction of rail lines connected it to markets.[7]

Agricultural patterns determined by the environment also distinguished the frontier from the rest of Texas. The eastern boundary of the frontier region in 1860 marked the limits of the cotton-growing South and the slave plantation system. Frontiersmen grew corn and wheat on small farms, and where limited markets and transportation were available, they used horse-drawn machinery. As long as these conditions persisted there would be no cotton or slaves in this region. Even if the threat to slavery posed by Indian attack was eliminated and railroads linked the area to markets, unfavorable climatic conditions on the frontier prevented the spread of the cotton culture. As careful observers of the day well knew, slavery could not go where nature would not let it, and nature prohibited the frontiersman from looking forward to a day when his region would be like the Lower South.[8]

This unique frontier environment created a distinctive relationship between the frontiersmen and the army. The army was an important and highly lucrative exception to the absence of a marketplace on the frontier. Frontiersmen sold their livestock, their crops, and their services to the army. They built and maintained forts, helped feed troops, and provided grain for animals. The soldiers in turn spent money in the small towns that sprang up near military posts. He may have had drawbacks as an Indian fighter, but the soldier supplied the bulk of the cash that raised the frontier economy a bit above the subsistence level.[9]

Frontier citizens, nevertheless, were outspoken critics of the government and the army. A cash economy did little good in a land where survival was so hazardous. Markets meant nothing if a man's family was murdered and his livestock stolen. When Indian raids increased, as they did from 1857 to 1860, citizens of those counties least protected by the army reacted with a stream of indignant letters to their governor, congressmen, and local newspapers. The second tier of counties behind the frontier also protested the ineptitude of the army. Secessionists seized upon another reason for Texas to leave the Union: its borders were not safe.

Despite a critical lack of manpower and mobility, the army did give some protection to areas immediately surrounding its forts. Fort Mason, for example, defended Mason, Llano, and Gillespie counties. South of Fort Mason, where Indian attacks were less severe than in the more exposed areas, settlers and soldiers never confronted each other in the years immediately prior to secession. Consequently, the army's reputation and standing in that region remained high.[10]

Such was not the case on the rest of the frontier and in other areas of Texas attuned to frontier needs. Here, Indian attacks not only affected attitudes toward the national government, they affected state politics as well. Since the army had neither enough men nor the right tactics to protect the frontier adequately, much of the burden of frontier defense fell on the state government and on state-organized Ranger battalions. Because the state treasury seldom had surplus funds, the governor found himself in a difficult position. The Republic of Texas and the state government prior to 1855 had been constantly in debt. Governor E. M. Pease had used the money obtained from the federal government when Texas relinquished its claim on eastern New Mexico to put the state on an even financial keel. Governor Hardin R. Runnels and his successor Sam Houston were reluctant to plunge the state back into debt by financing a large number of Ranger battalions, and were equally reluctant to seek higher taxes. They turned instead to the federal government and insisted that it pay for Texas troops to do the job the army should have done. This took time, and meanwhile the frontier often went without the protection of the highly mobile and efficient Rangers.

Woe be to the governor who allowed the frontier to be ravaged because he wanted a balanced budget! He lost not only the votes and support of the frontiersmen, but also the votes and support of Texans in the interior who remembered Indian attacks of the past, who suffered occasionally from lightning-fast Indian raids, or who had relatives and friends farther west. Frontier defense struck at Texans' deepest emotions. Tales of women and children murdered and of families robbed of their livestock and livelihood made attempts to balance the budget seem contemptible.[11]

No better example of the frontier's effect on state politics can be offered than the 1859 governor's race. Increased Indian attacks were to antebellum Texas governors what economic depressions have become to latter-day American presidents. They were events over which the governor had little control but which nonetheless greatly influenced his power, popularity, and chances of reelection. When Runnels was elected governor in August 1857, he and his Democratic party appeared at the apogee of their political power. They had after all just defeated Sam Houston, the single most popular campaigner in Texas history. Unfortunately for Runnels, the year 1857 also marked an upsurge in Indian attacks. The Comanches, pressed westward by advancing frontiersmen who drove other Indians into their territory, facing a declining supply of buffalo due to increased demand for buffalo hides among whites, and diverted from their usual raids into Mexico by the army's attempts to protect Mexico from attacks of Indians native to the United States, took advantage of the reduction of federal troops in Texas to raid frontier settlements with increasing frequency.[12]

Reservation Indians and homeless tribes like the Kickapoos often raided settlements independently of the Comanches. The Kickapoos had been forced from their agrarian eastern settlements by the westward movement of white civilization and now were almost as nomadic as the Comanches. Because of their contact with eastern traders, however, the Kickapoos enjoyed the advantage of being armed with the very latest weapons. Often equipped with better rifles than the army, they were a threat both to the settlers and to the Comanches whose hunting grounds they had appropriated. Joining the Kickapoos were remnants of other eastern tribes who also took advantage of the turmoil to raid the Texas settlements. Oftentimes they left the federal reservations in Indian Territory, slipped quietly across the Red River to raid in Texas, and then returned to the protection of their reservations. Many Texans also believed that Indians on the two reservations recently established in Texas on the Brazos River and on the Clear Fork of the Brazos took part in raids against settlers. Texans, therefore, demanded protection from attacks by reservation Indians as well as by hostile tribes.[13]

In December of 1858, settlers and the army clashed when the frontiersmen retaliated against Brazos Reservation Indians for depredations in nearby Parker and Palo Pinto counties. Taking matters into their own hands again the following May, some three hundred settlers led by John R. Baylor confronted both the Indians and federal troops at the Brazos Indian Agency. Baylor and his men declared that they were there to seize several Indians who had been raiding the area and demanded that the Indians be immediately removed from the state. A bitter exchange followed between the soldiers, the Indians, and the Indian agent on one side and the settlers on the other. Shooting began, and several Indians were killed. Baylor and his men then left, but were attacked on their way home by enraged Indians.[14]

In the wake of this incident came a long and vituperative exchange between the army and local citizens. Caught in the middle, Governor Runnels tried to make peace and at the same time retain the frontier vote. He failed in both endeavors. The army emerged from the affair persuaded that the settlers were the troublemakers and that complaints of Indian depredations were often exaggerated and unjustified. The settlers, on the other hand, were convinced that the army was the defender of the Indians and not of the frontiersmen. The War Department in Washington, D.C., was soon informed through official channels of the affairs in Texas, and the federal government found itself in a struggle with frontiersmen over the Texas reservations. All further appropriations or increases in troop strength for Texas were seen in the light of the incident on the Brazos Reservation. On the northwestern frontier, the army and the federal government did little to shed the negative image they had gained in the spring of 1859.[15]

As Indian raids grew in intensity so did demands for Ranger battalions and for the government to act on the question of reservation Indians. Frontiersmen and their sympathetic supporters to the east called for quick action on the part of the state government. No action taken by Runnels, however, could be quick. Removal of the Indian reservations from Texas required the cooperation of the federal government. Control of the Indians in Indian Territory rested with the army and with the secretary of war in Washington. Rangers cost money the state did not have, and getting money from the federal government to finance them took time. Eventually Ranger battalions would be sent to the frontier with the hope that the federal government would pay part of the cost at a later date. Eventually the tribes on the reservations in Texas would be removed from the state. Eventually the army would move to seal off the border along the Red River. And eventually both the Texas Rangers and the U.S. cavalry would strike hard at the Comanches. But in 1859 Runnels appeared a slow-footed and vacillating governor incapable of handling domestic defense.[16]

Frontier defense was only one of many factors which contributed to Sam Houston's political revival in 1859. Still, in no other area did Runnels suffer as precipitous a decline in popularity as along the frontier, and in no other section of the state was Houston's margin of victory greater. Houston's Unionism certainly helped his cause on the frontier. In areas where army forts were important, Unionism meant that the protection of settlers and the economy of a frontier society would not be threatened by secession. This was one reason Houston was able to narrow the gap in the German counties on the frontier despite his ties to nativist groups. Commentators then and now, though, have almost unanimously ascribed his dramatic rise in popularity along the frontier to Runnels's failure to deal effectively with the Indians.[17]

Houston proved little more effective in protecting the frontier than his predecessor. The army in Texas was still undermanned and still relied too heavily on its infantry. Impoverishment still haunted the state government; neglect still marked the course of the federal government. In fact, conditions worsened in 1859 when the bitter dispute over the speakership of the U.S. House of Representatives diverted congressional attention from the frontier. After the Republicans gained control of the House, partisan politics often denied Democratic Texas the appropriations it needed.[18]

Frontier problems in 1859 had two negative effects on Unionism in that region. First, Sam Houston, the most prominent and influential unionist in the state, owed a significant margin of his popularity and influence on the frontier to his promise to protect settlers from the Indians. When he could not fulfill this promise, his popularity diminished and with it the influence of his voice for the Union. If Houston could not be trusted to eliminate the threat of Indian attack, why should he be trusted when he sang the praises of the glorious Union? So went the secessionist argument on the frontier. Second, the repeated failure of the federal government to handle the Indian problem caused men to question the value of the Union. Stability and a good climate for economic expansion, which in frontier Texas meant protection from the raids of Indians and Mexicans, were prime reasons Texans had joined the Union. Now this protection seemed an idle dream. Unionism motivated by private concerns—by hopes of peace and prosperity—was no longer as great a force on the frontier in 1860 as it had been in 1845.[19]

Indian raids and the shortcomings of the federal government did not instantly convert all frontiersmen into secessionists. Not all agreed with Rip Ford, the prominent politician, editor, and Ranger leader, when as early as 1858 he declared: "There is no better principle established than, that when a government fails or refuses to protect its citizens the ties of allegiance are dissolved, and they have a perfect right to take care of themselves. In my opinion Texas has already had ample cause to sever her connection with the Union on this very head." Equally influential George B. Erath, a longtime Texan, spokesman of the frontier in the state legislature, and Indian fighter in his own right, pointed out that secession would not solve the Indian problem. In fact, if Texas seceded the Indians would be able to retreat across the border into a foreign country. The inability of Texans while they were citizens of the Republic to pursue Indians into United States territory had been a constant problem. Erath did not want it repeated. He argued that a better course of action than

secession would be to remember Texans' emotional ties to the Union
and to trust that a change in administration at the state and national
levels would ease the Indian situation.[20]

Despite Erath's arguments, Indian troubles drove a wedge into
what should have been the impenetrable block of Unionism on the
frontier. If Indian raids had not increased in intensity in the years
immediately preceding the secession crisis, if the army and citizens
had stayed on better terms, or if the Republicans in the House of
Representatives had not denied appropriations to Texas for defense,
the frontiersmen would have had every reason to oppose secession.
It was not a land of large slaveholders and never would be. It depended upon the army both for protection and for the money the
army put into the local economy. Most frontiersmen were from cultural groups with strong emotional ties to the Union. It was the Indian menace that put the seed of doubt in frontiersmen's minds.[21]

Indian threats and the issue of frontier defense allowed John
Marshall and other states' rights leaders to begin to bind the nonslaveholding western portions of Texas to the slaveholding east. As
editor of the Austin *Texas State Gazette* and state chairman of the
Democratic party in the late 1850s, Marshall premised his attacks
on the North not only on the abstract principle of southern rights
but also on the pragmatic conviction that union with the North was
a threat to the safety and property of every white Texan. The *Gazette* editorials seized upon the fires in North Texas in the summer
of 1860 to raise to a hysterical level rumors of abolitionist plots to
free the slaves by promoting anarchy. The Texas Troubles struck
even the frontier. In Parker County, where there were few slaves,
cases of arson and attempted assassinations were reported in the
town of Weatherford. The office of the Weatherford *Whiteman* was
burned and the fire blamed on incendiaries. Stories of abolitionist
conspiracies to aid the Indians circulated freely.

Such incidents were used by the *Texas State Gazette* to substan-
tiate its argument that a Republican administration direly threatened the frontier. Not only would a Republican president and Congress deny the frontier the men and money it needed for protection,
but they would turn the northwestern frontier of Texas into another
"bleeding" Kansas. Abolitionists would be allowed, even encouraged, to move into northwest Texas and turn it into a free state.

As if such threats were not enough, Marshall and his assistants
at the *Gazette* reported every Indian incident and every failure of the
army to protect the frontier. Abolitionist plots were things of the future and of small consequence compared to the Indian raids of the
present. The *Gazette* argued that just as federal action or inaction

threatened the slaveholding lands, it likewise threatened the frontier. All southerners, all Texans should unite against the tyranny, the neglect, and the abuse of power that would be inevitable in a Republican-dominated government. For Texans the Union would become more dangerous than advantageous.[22]

In the midst of Indian depredations, the Texas Troubles, and attempts to gain financial support for the state's military forces, the presidential election of 1860 afforded the frontiersman a clear opportunity to register his dissatisfaction with the current state of affairs. Political parties barely existed on the frontier. Local candidates ran on their standing in the community, not on partisan ties. Statewide races were won or lost on specific issues. The one exception on the frontier was in the German counties. Like German counties farther east, they had moved into the Democratic camp when threatened by the Know-Nothings, and they remained there until the Civil War. With this exception, 1860, which would be the first presidential election year when the votes of many frontier counties were recorded, should have been an ideal time for the Opposition party to win converts. The appeal of the Union which the Opposition party trumpeted should have been persuasive. Instead, the Opposition did worse on the frontier in 1860 than it did in the state as a whole.

Sam Houston's party was handicapped by lack of internal unity and by the Opposition party's limited ties to nationwide organizations; lack of a popular candidate also hurt. Its promise to vote for the candidate who stood the best chance of defeating Abraham Lincoln drew skepticism from some voters. This explained why the Union Electoral ticket received only 25 percent of the statewide vote. Yet along the frontier, where the Opposition party had done so well in 1859, its percentage of the vote was even less. In fact, in counties north of Fort Mason, the Union ticket, for which Sam Houston campaigned, did almost as poorly as had Hardin Runnels's Democrats in 1859. Fusionists received only 16 percent of the vote in this region. Clearly, Houston and the Opposition party had fallen out of favor with frontiersmen.[23]

A vote for Breckinridge, however, was not necessarily a vote for secession. Breckinridge's political managers in all parts of Texas went to great pains to present him as moderate and to disassociate him from such well-known political radicals as William Yancey of Alabama. Moreover, it was only in the closing months of the campaign that the Fusionists focused on the issue of union versus disunion. The isolated frontier counties, with the exception of those nearest Austin, were largely insulated from this debate. Instead, frustration with Houston and other Fusionists' poor records on frontier defense coupled with disatisfaction with the role of the federal government on the Texas frontier caused the frontiersmen to reject Opposition party spokesmen's calls for a vote for the Union.[24]

With the election of Lincoln, however, it became apparent that many frontiersmen in the counties above Fort Mason were indeed ready for secession. John Baylor, the leader of the Texan attack on the Brazos Reservation in 1859, was one of those prepared for rupture with the Union. Baylor had been an Indian agent in the mid-1850s and had led volunteers against the Indians on numerous occasions. Since the confrontation between the settlers and the army on the Brazos Reservation, he had become one of the most vocal critics of federal Indian policy. The army's defense of the reservation Indians and the reluctance of the federal government to take whatever steps were needed to safeguard the frontier convinced Baylor that the Union offered frontiersmen no special safeguard.

Even before the election Baylor felt that Texas should secede if Lincoln won and began to discuss with Oran M. Roberts, the future chairman of the Texas Secession Convention, possible methods of removing the state from the Union. In the fall of 1860 Baylor became an associate editor of the Weatherford *Whiteman*, using the newspaper and his reputation to aid the cause of secession. Dedicated to "the frontier and its defense," the *Whiteman* avidly supported Breckinridge for president. Throughout the campaign the newspaper's editors vehemently attacked the federal government, once proclaiming that "For three years past the frontier people have begged, prayed and supplicated both State and Federal Governments for protection, and the Federal government had displayed a cold blooded indifference to our condition that would do credit to the Czar of Russia."[25]

John Baylor and his brother George were as militant secessionists as could be found in the state. Their entire lives and careers had been focused upon ridding Texas of Indians, and they tried to ruin and remove from power anyone who stood in their way. They were as rabid on the topic of Indians as any Southern fire-eater discussing abolitionists. When the federal government impeded their cherished dream, they retaliated. When the Republicans blocked aid to the Texas frontier, they condemned them. If "the federal government, while but partially under the control of these our unnatural and sectional enemies, has, for years, almost entirely failed to protect the lives and property of the people of Texas against the Indian savages on our border," then what could be expected if the executive branch were in Republican hands? For the Baylors the answer was obvious: conditions would only worsen. If the imbalance between North and South continued to tilt in favor of the North and if the Republican party continued to grow in strength, the Texas frontier would be menaced by the Indians for years to come. The only solution to the problem was secession.[26]

George Erath, like John Baylor, had lived on the frontier for many years by 1860, but he did not agree that secession was justified. He did not object to the idea of secession—secession, he conceded, was the natural right of any state. He objected to the practicality of secession. A split with the Union was neither justified by events nor in the best interests of the people of Texas.[27]

Both Erath and the Baylor brothers either opposed or supported secession on pragmatic grounds. This was not true of all frontiersmen. Germans like Edward Degener and Hermann Speiss were nationalists who viewed with dismay any attempt to break up the magnificent Union. Reading W. Black of Uvalde County was a prominent frontiersman who supported the Union on principle; doubtless there were others to whom principle was as important as practicality when deciding for or against secession.[28]

Nevertheless, a pragmatic view of its unique local conditions seems to have been almost entirely the dominant force behind the frontier's decision to support or oppose secession. The extent of Indian depredations, the importance of military forts to the economy and for local protection, and the probability that the frontier would be neglected by a Republican administration dominated public debates on secession.

Along Texas's northwestern border few would oppose secession. The only opponents lived in the northernmost frontier counties, those counties especially vulnerable to raids from the federally controlled Indian Territory and those in which Erath's argument that restoring Texas and the United States to the status of two separate nations would give the Indians a safe harbor in a foreign land had the most cogency. Along the southwestern frontier would be found an equally disproportionate number of antisecessionists. Here Indian problems had been slight in comparison with the northwest, and Germans and Mexicans exerted a cultural influence against secession. The forts were seen as critical to the local economy and safety, and articulate and highly vocal nationalists argued for the sanctity of the Union. In no other region of the state was there such overwhelming opposition to secession. Frontiersmen thus stood in sharp contrast to one another. Their extreme range of opinions, however, sprang from a common origin—a practical assessment of the value of the Union.[29]

Although frontier citizens as a whole represented only a miniscule portion of the state's population, these practical assessments of the Union would have broad-ranging effects. Events on the frontier were not confined solely to the frontiersman: frontier issues quickly became statewide issues. Most Texans felt a kinship for the frontiersmen. They remembered what it was like to live on the frontier, or they had friends or relatives living exposed to the Indians. The importance of a fort to the local economy was an issue restricted to particular counties. People in McLennan County cared little that Fort Mason boosted the economies of distant Mason and Gillespie counties, but they cared a great deal that counties up and down the frontier had suffered repeatedly at the hands of the Indians and that the federal government had done little to prevent it. In turn, frontier failures attributed to the Republicans and the federal government gave cogency to secessionist rhetoric. One reason Texas had joined the Union was to secure its borders and gain stability. The frontiersman's unique setting should have made him a unionist. Instead, in 1861 the desire for security and stability turned many against the federal government and was used to buttress secessionist arguments that a Republican-dominated nation was a nation so decayed that it could not be restored to its original pure form. Secession's propagandists argued that a southern confederacy offered the promise of the United States in 1845 without the drawbacks of the Union in 1861.[30] Once again, a group that should have helped block secession did not. The issues which propelled the northwestern counties to enthusiastically endorse secession became part of the impetus that moved all of Texas out of the Union.

7

The Debate over the Union

Secession seemed to come upon Texas in November of 1860 like a sudden storm. Few Texans had considered the presidential election of that year as simply a referendum on the future of the Union. No widespread call for secession existed before the November election. Yet with the news of Abraham Lincoln's victory came thunder, lightning, rain. Within four months Texans would join the process of dismantling a nation that had survived for over seven decades.

Such rapidity of action, occurring with little warning, seemed baffling. True, antebellum Texas had grown steadily more like the Lower South and it was natural that Texans identified with and to some degree followed the lead of citizens of the older cotton-growing states. Texans who were part of the Upper South culture shared all southerners' worries about Republican threats to slavery and the character of the nation. German and Mexican Texans did not have such pronounced fears of Republican threats to slavery and the nation, but for reasons of their own they often followed the lead of other Texans. Frontiersmen did not have the same pragmatic attachment to the Union they once did. Political parties and ideological beliefs allowed and in some cases encouraged the development of secession sentiment.

Still, these things alone did not cause secession; they merely set the stage for the secession crisis. It is clear that by December the crucial questions had changed. Texans were no longer being pulled along by their ties to the Lower South, nor were they simply reacting to outside events. Their actions were not just a logical extension of their past experiences, environment, or culture. Instead, Texans were in the midst of a violent and swirling debate about the value, importance, and nature of the Union, a debate in which leaders of different political factions attempted to convince the public of the wisdom of their particular policies.[1]

In retrospect, the result of this debate about the Union was not without precedent. In particular, the experiences of frontiersmen, Germans, and Mexicans in the 1850s offered clues to the pattern of the secession movement in 1860–1861. For the frontiersmen, a particularly compelling event, the failure of the U.S. Army and other governmental institutions to adequately protect them from Indian attack, brought into focus all their doubts concerning the nature of the Union and made that Union seem less desirable. To ethnic Texans, the dominant Anglo-Saxon and southern society had demonstrated by 1860 that diversity of opinion on issues regarded as vital would not be tolerated. In the secession crisis itself, Lincoln's election jolted Texas's old bond to the Union so severely that tradition and habit could not prevent the growth of secession sentiment. Once in motion, secession captured the support of a group near the political center, men who continued to arouse public prejudice in favor of secession because their opponents could not provide a viable alternative or did not have the energy to resist. As this group grew in numbers, public prejudice in favor of secession, an issue increasingly seen as vital to society, solidified to the point that dissent proved costly if not impossible.

Such dominance by secessionists seemed impossible as late as mid-1860 when Texans were overwhelmingly unionists. They were unionists of different types, though; the fact that they were neither homogeneous nor constant but instead fell into groups determined by partisanship, ideology, culture, environment, and personal aspirations explains why secession could have occurred so rapidly.

Of course, it would be difficult to characterize some Texans as unionists in any sense of the word, and at one extreme of the political spectrum stood a few outspoken and longtime exponents of southern rights. Primarily Democrats, men like Guy Bryan and John Marshall stressed the duty of the nation to the citizen and looked upon the nation as valuable only for the functions it could perform. These extremists were almost always part of the plantation South, in reality or in their aspirations. Their philosophy, however, had been soundly rejected in 1859, and they were to be largely left out of the political power structure that emerged after 1860.

In 1859 and 1860 a second, much larger group, closer to the political center, proved decisive. In 1859, U.S. Representative John H. Reagan, the group's leading figure, won a sweeping victory as a unionist. In 1860 partisan squabbles in the Republican-dominated House of Representatives seemed to convince him that a Republican-controlled executive branch would be disastrous for the South. He advocated secession in October of 1860 after he was sure that Lincoln would be elected. Yet he still hoped to preserve the Union if certain conditions were met—if southern rights and the security of southern society and property were not threatened. Like Reagan, most members of this second group were Democrats, but Democrats who placed value on the Union as a thing of worth in and of itself. They had revered the Union because of tradition and habit, and because they identified their own destiny with the history of the nation, its flag, its founding fathers, and its Constitution. Most members of this group were either part of the plantation culture or becoming part of it, but Democrats from other cultural groups, such as Charles De Morse and Ferdinand Lindheimer, also joined Reagan in support of secession in the fall of 1860.

Beyond Reagan and the moderate secessionists, but still in the middle range of political opinion, stood a third group. Also substantial in number, this group was best represented by men like Sam Houston, James W. Throckmorton, and Ferdinand Flake. Until March of 1861, they opposed not the right of secession, but only its necessity and wisdom. Pointing out that to secede because Abraham Lincoln had been elected president violated the cherished concepts of democracy and majority rule, this group consistently maintained that southerners would be protected by the Constitution. As might be expected by their reliance upon the Constitution, members of this group were typically long-standing opponents of the states' rights Democrats and had a much more deep-seated regard for the Union and its premier symbol, the Constitution. With few exceptions, members of this group came from outside the plantation culture and had no aspirations to be great planters; the exceptions to this rule were usually planters with large landholdings and a Whig tradition. Most members of this group acquiesced in secession in the spring of 1861.

On the opposite extreme from the fire-eaters resided a fourth group who placed no conditions on their Unionism and who never accepted secession. Led by men like George W. Paschal and U.S. Representative A. J. Hamilton, this group, although few in number, remained highly vocal and prominent until after Texas joined the Confederacy. All members of this group had abandoned the Texas Democratic party by 1859 and most regarded the Union as inviolate and eternal. Tradition, habit, self-identification with the history of the nation, and a belief that no system of government could function as well as the present one made these men uncompromising opponents of secession. Seldom from the plantation South, they typically came from the urban North, Upper South, or Germany.

Debates over the wisdom of secession became a political and ideological conflict between these four groups. In this conflict, moderate secessionists like Reagan, aligned with militant secessionists, had substantial advantages over their opponents. Momentum generated by the secession of six other cotton-producing states and unity of purpose gave them strength. The advocates of secession obscured the potential for war and astutely used the Democratic party organization while appealing for bipartisan support. The very nature of the political system aided them: they could turn a small local majority in the county elections of secession delegates into a large majority in the statewide convention.

Moderate unionists like Throckmorton and militant unionists like Paschal were not without some leverage of their own. They were blessed with some of the most gifted leaders and public speakers in the state. Their faction controlled the executive branch of the state government. They had a noble cause—the preservation of the Union. They used the logic of the importance of the federal government to the frontier to aid them in that area and the dire threat of civil war to counter the rashness of the southern radicals. In the German, Mexican, and Upper South citizens of Texas they had a group who together were a majority of the state's people and in whose cultures slavery had less value than in the Lower South. Unionists had strong principles, pragmatic arguments, and cultural prejudice on their side. Yet they lost.[2]

Organized attempts at secession really began in Texas in October 1860, when it became clear to many that Lincoln would be elected. Lincoln's imminent election convinced Texas Supreme Court Justice O. M. Roberts, U.S. Representative John H. Reagan, and a few other Texans with whom they corresponded that secession must occur. Neither Reagan nor Roberts wanted secession to be accomplished by the machinations of a secret organization like the Knights of the Golden Circle. Instead, they favored free and open discussion of the merits of the Union and then the expression of the will of the people in a convention. For these two lawyers, secession was not to be a chaotic social revolution but a well-considered legal step which would preserve and promote stability.[3]

Within a few days of news of Lincoln's election reaching Texas, modest efforts to achieve secession began. No concrete plan of action was called for, but there were public meetings to discuss the implications of Lincoln's election and calls for the legislature to meet in special session as the first step toward resistance to "Black Republican rule." From the middle to the end of November there was a good deal of excitement around the state. Texans were faced with two decisive questions. First, should they resist the legal and proper election of a president of the United States who had not yet had an opportunity to abuse his power? Second, if they did choose to resist Republican rule, should they act separately or in cooperation with other southern states?[4]

For Judge Roberts, State Comptroller C. R. Johns, State Treasurer C. H. Randolph, State Attorney General George Flournoy, John S. Ford, George Baylor, and a small number of other leading Texans who assembled in the office of the attorney general soon after hearing of Lincoln's election, the answers to these two questions were obvious. Texans should resist Republican rule and should move toward separate and immediate secession. Their only problem was one of tactics. Only the state legislature could legally call for a convention of the people. Only the governor could convene a special session of the legislature. If the secessionists wanted to act before the next legislative session they would have to act through Sam Houston, their obstinate and Union-loving governor, or they would have to find an extralegal method of assembling a convention.[5]

For unionists and conservatives the questions were not that simple. As Thomas F. McKinney put it in a letter written to his friends and business associates Thomas Jack, W. P. Ballinger, and Guy M. Bryan: "Certainly the people of the North have a constitutional right to elect Mr. Lincoln in a constitutional manner just as much as we had to elect Mr. Breckinridge, but according to the doctrine of some of our friends if we elect Mr. B. we will fight to sustain the constitution and if Mr. Lincoln should be elected we will fight to violate the constitution. This seems to me utterly wrong and in addition great injustice to our millions of friends who have battled so nobly and so generously for us and our constitutional rights at the North." McKinney went on to recommend that the southern states meet in a convention, and he expressed the hope that with time, secessionist ardor would cool.[6]

In McKinney's letter could be found the crux of the strategy used by unionist leaders Pease, Paschal, Throckmorton, and Houston in the closing weeks of 1860. They pinned their hopes on the passage of time and the strength of their constitutional arguments. They insisted that the southern states should act in concert, not independently. Unionists viewed the secession crisis in Texas as momentary hysteria caused by the excitement of the presidential election and the rhetoric of demagogues. They hoped that in time the outcry for some type of resistance to Lincoln's election would lessen. Adopting this strategy, Governor Houston repeatedly refused to call the legislature into a special session for the purpose of organizing a convention to consider the relationship of Texas to the federal Union. Houston hoped that in less passionate times the argument that Lincoln had been constitutionally elected would be heard.

Even the most ardent unionist, however, was forced to concede that there was a general belief among the public that something must be done. To this end unionists stressed cooperation with other southern states. Seizing upon a by then defunct call by South Carolina for a convention of the southern states, Houston argued that such a step was appropriate. If Texas seceded, it should not do so alone. Seceding separately would leave it at the mercy of the United States government, and the fate of South Carolina during the nullification controversy of 1832 might be the fate of Texas in 1861. Instead, the South should secede as a unit. Besides, cooperation had the added advantage to the unionists of slowing down secession. To the question of immediate secession the unionists answered no. They insisted upon the constitutionality of Lincoln's election and pointed out that he had done nothing to harm the South or justify revolution. They hoped that with the passage of time the passions of the moment would fade. By conceding that the South should meet in a convention, however, they admitted the potential threat posed to their society by a Republican president. The moderate unionists made it clear that they would resist the coercion of southern states by a Republican president and insisted that they would not submit to Republican tyranny. Their position was that in November and December of 1860 neither revolution nor secession seemed justified.[7]

Public ardor for secession, instead of cooling with the passage of time as the unionists had hoped, seemed to quicken as the year's end approached. As was true of the Texas Troubles the summer before, news of northern atrocities—in this case the election of a Republican president—and news of how some Texans were reacting to that atrocity spread across the state. As the word went out that Texans in Marshall, Galveston, and Austin were hoisting the Lone Star flag, calling for the governor to convene the legislature, and declaring in favor of immediate secession, Texans in Dallas, Waco, and San Antonio were inspired to do likewise. Instead of running out of steam, secession had gained momentum by the end of 1860.[8]

Governor Houston, however, still refused to call the legislature into session. In a letter explaining his position he declared, "So long as the Constitution is maintained by the 'federal authority,' and Texas is not made the victim of 'Federal wrong' I am for the Union as it is." Warning of the awful potential of a civil war, Houston argued that because it was his duty as governor to uphold the Constitution he could not convene the legislature for the purpose of beginning a revolution. As an alternative, Houston proposed taking advantage of a resolution passed by the state legislature in 1858 calling for a convention of the southern states when the governors of those states deemed such a convention necessary. To this end Houston wrote all of the governors of the Southern states on 28 November.

Nothing came of this attempt at diplomacy, and the pressure for Houston to assemble the legislature intensified.[9]

Responding to the growing public pressure in favor of secession, Judge Roberts, John Ford, several members of the state legislature, and other prominent Texans who had journeyed to Austin to petition the governor to convene the legislature decided to issue a call for a convention independent of the governor. Ironically, the same men who drew up resolutions in favor of the annexation of Texas in 1845 were now taking the first concrete step toward dissolving those ties. The call for a convention was of doubtful legality, but, as was true of the vigilante committees of the past summer, it was thought that extraordinary times justified bending the letter of the law. Instead of waiting for the legislature to call a convention and determine the procedure for electing delegates, a small handful of self-appointed leaders took over this responsibility. In doing so they insisted that "the insults, threats and aggressions which have been directed at the honor, the equality, and the happy social existence of the people of Texas and the South for the last forty years, have reached a climax," and that in such a situation they as a sovereign people had the right to call a convention independent of the governor or state legislature.[10]

According to the plan adopted, the election of delegates was to be based upon the districts in the state legislature's lower house. Each district was to elect twice as many delegates as representatives to the state legislature. The date for these elections was fixed at 8 January, and the convention was to assemble on 28 January. On 3 December the call was printed in major newspapers across the state, and new pressure was applied to the unionists.[11]

Secessionists now had both a clear set of goals and a method to achieve these goals. They wanted Texas to secede separately and then to join a southern confederacy. Unionists likewise had a clear goal—the preservation of the nation as it was then constituted—but they were never able to unite on a method to counter the tactics of the secessionists. Some unionists advocated simply ignoring the call for the convention, still entertaining the vain hope that the simple passage of time would aid their cause. A few moved to seize control of the delegations to the convention and actively campaigned for election. Some, like Sam Houston, took a partial step toward bowing to majority opinion. After putting off demands that the legislature be called into special session, on 17 December, Houston finally called for a special session to meet the following month. Its purpose was to consider the relationship of Texas to the federal government. Houston stipulated that any action affecting federal or state relations must be submitted to the vote of the people. He evidently hoped that he would have a better chance of influencing the people as a whole rather than the secessionist leaders meeting in an extra-legal convention.[12]

Houston, Throckmorton, Paschal, and other unionists also con-tinued their constitutional arguments. Paschal insisted in 1861 that secession was unconstitutional and was to press his point until it was upheld by the United States Supreme Court in *Texas* v. *White* (1869). Throckmorton and Houston were not as adamant as Paschal. Secession might be unconstitutional, but certainly revolution for the right cause was not. Instead, they insisted that until the Consti-tution was violated the South should not act, and they held out the hope that Houston's scheme of a southern convention might lead to some constitutional adjustment between North and South.[13]

By the new year, hopes of a constitutional adjustment, indeed hopes for the preservation of the Union in any form, had begun to fade. Time, instead of being the ally of the unionists, had proven to be the friend of the secessionists. After South Carolina seceded on 20 December, five other states of the Lower South departed the Union in rapid succession. This made the concept of cooperation a dead issue for the unionists. The states with which they had advo-cated cooperation were already out of the Union and were beginning to form a new confederacy. As the immediate secessionists argued, in a pragmatic sense they were the real cooperationists. The sooner Texas left the United States, the sooner it could join the new nation being built of southern states. Those who opposed rapid secession were in fact opposing the formation of the South into a united front to oppose northern aggression. The secession of the other states along the Gulf Coast meant, too, that with Louisiana out of the Union, Texas was virtually isolated from the United States. Only along the narrow border with Arkansas did Texas still touch a state that re-mained in the Union. In other southern states during the secession crisis a strong middle group of cautious citizens favored cooperative action among the southern states and continued to hope for some adjustment of the difficulties between North and South. They feared that if their states acted precipitously they would be left isolated. By the time the Secession Convention of Texas met, the fears of isola-tion and the desire to cooperate with other southern states favored the secessionists, not the cooperationists or unionists.[14]

Time and the momentum generated by other seceding states were not the only things working in the secessionists' favor in the last days of 1860. Unionists had always relied heavily upon the Con-stitution as a guarantor of stability and prosperity. In their successful campaigns of 1859 the Constitution had been their byword. The reputation of frontier states for lawlessness notwithstanding, most Texans had a profound respect for law and for established procedure. The Constitution, as the highest of all laws, had a special appeal. In 1859, while the Opposition party was running on a platform of law and stability, the Democrats were associated with the slave trade and filibustering. Both of these were clearly perceived by voters as being illegal and socially disruptive. This perception had contributed greatly to the victory of the Opposition in 1859. In 1860 and 1861 unionists once again attempted to invoke the law and the Constitution by arguing that Lincoln was legally and constitutionally elected and that until he violated the Constitution there was no ground for secession. Their argument failed in the winter of 1860–1861, but it was not because the majority of Texans had suddenly abandoned their conservative reliance upon the law. The purpose of law was stability and order. Over time the law or individual laws such as the Constitution had become revered as things important in themselves, but nonetheless, laws represented a search for order. When order was threatened, action outside of the law or in violation of established principle seemed justified. In the winter of 1860–1861, the election of a Republican seemed such a threat to internal order that many Texans believed themselves justified in rejecting the Constitution and the Union and in taking the radical step of moving toward secession outside established legal procedures. Still, Texans were careful that the movement be led by the best people of the community. Internal orderliness and stability had to be preserved even while Texans were taking radical steps to meet an external threat. F. B. Sexton, chairman of the state's Democratic convention in 1860, caught the spirit of the times when in December he wrote to O. M. Roberts describing a recent secession meeting: "The sober, reflecting, sterling men of the country were present and no division of feeling existed." Secession might have been a radical step, but the movement was not led by radical men.[15]

One of the supreme ironies of the secession crisis in Texas was that, just as unionists had counted on the passage of time to erode the impact of secession, they also counted upon Texans' faith in the law and the Constitution to prevent any radical departure from established procedure. In both cases unionists did not realize that time and the concern for order were on the side of the secessionists. The path toward perceiving Republican rule as a threat to established procedure and internal order was long and tortuous. As early as 1856, the Republican party had been portrayed in Texas as a revolutionary sectional party dedicated to the destruction of slavery and southern institutions. Turmoil in Kansas reinforced this image, as did the personal liberty laws passed by several Republican-controlled states. These laws, because they directly countered the constitutionally sanctioned principle of returning fugitive slaves, helped prove to southerners that Republicans would violate all established procedure and law to achieve their goals. As has been shown, the events of 1859 and 1860 convinced Texans all the more that Republicans represented chaos and the most narrow of sectional views. Still, most Texans' worries about Republicans were balanced by attachment to their nation. Lincoln's election tipped the balance in favor of secession. A democratic system of government rests ultimately upon the belief of the public that all political factions will observe the basic rules of the system. Since a large number of Texans were convinced that the Republicans would violate both laws and established procedure, Lincoln's election put what these Texans regarded as a revolutionary party dedicated to an inevitable conflict between North and South in control of the executive branch of the national government. From this perspective, secession was less dangerous than remaining in the Union.[16]

Obviously such an argument was undermined by the prospect of war. Because the desire for stability and order played an important role in causing secession, secessionists were forced to disavow that in moving to preserve order they would provoke society's ultimate plague—a civil war. A few realists like Rip Ford knew that secession was actually a revolution whose probable result would be war. Most secessionists, however, denied the warnings of Sam Houston that secession would mean a long and bloody civil war in which brother would kill brother. They argued that the North would leave the South in peace because northerners either accepted the legality of secession or they feared the combined strength of the southern people. If a war did occur, most secessionists predicted it would be of short duration and of little consequence. R. W. Loughery enunciated one version of this theory when he wrote in the *Texas Republican*: "The prompt action of the Cotton States will compel the border States to take a decided position, and this will prevent Civil War, for whenever the Slaveholding States are united, and determined upon resistance, coercion is out of the question." As late as 23 March 1861, Charles De Morse still expected peace and held out a hope shared by many Texans that if the Union could not be reconstructed along lines more favorable to the South, then the two regions could at least exist as friendly neighbors.[17]

Not all secessionists were as sanguine about the prospects for peace. Depressed by the situation which faced him, John Reagan wrote the Nacogdoches *Chronicle*: "The sad alternative is now submitted to us of the unconditional submission to Black Republican principles, and ultimately to free negro equality, and a government of mongrels or war of races on the one hand, or secession and the formation of a Southern Confederacy and a bloody war on the other." It was a difficult time for Reagan. He saw the stability of southern society threatened by any action the South took. For him, however, the threat of an internal race war provoked by the actions and principles of the Republicans was greater than the possibility of war between North and South. Each was in a way a civil war, but a war between races living side by side was more to be feared than a war between the same race separated by state boundaries. Reagan's views seem to be rather exceptional and were perhaps a result of his own inner torment over secession.[18] Most Texans regarded the possibility of war as did the merchants of Marshall. Taking advantage of the situation for a little eye-catching advertising, one merchant's ad held out the promise of cheap prices:

GREAT WAR
The War is Not to be Avoided!

Messrs. Cohen & Bredig
Have Declared a Great War
against the
Merchants of Marshall

The threat of war troubled some farsighted souls, but most Texans, like the merchants of Marshall, took the threat lightly and denied that secession would cause a long and bloody civil war.[19]

By the first day of the new year secessionists' tactics, perceptions of the evilness of Republicans, and the pull of the Lower South appeared to make secession unstoppable. Those who still looked askance at secession, however, were worried but hopeful. They believed that the majority of Texans remained unionists at heart. In a way that was true, but they did not realize that by the eve of the election of delegates to the Secession Convention the pillars of traditional Unionism in Texas were crumbling. A plantation culture made some members of the Opposition party secessionists. Partisan politics and personal ideology made some Upper South Texans and ethnic Texans reluctant secessionists. Along the frontier pragmatic considerations made Texans both unionists and secessionists. Even among businessmen and the commercial elements in Texas that profited most from a strong central government and a favorable business climate, secession was making headway. Again and again leading Texans who had long loved the Union reached a personal crossroads. Some declared for secession. Their followers did likewise. With each new division the cause of the Union weakened and moderate secessionists added to their numbers.[20]

Of most importance to this process of disintegration and growth was the demise of the fragile coalition which had brought the Opposition party victory in 1859. The major defectors were East Texas Whigs, who, like other opposition groups in the Lower South, joined with the Democrats to make secession a bipartisan effort. Actually, the process of detaching the Whigs from the Opposition had begun with the 1859 congressional campaign in the First District when William B. Ochiltree thought John Reagan too moderate a defender of the South and combined with like-minded Whigs and states' rights Democrats to oppose his reelection. In the state elections of August 1860 the Democrats, with the help of East Texas Whigs, rebounded from their losses of the previous year and swept every election. Later in the fall, for the first time in the decade, Whig or Opposition party presidential candidates were to get less than 40 percent of the vote in almost every East Texas county. Even before the secession movement got underway, the Opposition party's strength in the state legislature and among the voters was cut almost in half.[21]

After news of Lincoln's election was confirmed the *Texas Republican*, the mouthpiece of the Democratic party in the upper portion of East Texas, exulted: "From every portion of our State, from which we have heard, where intelligence has been received on Lincoln's election, there has been manifested but one feeling, one sentiment, and that is that the people of Texas will never consent to Black Republican domination. All party divisions and distinctions have been laid aside, and for once we are united." The *Texas Republican* exaggerated the extent of unity. Even in Marshall the *Harrison Flag* continued to support the Union and advocate cooperative action by the southern states, not immediate secession. The *Flag*'s traditional constituency, however, seemed to be undergoing the same internal crisis as the Democratic followers of John H. Reagan. Secessionists in East Texas and along the lower Brazos and Colorado rivers had the added incentive of slavery's direct tie to their economic prosperity. The fruits of the slave labor system lined their pockets with gold and encouraged their enthusiastic and unanimous endorsement of slavery. In these regions the election of a Republican president not only threatened internal stability, law and order, and racial harmony, but also prosperity and economic growth. Even so, some East Texas Whigs like the editor of the *Flag* continued to oppose secession.

As the impetus from the other southern states increased, the majority of the Opposition party members in plantation regions joined the secessionists. In fact, the party there almost vanished, and those who did oppose secession did so as individuals rather than members of a group.[22] Opposition party structure was also weakened in other portions of the state, but outside of the plantation counties the party survived. It survived because in other sections, from the very beginning, the Opposition party had drawn strength from Unionism.[23]

Unionism sprang not just from different economies or ideologies but from habit—a habit engrained in cohesive cultural groups outside the guidelines of a Lower South society. Unfortunately for the unionists, ties to the Democratic party and an ideology that stressed individual rights and the responsibilities of government often overrode the habit of Unionism.

Texans from the Upper South were the most important and numerous cultural group with the habit of pronounced and persistent Unionism. Those areas of the state which most resembled Tennessee, Kentucky, and Missouri had always been the least inclined to take a militant stance in defense of southern rights. In January 1861, there was even talk that some counties in North Texas planned to secede from Texas and form a new state if Texas left the Union. As in the case of the Opposition party, however, the once solid facade of support for the Union cracked in North Texas. North Texans divided more or less along party lines, with Democrats reluctantly supporting secession and Opposition party members continuing to oppose such a radical cure for the sectional ailments of the times.[24]

Whether this split on secession developed because of partisanship or grew naturally from ideological differences between parties remains difficult to determine. Some North Texans undoubtedly supported one group or the other because of party loyalty or devotion to a particular party leader. Others may have supported or opposed secession because they viewed the issue as an advantage or disadvantage to their particular party. Not even the most convinced secessionists argued that the vying for political dominance between two well-balanced parties ended in North Texas during the secession crisis, and it was clear to both sides that secession gave the Democratic party the unity and strength it had lacked since the halcyon days when it had battled the evil Know-Nothings. Still, only because upper southerners had varying conceptions of the value and importance of the Union could secessionists and the Democratic party leaders split their ranks. Many North Texans were conditional unionists— unionists only so long as it suited their interests or ideology. North Texans' interests were threatened by the apparent goal of aboli- tionists to incite slave rebellions in Texas. Slavery had relatively little economic importance in North Texas, but racial harmony and the perpetuation of a social order resting upon white supremacy had a good deal of importance. If one right was abrogated, or even chal- lenged, by a sectional party in control of the national government, then all rights, all laws, were vulnerable. In the eyes of exponents of this theory, Republicans were radical revolutionaries—fomenters of social discord who displayed a marked ability to disregard the Con- stitution when it suited their purposes. Such theories were even easier to accept if the value placed upon the Union rested, as it did for most Democrats, upon notions of the Union as the guarantor of liberties, as the fount of law and order, and as a vehicle to achieve national greatness, and not upon notions of the Union as a mystical thing of great intrinsic value.[25]

Although North Texas was the only area of the state in which Upper South culture was clearly dominant, the area around the capi- tal city of Austin also closely resembled Tennessee and Kentucky. Austin area residents' past culture, present economic reality, and prospects for future growth were distinctly upper southern, and through 1859 self-interest and ideology made the farmers and city folk of the counties surrounding Austin bastions of Unionism. Un- like North Texas, however, Austin as the capital city of the state contained a goodly number of vocal advocates of southern national- ism. Chief among them was John Marshall, editor of the *Texas State Gazette* and chairman of the state's Democratic party. Through the years leading up to secession, Marshall had worked consciously and deliberately to bridge the gap between the planter-slaveowning re- gion of Texas and the farmer-nonslaveowning portion of the state. By insisting that slaves should be available to every white man and that slavery stimulated the entire economy, he linked the selfish in- terests of all free Texans to the perpetuation and growth of slavery. Aiding Marshall in his attempts to convert the state to a southern point of view were numerous politicians who resided periodically in Austin. H. R. Runnels, F. R. Lubbock, and O. M. Roberts all clearly articulated the southern point of view in public and private. Joining them were a host of lesser-known state officials. The Austin area, then, while in character much like North Texas, had within itself a greater potential for support of secession.[26]

With the election of Lincoln Unionism was called into question in Austin and surrounding counties, and by 7 January, secessionists and unionists stood at near parity. Austin, in fact, became the nerve center and headquarters of both the unionists and secessionists in Texas. It was from Austin that O. M. Roberts and his associates issued the call for a secession convention. It was from Austin that Sam Houston, George Paschal, A. J. Hamilton, and E. M. Pease tried to prevent or at least slow down the movement. Interestingly enough at this critical juncture, John Marshall, who had done so much to promote extreme southernism, was absent from the state. Leadership in the secession crisis fell into more moderate and conservative hands. The reasons for the growth of secession spirit in this Central Texas area were similar to those that affected North Texas. Conditional unionists considered both their rights and their safety threatened by a sectional party which could, as the past had demonstrated, foment slave rebellions in Texas. These conditional unionists could look upon the Republicans as a threat to law, order, and established custom within the United States. Moreover, the growth of secessionism in the Austin area was aided by factors not applicable to North Texas. Critics of the U.S. government's frontier policy had been bombarding the citizens of Austin with their views for almost two years. Some of the most enthusiastic responses to secessionist speakers came when the argument was brought forward that federal neglect of the frontier justified secession. At the same time, the very presence of such articulate and popular secessionist leaders as O. M. Roberts, Rip Ford, and George and John Baylor generated a following for secession. Given all these factors it is a bit surprising that the unionists remained as strong as they did in the Austin area.[27]

Among ethnic Texans a similar fracturing process occurred. Since the uniformity inspired by the threat of Know-Nothingism, Germans had come to support a variety of candidates and issues. Until the fall of 1861, however, they, like the citizens of Texas from the Upper South, had firmly believed in the worth and value of the Union. By January of 1861 this had changed. At this point most Germans were ideologically kin to other Texans. In particular they followed the model of Texans from the Upper South. Slavery had very little impact on their daily lives, but they accepted slavery and the necessity of white supremacy. Republican threats to law, order, and established procedure disturbed German leaders as profoundly as they disturbed John H. Reagan. Strong partisan ties linked Germans to the Democrats who now led the secession movement. Secessionists had stood by Germans a few years earlier in their struggle against the Know-Nothings, while their unionist opponents had often been leading Know-Nothings. The Know-Nothing movement had also convinced Germans like Ferdinand Lindheimer of the necessity of conforming on issues widely supported by other Texans. The growing popularity of secession influenced Germans to conform to the dominant trend. Finally, some Germans, particularly those who had lived in Texas for some time, were philosophically attuned to parochialism and not nationalism. For these reasons many Germans accepted secession in January 1861. Other Germans, however, continued to reject secession. After 1857 a significant number of them had supported the political faction led by Sam Houston, despite the ties of many in this faction to the Know-Nothing party. Other Germans detested slavery and, while not always speaking out publicly, saw little reason for seceding and possibly fighting a civil war for an institution which they disliked and was of little personal benefit. Still other Germans, particularly those isolated on the frontier, valued the protection of the U.S. Army and understood the important contribution the army made to the local economy. Finally, a large number of politically attuned Germans were either conservatives or nationalists. Many conservative Germans feared the anarchy of secession and civil war more than they feared the imminent peril of Republican control of the executive branch of the national government. Nationalists not only had a mystical attachment to the nation as a whole, they valued the Union in a pragmatic sense. Urban merchants, for example, thought the Union good for business and the economy. So by January, German Texans, like Texans from the Upper South, were divided into two fairly distinct camps—one at least acquiescing in secession, and the other continuing to oppose such a drastic step.[28]

Among Mexican Texans, the only other major ethnic group in the state, there had never been a strong bond to the Union. Mexicans were motivated more by personal ties and an attachment to their place of birth than they were by ideological ties to the Union. The center of power among Mexican Texans was still the old upper-class families or their American replacements. This upper class held Sam Houston in high regard and supported his party in 1859 despite his former association with the Know-Nothings. Know-Nothingism, however, had left Mexicans, like Germans, with a distaste for many leading unionists and a fondness for many secessionists. Know-Nothingism, too, had taught them the lesson of conformity on basic issues. Finally, Mexican Texans felt a deep loyalty to Texas. It was their homeland. They had supported this homeland in the revolution against the Mexican government in the 1830s. They would support Texas in its revolution against the United States government in the 1860s. Some Mexican Texans, because of personal regard for

Sam Houston or because of a vendetta against the established classes in Texas, would oppose secession. Most Mexican Texans would at least acquiesce in secession.[29]

Old bonds that held Texans together in support of the Union—the bonds of party and of cultural groups—snapped between October of 1860 and January of 1861. Groups dedicated to the conservation and growth of the Union throughout the 1850s now abandoned their traditional stance. Left without the institutional support of a party, unionists in the east could only act as individuals. Unionists in the west still retained a semblance of party structure, but unanimous support for the Union by Texans from Germany and the Upper South was gone. Gone, too, was the allegiance many Mexican Texans had rendered the Opposition party. In these changing circumstances, secessionists were the only virile, growing force on the political and social scene. Their very vitality attracted some adherents. They grew in power, while those attempting to delay the plunge toward secession possessed only decayed and diminished influence.[30]

Not even pragmatism or cautious self-interest could stop this growing vitality. Across the entire South antisecessionists often drew strength from the urban commercial and manufacturing classes—those involved in the manufacturing, merchandising, and transporting of goods and agricultural products, as well as those who supplied legal and financial services necessary to ensure the smooth flow of commerce. For those integrated into the national economy, the forces of the marketplace encouraged preservation of the Union. It was to the advantage of dock workers as well as cotton factors that the flow of cotton from Galveston to New York or New Orleans continue. Both those who worked in and those who owned the small tool-producing companies in Dallas, Galveston, and Houston wanted their access to raw materials unimpeded by a division of the Union and consumer demand for their finished product undiminished due to a downswing in the economy caused by sectional tension.[31] Large planters and farmers were equally involved in commerce, but the essential difference between them and the strictly commercial classes was that they owned their land. If they were relatively free of debt or if the payment of debts were suspended, planters and farmers could live off the products of their fields. The urban commercial classes depended upon a cash economy for survival. A toolmaker with a home garden might get by on reduced wages, but he depended more directly for his subsistence upon the money he earned for his labor. A factory owner might survive for a while on his surplus capital, but Texas manufacturers were small-time operators with little surplus capital, and they depended upon continuity of production and sales for their livelihood. Pragmatic considerations seemed to dictate that the commercial classes in Texas would oppose secession.[32]

William Pitt Ballinger captured the conservative nature of the commercial classes when he noted in his diary on 30 December 1860: "This year closes I fear most ominously—This govt. will be overthrown and the Union destroyed. I hope for the best and it may be that public order and prosperity will not be weakened and that security will be given to the institution of slavery—But I have strong fears to the contrary, and my best judgment is that we are doing an unwise and maybe a fatal thing." Ballinger's diary entry illustrates the difficult position of the commercial classes of Houston and Galveston. They both feared that secession would create chaos and be bad for business, and hoped that slavery and the cotton economy of which they were a part would be made secure by secession. Torn by these doubts, the commercial classes of the Lower South region of Texas bowed to the will of the majority in their region and tacitly supported the disruption of the Union. But they lacked fervor and enthusiasm. Again, Ballinger caught their spirit when he wrote, "I have no heart in the cause—Its responsibility and its glory I leave to others."[33]

Galveston and Houston were unique in Texas; while the Lower South culture was perhaps dominant there, it was by no means omnipotent. These port cities had an international, or at least a national, flavor. They were Texas's window on the world. This was not true of the other major commercial centers of the state. In Marshall, Jefferson, Austin, and San Antonio, cultural ties were clearer and so too were the attitudes of the commercial classes. Marshall and Jefferson were breakpoints in the shipping of goods and agricultural products in and out of prosperous northeast Texas, a region of large plantations and high concentrations of slaves. The wealth and interests of the area were reflected in the size of the Whig and Opposition parties—groups that drew support because of their backing of internal improvements and their dedication to stability. Here a few merchants seemed reluctant to accept secession, but on the whole the commercial classes, including the great planters of the area, enthusiastically endorsed secession. Judging from the speeches and editorials of the closing days of 1860 and the first weeks of 1861, the reasons for this enthusiasm were much like those of other Lower South areas: the density of slave populations reminded whites of the necessity of controlling the black race, and Republicans were clearly perceived as a threat to law and order. Slavery's contribution to the economic system was repeatedly stressed, and the demand for cotton in Europe was trumpeted far and wide. It was argued that Texas had no choice but to go with the other states in the cotton-growing South. Of particular appeal to the commercial classes was the suggestion that secession be accompanied by stay laws that would prevent the collection of debts in the tumultuous days following secession. Far from opposing secession, the commercial classes in this most distinct Lower South region of the state supported it with their time, money, and votes.[34]

In urban areas more clearly the domain of the Upper South, or of a mix of upper southerners and ethnic Texans, commercial classes usually opposed secession. Ben Epperson, who clearly spoke for the economic interests of Red River and Lamar counties, opposed secession both for philosophical and pragmatic reasons. In Austin many of the leaders of the Union Club in the 1860 presidential election were merchants or financiers. Leading bankers and merchants like John M. Swisher, John Hancock, and Swante Palm continued to oppose secession through January of 1861. In San Antonio and in Rio Grande City, places whose economic prosperity was greatly enhanced by military expenditures, the commercial classes provided a bedrock of Unionism. In regions where the dominant cultural and economic order were not that of the Lower South, the preponderance of the commercial classes remained unionists.[35]

Taken as a whole the commercial classes of Texas were small in number. They represented, however, a concentration of wealth and an array of talent which made them a potent political force even in antebellum days. Their united support of the Union could perhaps have slowed the building momentum of the secessionists. Such support did not materialize. Despite the fairly widespread consensus that secession might be bad for business, commercial classes were not so much motivated by pragmatic monetary concerns as they were by their cultural ties. The same forces that moved Upper South Texans, Lower South Texans in the Opposition party, and ethnic Texans to abandon the cause of the Union also operated upon the commercial classes. Outside East Texas and the Gulf Coast, pragmatism seemed to help sustain the dedication of the commercial classes to the Union. Pragmatic concerns, however, seem to have been unimportant in East Texas and of only moderate importance along the Gulf Coast. The net result was that instead of the commercial classes binding together in opposition to secession, they, like so many other potentially powerful unionist groups, were split asunder.[36]

On the frontier, however, pragmatic concerns were of supreme importance. Survival dominated politics on the frontier. If the U.S. Army offered protection from the Indians as well as the important economic stimulus for the area, then the Union was a benefactor, but if the army failed to protect the citizens of the frontier and was of only minor importance to the economy, angry citizens often retaliated by expounding the virtues of secession. As was true of all the other pillars of the Union, by January 1861, the frontier had divided loyalties. That portion of the frontier above Fort Mason had continuous problems with the Indians from 1856 to 1861. In fact, as the Secession Convention prepared to meet, it was reported that a band of 900 Indians was raiding the frontier. In the eyes of the settlers in the area around Parker and Palo Pinto counties, the federal government had done little to alleviate this menace. Rather, by siding with the reservation Indians of the upper Brazos, it had prevented the settlers from striking at what they considered to be the source of many Indian depredations. The army, in turn, had come to dislike and distrust the frontiersmen. On the eve of the Secession Convention, secessionists had taken up the cudgels of the citizens of Parker and Palo Pinto counties and were scourging the federal government for its failure to do its duty and protect the settlers of western Texas. South of Fort Mason conditions were different. Indians had caused fewer problems in the years immediately preceding secession. The army posts contributed greatly to the local economy, and on the whole relations between the army and the settlers were good. The army was clearly perceived as being an important deterrent to Indian attack. Here, too, many of the settlers came from Germany. Some were German intellectuals who had fled their country because of the 1848 revolution. They now opposed slavery and supported the nation with the same fervor they had focused on changing Germany. For pragmatic as well as cultural reasons, then, the southern portion of the frontier remained unionist. The force of this Unionism, however, was blunted by the outspoken secession rhetoric of frontiersmen north of Fort Mason. Once again a cohesive group capable of swaying public opinion was fractured by the time of the secession crisis.[37]

By 8 January 1861, when most delegates to the Secession Convention were selected, not only were the partisan and ideological props of the Union shaken, but so too were its cultural and pragmatic supports. An additional pressure that helped bring the temple tumbling down was supplied by the tactical success and organizational strength of the secessionists and the tactical failure and organizational weakness of the unionists.

Unionists in Texas had long relied in their political canvasses not on organization, but on personalities and issues. One of the founding precepts of the Opposition party in 1858 had been a rebellion against the convention system and the domination of politics by a hierarchically organized party. Following this principle, the Opposition party was always loosely structured, and its strength was in local groups. Its leadership came from a talented few who either lived in Austin or journeyed there as state senators or representatives, but there was no permanent central committee and no network of organizations that could be called into service to campaign against secession. Secessionists, on the other hand, had the friendship and organizational ties of the Democratic party to aid their cause. It was no accident that the leaders of the call for the convention were Democrats who not only were leaders in their own party but had also been elected to the offices of state supreme court justice, state treasurer, and state attorney general. Their offices gave their actions the aura of legitimacy. Their positions in the party gave them access to all the local Democratic organizations and Democratic newspapers. They could and did formulate a statewide movement to elect secessionists to the Secession Convention. Unionists, on the other hand, had a shattered party in the eastern half of the state and poor organization elsewhere. As in the presidential election of 1860, they were too late in deciding upon a program to combat their opponents, and they never achieved united group action.[38]

At first, unionists attempted to ignore the movement in hopes that with time it would dissipate. When the Secession Convention was called, they treated the entire maneuver as illegal. In most counties, like Travis County, unionists simply refused to vote for delegates. In other counties, such as Comal County, unionists supported candidates who promised to support secession only as a last resort. It was only in Collin County, a few other North Texas counties, and in Williamson County that unionists made an organized attempt to elect delegates to the convention. At no time was there a systematic statewide attempt to ensure that unionists would have a voice at the Secession Convention. In fact, at no time prior to 8 January was there a concerted statewide drive to prevent secession. Whereas the secessionists were well organized and consistently applied workable tactics, the unionists were fragmented and inconsistent in their approach to the secession movement.[39]

From mid-October to the close of 1860 moderate secessionists added to their numbers as more and more moderate unionists converted. Five basic reasons caused this change. First, secessionists offered a clear solution to a widely perceived problem. Second, unionists had no such solution and relied instead upon the traditional attractions of the Union. Third, such reliance upon the tradition was increasingly out of step with a public galvanized into action by the election of Lincoln and the secession of the other cotton-growing states. Fourth, in effect, each traditional stronghold of the Union—non-Democratic political groups, non–Lower South cultural groups, and places where Unionism aided prosperity and survival—split into two camps; old coalitions which had brought unionist victories in the past could no longer be assembled. Finally, the secessionists used superior tactics and developed a more coherent strategy. As a result, on 8 January 1861, secessionists won an overwhelming majority of delegates to the Secession Convention. That convention, together with the state legislature, would enhance the legitimacy of secession. That legitimacy in turn would make it most difficult for unionists to convince the public to reject secession in the 23 February 1861 popular referendum. In the early months of 1861, secession grew while Unionism decayed.

8

Legitimizing Secession

On 7 January 1861, Governor Sam Houston took time out from his efforts to protect the Texas frontier from a sudden upsurge of Indian attacks and wrote a long letter to J. M. Calhoun, a representative from the state of Alabama. Calhoun's mission was to convince Texans of the wisdom of secession, and he particularly tried to persuade state officials to speed the course of secession. Calhoun asked the state's leaders to speak for Texas. In a classic defense of popular sovereignty Houston replied that only the people themselves could speak for Texas. And as he said, "A fair and legitimate expression of their will, through the ballot-box, is yet to be made known. Therefore, were the Legislature in session, or were a legally authorized Convention in session, until the action taken is ratified by the people at the ballot-box, none can speak for Texas."[1]

Houston thus put his finger on the central problem of the secessionists. Who legitimately spoke for the people of Texas? If the people's elected governor spoke for them, secession was doomed. If they must wait upon "a legally authorized Convention," secession was slowed. Even such a convention or the state legislature could not give absolute legitimacy to secession; that could only be achieved by a popular referendum. Secessionists then were faced with the problem of both achieving secession quickly and establishing its legitimacy.

Legitimacy, or at least the semblance of legitimacy, was essential. Throughout the secession crisis, in both their public utterances and private correspondence, secessionists insisted they were acting according to law, tradition, and precedent. They insisted that they had the support of not only the majority of Texans, but of the "best" people of the state. Perhaps this concern with legitimacy sprang from the realization that more reluctant secessionists would not join a movement tainted with radicalism or illegality. Expressions designed to prove the legitimacy of their actions were too common, however, just to be propaganda. In part, the desire for legitimacy arose from insecurity. Secessionists were convinced that they must act quickly in order to preserve and protect their society; they also wanted to repay the North's insult of electing Abraham Lincoln by seceding before his inaugural on 4 March. This haste made them vulnerable to unionists' charges that they were revolutionaries and demagogues acting rapidly in order to take advantage of temporary public hysteria. Self-doubt enhanced the sense of insecurity bred by unionists' criticism. Most secessionists felt at least a twinge of reverential devotion to the Union. That residual twinge must have at times engendered guilt and concern for what the rest of the world and future generations would think of their actions.

Besides, most secessionists had habitually acted according to law and precedent. Even the examples of vigilante justice so common in 1859 and 1860 were justified as cases in which security and order demanded swift action. Order: that was the key. The perception that Lincoln's election meant inevitable social and political disorder helped cause secession. Certainly, defenders of order have sometimes acted disorderly. For secessionists to do so, however, was to ignore the lesson of the elections of 1859 when the public had turned the promoters of disorder out of office. Such stupidity might have characterized a few fire-eaters, but not the larger group of moderate secessionists. John Reagan was a lawyer and a judge, not a revolutionary, and he was too shrewd a politician to act radically. Secession was a momentous and revolutionary act, but because of political issues, unionists' criticisms, self-doubt, and an instinctual reliance upon law, this revolutionary act had to seem to occur for legitimate reasons in a legitimate manner.[2]

Secessionists gained the legitimacy they sought when most of the organized counties in the state elected delegates to the Secession Convention called by O. M. Roberts and other secessionists. They gained legitimacy when the state legislature recognized the convention as the legal voice of the people of Texas. That convention's reasonable debate and overwhelming vote for secession lessened the taint of radicalism. Even the convention's orchestration of the takeover of all U.S. military installations in Texas and its attempts to join Texas with the Confederacy enhanced legitimacy. Forcing opponents out of positions of prominence and the intimidating acts of such groups as the Knights of the Golden Circle silenced many critics, and their silence made secession seem the only alternative. Still, as Houston had insisted in his letter to Calhoun, until the popular referendum on 23 February, secession could not be totally legitimate. By that date, however, secessionists had almost turned the tables on the unionists. Not secession but opposition to secession was rapidly becoming illegitimate.

On or about 8 January 1861, the first step in this process of legitimization began. On that date (or in some counties, a few days earlier) delegates to the Secession Convention stood for election. Candidates were nominated and elected informally at the discretion of each county. Elections were supposed to be ordered by the chief justice of each county, but in some counties other local officials took charge. Nominees were often selected at public meetings, usually arranged by secessionists, and this process seldom produced candidates that offered a clear choice between secession and the Union. In some counties unionists were probably prevented from running. In other cases unionists chose not to run because they considered the whole process illegal and feared their participation would impart de facto legality to the convention. Perhaps for that reason the voting was very light, but 92 of the 122 organized counties did select delegates in some fashion.[3]

After the county elections unionists charged that the selection of delegates was illegal and did not represent the will of the majority. They insisted that secessionists had tricked the public or that they had intimidated unionist voters. This might have been true in some plantation counties where remaining evidence suggests fraud or use of force. In many cases, however, the delegates were secessionists because the unionists did not go out and campaign for a spot on the delegation. A less biased and more secret election in which unionists had competed might have produced more unionist delegates, but probably would not have changed the convention's vote in favor of secession. It might have been, however, a much closer vote.[4]

On 21 January, a week before the newly elected delegates to the Secession Convention were scheduled to begin meeting, the special session of the legislature called by Governor Houston met in Austin. Texans had besieged the governor with calls for a special session as soon as the news of Lincoln's election became well known. Houston, hoping that time would cool the passions of secessionists, had delayed calling the special session until after moves were afoot to call a secession convention despite the opposition of the governor. On 17 December, Houston called for the legislature to meet in January, hoping that it would help him thwart the rise of secession sentiment. He hoped in vain.

In his address to the extra session Houston focused on the need for better defense against Indian attack and asked the legislators to help him organize a convention of southern states that could work cooperatively to insure their rights within the Union. Houston advised against immediate secession and reminded them of their lofty duty to give wise counsel to the people of Texas. Despite the governor's hopes, advice, and reminders, the state legislature moved quickly to support the Secession Convention. One of its first acts was to repeal the joint resolution of 1858 which had called for a convention of all the southern states to consider their relationship to the federal government. It was upon that resolution that Houston had based his call for cooperative action instead of immediate secession. Next, by joint resolution the Senate and the House validated the convention to be held on 28 January and the selection of delegates to that convention. The legislature pointed to the Texas Constitution's Bill of Rights, which reserved ultimate power for the people, and insisted that the people had used this power in the organization and selection of delegates to the Secession Convention. The leglislature bowed to the wishes of the governor, however, and provided that any action of the convention must be ratified by a popular referendum. Houston did not approve this joint resolution until 4 February and with his approval he issued a protest against any assumption of power by the convention beyond that specifically delegated by the people and the legislature to the convention. As in so many other cases in the secession crisis, all sides displayed an amazing respect for the letter and the intent of the law. Not even a sense of urgency could move either side to operate without the sanction of law.[5]

After passing another joint resolution rejecting the federal government's right to use coercion against any of the states, the legislature offered the use of the House chambers to the delegates to the Secession Convention. There, on 28 January 1861, slightly fewer than 180 Texans met and immediately began to take concrete steps to sever the bonds between Texas and the United States.[6]

These delegates were not average Texans, but neither were they the richest planters. Over 90 percent of the members had been born in the South. Almost 72 percent owned slaves, but only thirty-five of the members owned more than twenty slaves. Lawyers were the single largest group, making up more than 40 percent of the membership. Farmers and planters were next, with 35 percent of the membership. Most members were not rich, but the majority were certainly well off financially and had a background of community leadership. As Reagan and Roberts had hoped since the previous October, the convention represented the best men of Texas—not the richest slaveholders, for there were few of those present, but the prosperous farmers, lawyers, and small planters who dominated the economic, political, and social life of much of Texas.[7]

Like the state legislature, the convention wasted little time getting to the business at hand, and within a week passed by overwhelming consent various measures designed to take Texas out of the Union and into a new southern confederacy. On Monday, 28 January 1861, at 2:00 P.M., the convention was called to order and a prayer offered by Bishop Alexander Gregg of the Texas diocese of the Episcopal church. Oran M. Roberts was elected president and took the chair saying, "I bow to the sovereignty of the people of my state. All political power is inherent in the people. That power, I assert, you now represent." After the elections of secretaries a Committee on Credentials was appointed and the meeting adjourned until 7:30 that evening. During the evening meeting additional officers were elected and discussion began about a Committee on Federal Relations. Most important matters, though, were reserved for the next day.[8]

On the afternoon of the 29th, delegates left little doubt what the result of the convention would be. After a report on credentials and a decision to seat all contested delegations but to limit their votes to the number to which their districts were entitled, the president appointed a Committee on Federal Relations. John A. Wharton of Brazoria County, one of the members of this committee, stood and offered a resolution. Wharton, the son of William H. Wharton, a prominent leader of the movement for independence from Mexico, followed in his father's footsteps and asked the convention to declare their independence from the United States. Wharton asked the convention to agree "that without determining now the manner in which this result should be effected, it is the deliberate sense of this Convention that the state of Texas should separately secede from the Federal Union." George M. Flournoy moved for a vote on Wharton's resolution and without debate the convention voted 152 to 6 in favor of separate secession. That vote killed any remaining chances of cooperative action as favored by Governor Houston and indicated how few unionists had been elected to the convention.

Little else was accomplished on the 29th except the vote on Wharton's resolution, but on the next day the convention was busy and, for once, contentious. A standing Committee on Public Safety was appointed by the president and then, after the appointments of a few more committees, the convention invited John McQueen, the commissioner from South Carolina, to sit with the president during the rest of the convention. Although there was some objection to the seating of McQueen, the convention had been relatively quiet up to that point. When the specific wording of the Ordinance of Secession and a resolution to join Texas to the Confederacy were taken up, debate intensified. Several resolutions concerning the formation of a southern confederacy were offered, but all were tabled. Then Thomas

Jefferson Chambers, the chairman of the Committee on Federal Relations, submitted the ordinance drafted by his committee. Section I of the ordinance read:

> Whereas, the Federal Government has failed to accomplish the purposes of the compact of union between these States in giving protection either to the persons of our people upon an exposed frontier or to the property of our citizens; and whereas the action of the Northern States of the Union, and the recent development in federal affairs, make it evident that the power of the Federal Government is sought to be made a weapon with which to strike down the interests and prosperity of the Southern people, instead of permitting it to be as it was intended our shield against outrage and aggression: Therefore We the people of the State of Texas in Convention do declare and ordain that the ordinance adopted by our Convention of delegates on the 4th day of July, A.D. 1845, and afterwards ratified by us, under which the Republic of Texas was admitted into the union with other States and became a party to the compact styled "The Constitution of the United States of America" be and is hereby repealed and annulled; that all powers which by said compact were delegated by Texas to the Federal Government are revoked and resumed; that Texas is of right absolved from all restraints and obligations incurred by said compact and is a separate sovereign State.[9]

Besides illustrating a lawyer's proverbial ability to obscure the obvious with excessive rhetoric, Section I reveals that secessionists relied upon a legal doctrine often called the Compact Theory of Government. According to this doctrine, which had been present in various forms throughout the nineteenth century, the people of each state, not the people of the entire nation, were the ultimate sovereign power. Since the people of the state delegated power to the federal government but retained their sovereignty they could take back the powers they delegated. Secession, therefore, was legal. The validity of this theory and its use in Texas is not important. Instead, its importance is that it reveals once again the secessionists' need to act legitimately and legally. Secession, it was argued, was not revolution. It was the exercise of the rightful constitutional functions of each state.[10]

Section I of the Ordinance of Secession inspired little debate and was eventually passed with only minor changes in wording. Such was not the case for Section II, which stated: "This ordinance shall be submitted to the people of Texas for ratification or rejection by the qualified voters on the 23rd day of February A.D. 1861, and unless rejected by a majority of the votes cast shall take effect and be in force on and after the 2nd day of March, A.D. 1861." After the reading of the ordinance William B. Ochiltree, one of the members of the Committee on Federal Relations, offered a minority report which called for the deletion of Section II. No decision on the majority and minority reports was made that afternoon, and the convention adjourned until 7:30 that evening, when it met in secret session.[11]

All that evening and all the next day the convention debated the wisdom of submitting the Secession Ordinance to a popular vote. Finally, on the afternoon of 31 January, a motion by John Gregg to strike the second section was brought to a vote. Gregg's motion lost by 145 votes to 29.[12]

That evening, after still more debate about the Secession Ordinance, the convention passed a resolution to vote the next day at noon with no debate. A few minor amendments were passed. John Reagan and four other members of a committee who had met with the governor delivered a letter from Houston to the convention. In his letter, Houston said among other things, "I can assure you, gentlemen, that whatever will conduce to the welfare of our people will have my warmest and most fervent wishes, and when the voice of the people of Texas has been declared through the ballot box, no citizen will be more ready to yield obedience to its will or risk his all in its defence than myself. Their fate is my fate. Their fortune is my fortune. Their destiny my destiny, be it prosperity or gloom, as of old I am with my country." The convention then adjourned to await the vote on 1 February.[13]

Early the next morning, Judge Roberts dispatched Joseph Smith, an old friend of the Governor's, to convince him to attend the vote on the Secession Ordinance. Public notice of the noon vote had been posted and various dignitaries had been invited, but it was particularly important that the Governor, the most visible symbol of opposition to secession, be present and give at least tacit approval of the legality of the convention's actions. Later that morning, a committee of convention members waited on the Governor, who had agreed to attend. Slightly after 11:00 A.M. the committee escorted the Governor to a seat on the right of Roberts.

If Houston still entertained hope for the Union, the scene that greeted him surely dashed those last hopes. Warm applause marked his entrance, but it was clear that he was not at center stage. Almost every person in the crowded hall had one thing in mind: secession. Members of the state legislature, prominent local citizens, heads of various state departments, a group of Travis County ladies ready to present a new Lone Star flag, and the delegates themselves all were caught up in a momentous event. The noise and babble that had accompanied Houston's seating in the hall died down. Onlookers sat down in their chairs and quietly made themselves ready for a spectacle. Noontime had arrived. It was time for the vote.[14]

Out over the now silent crowd rolled the sound of the secretary of the convention reading the proposed Ordinance of Secession: "Whereas, the Federal Government has failed to accomplish the purposes of the compact of union. . . ." Then, in alphabetical order, the secretary began to call the names of the delegates: L. A. Abercrombie, W. S. J. Adams, W. A. Allen. Some stood and explained the reasons for their vote. Most simply said aye. Thomas P. Hughes of Williamson County was the first to vote no. He was joined by only seven others, among them James Throckmorton. When it was his turn, Throckmorton rose from his seat and said, "Mr. President, in view of the responsibility, in the presence of God and my country —and unawed by the wild spirit of revolution around me, I vote no." The crowd, which had remained fairly quiet during the voting, erupted. Some cheered and clapped; perhaps even ardent secessionists admired Throckmorton's courage. More of the crowd hissed. Throckmorton again rose from his seat and addressed Judge Roberts: "Mr. President, when the rabble hiss, well may patriots tremble." Loud and long cheering broke out. Perhaps the temple of the Union to which men like Throckmorton constantly referred still had some hold on Texans' minds and hearts. Perhaps they only admired his courage all the more.[15]

After a strong remonstrance from the president the crowd calmed down and the voting continued. When it was over the tally stood 166 members in favor and 8 opposed: secession had been passed by the convention. On the motion of John Reagan the ordinance was ordered engrossed on parchment for the delegates' signatures that evening. The ladies gave their flag to George Flournoy, who with flamboyant oratory presented it on their behalf to the convention. John Wharton accepted the flag for the convention and in gallant southern fashion thanked the ladies of Travis County for their expression of patriotism. The flag was draped across the president's stand. Loud cheering broke out once more. The group adjourned until evening. As he was about to depart, O. M. Roberts turned to Houston and remarked, "General, I am pleased to see you here today." Houston, showing no excitement and perhaps again worried about the future, responded, "I hope we will have many happy days yet." Most, however, left the hall amid cordial greetings, certain they had done the right thing. The joyous spirit of the moment carried them out of the hall and on through the next few months until it was replaced with the reality of the war Houston foresaw.[16]

After the election of delegates in early January, certainly after the passage of Wharton's resolution early in the convention, few questioned that the events of 1 February would occur. The convention's rejection of cooperative action, rejection of waiting upon an overt act of aggression by the North, and large vote in favor of separate secession were all expected. Its decision to take the matter before the public for a final judgment was another matter. On the last day of the first session of the convention, John Henry Brown, anxious to justify his vote in favor of a popular referendum, had it read into the journal that while he himself was in favor of secession proceeding unhindered by a time-consuming popular vote, "from the provisions of the call, the positions taken by many delegates in the canvass in favor of referring, and the more important fact that so many pains were taken to mislead the people before the election, and unfairly prejudice them against the proposed convention, I believe that sound public policy and future harmony among the great mass of the people dictate that the question should be fairly passed upon by the people of the State divested of all extraneous issues."[17]

Brown's statement and those of others indicate that the desire for secession to be regarded as totally legitimate motivated the inclusion of the provision for a popular vote. In many counties the published call for election of delegates to the convention had mentioned that the action of such a convention would have to be ratified by the public. This inclusion of public ratification also sprang from insecurity about the extralegal nature of the call for a convention, an insecurity heightened by unionist criticism. In addition, both the state legislature and Governor Houston had mentioned the necessity of a referendum in their acceptance of the convention. Finally, the popular referendum was included in the final Secession Ordinance because, since 1845, that had been the normal procedure for deciding any major question. If a popular vote had been necessary for annexation, it followed that a popular vote was necessary for secession.[18]

Besides, secessionists were confident of victory in any popular election. As Brown went on to say, "Thousands of true and honest men having had more or less hope of some adjustment, and others, under mistaken views as to its practicability having favored a combined movement of the whole South before separation, now that all these plans have failed and separate State secession is demonstrated as the only safe course, desire to record their votes in favor of secession." The election of delegates in favor of secession from across the state, the show of popular support in Austin, and the growing sense that they had done the right thing convinced secessionists that the public would support them. They waxed in power while the unionists waned.[19]

On the evening of 1 February, after voting that Edwin Waller, the only signer of the 1836 Declaration of Texas Independence among the delegates, sign the ordinance after the president of the convention, the delegates signed this new declaration of independence in alphabetical order. After the signing the chaplain asked a blessing on their action, and the convention went into secret session. During the secret session the convention agreed upon procedures for the 23 February referendum. The most significant feature agreed upon was that each ballot was to be marked "For Secession" and "Against Secession"; that way there could be no confusion as to the will of the public. Language difficulties were another potential cause of confusion, so the delegates voted that one thousand copies of the Ordinance of Secession be printed in both Spanish and German.[20]

Saturday, 2 February, the convention again met in secret session. Their first important item of business was a resolution allowing the Committee on Public Safety to order the takeover of any federal property within the state of Texas. By a vote of 159 to 5, delegates granted this extraordinary power to a small group of Texans.[21]

Next, the convention approved a lengthy "Declaration of Causes which Impel the State of Texas to Secede from the Federal Union." Drawn up by John Henry Brown, George Flournoy, John Wilcox, M. D. Graham, and A. P. Wiley, the document attacked the North for challenging white supremacy and for allowing the rise of a sectional party in its midst. One by one the other sins of the North were listed: invasion of southern soil, spreading of sedition and servile insurrection, impoverishment of the southern states by biased legislation in the U.S. Congress, failure to protect the Texas frontier from Indian attack, "and, finally, by the combined sectional vote of the seventeen non-slave-holding States, they have elected as president and vice-president of the whole confederacy two men whose chief claims to such high positions are their approval of these long continued wrongs, and their pledges to continue them to the final consummation of these schemes for the ruin of the slave-holding States." After a positive defense of slavery the authors then added the telling phrase, "By the secession of six of the slave-holding States, and the certainty that others will speedily do likewise, Texas has no alternative but to remain in an isolated connection with the

North, or unite her destinies with the South." Judging from this document, then, secession occurred because of the perceived sins of the North, the election of Lincoln, which demonstrated that these sins would continue and would become more detrimental to the South, a desire to defend slavery, and the leadership of the six states of the Lower South.[22]

Determined that their reasons for secession get a fair hearing and anxious for a favorable vote, the convention ordered printed 10,000 copies of the declaration in English, 2,000 in German, and 2,000 in Spanish. The convention then adjourned until 7:30 that evening, when it was to take up the last important item of business: joining the Confederacy.[23]

Saturday's evening session accomplished little. Delegates argued over whether it was best to immediately send delegates to the convention of the six other seceding states then meeting in Montgomery, Alabama, or to wait until after the 23 February referendum. Sam Houston had argued from the beginning that the convention's powers were narrowly defined. Delegates had been selected to consider the relationship of Texas to the federal government and that was all. Evidently many members of the convention considered his argument valid, because resolutions to send delegates to Montgomery were introduced from the second day of the convention on, and none made it to a vote. The evening of 2 February was no exception, and the convention adjourned until Monday.[24]

Texas nationalism might also explain the convention's difficulties in agreeing to send representatives to Montgomery. Houston said he preferred resumption of separate independence instead of secession and joining a southern confederacy. Evidently this sentiment was shared by a few others, but it was never a potent force in the secession crisis; indeed, it may have been only a ploy used by unionists like Houston to slow the process of secession. For one thing, most Texans in 1861 were relative newcomers to the state and had no ties to the Republic. The state's population had tripled since 1850, and among new immigrants the bonds to their old states were stronger than the bonds to the Republic. Besides, separate independence was impractical. As F. R. Lubbock pointed out in his memoirs, "Had she [Texas] desired to desert her sister States of the South in this hour of need and peril (which she did not) and resume her former station as a republic, it was realized that she could not preserve a neutral attitude and maintain herself in that condition." Certainly the leaders of the Secession Convention had no notion of resuming separate independence. In the "Address to the People of Texas" which was written at the close of the second session of the convention, John Henry Brown, Pryor Lea, and John Stell summed up in lawyer-like prose the movement for separate independence:

> In this state, the public mind was exercised by the question of our final separation from all other States; but the idea of such a result had no favor; and the apprehension of it was used as an argument against secession while the objection was met by the assured policy of a seceded confederacy. Hence, with rare exceptions, the advocates and opponents of immediate and separate secession of this State commenced and prosecuted the canvass, differing on the leading proposition of secession, but uniting in opinion that consummated secession should result in confederation as an incident. So the decisive issue was on secession.

As this quote indicates, secessionists and unionists alike were nationalists, but they were not all Texas nationalists.[25]

Secessionists wanted to build a new nation; unionists defended an old one. Both acted for similar reasons. Texas alone could not fulfill the functions of a nation, nor did it encompass the heritage and destiny of an American nation. The history of the Republic of Texas clearly demonstrated that Texas could not protect its frontiers and provide a stable climate for economic growth. The ease with which Texans had given up their nation in 1845 demonstrated the shallow hold it had on their minds and spirits. Unionists argued that the Constitution, the flag, the memory of the founding fathers, the history of the country until 1860, and the destiny of the United States to grow in prosperity and prestige were among the most sacred features of life. They further argued that individual prosperity and safety were most secure in the Union despite the ascendancy of the Republicans. One of their frequent charges against secession was that it would end slavery, not protect it. Secessionists disagreed with unionists about the pragmatic benefits of the old Union, but the less extreme group typified by John Reagan retained a reverential attitude toward the Union. Members of this group were not anarchists. They were not destroyers of a nation. They were attempting to build a new nation as much like the old as possible. This new nation would better protect slavery and the Texas frontier, but because it would have laws and a constitution almost identical to the United States it could be legitimately regarded as a child of the old ways. Secessionists argued that the destiny of Americans took a new direction with the formation of the Confederacy, but retained its basic character. Again to quote the address of Lea, Brown, and Stell, "The

Convention found that the constitution for the provisional government of the Confederacy was well adapted to the emergency, without departing from any essential principle of the Union constitution." Essentials of an American nation would remain after secession. For the unionists of February 1861, that could not be entirely true. The United States was important in and of itself. It was not just a pragmatic shield from foreign attack or a promoter of domestic prosperity. It was not just the vehicle for the achievement of American destiny. The Union had a character and an attachment that could not be transferred from one government to the next. It had been legitimized by time, memorable events, and long-dead heroes. Those were things the Confederacy could never have in the 1860s.[26]

Still, Texas was to become a member of that Confederacy. On Monday, 4 February, the convention met for the last time before the secession referendum and finally began to address the questions raised by the creation of a new nation. After the proposal of many resolutions and amendments, by a vote of 102 to 38 the convention resolved to elect seven delegates to represent Texas at Montgomery "in order that the views and interests of the people of Texas may be consulted with reference to the constitution and provisional government that may be established." A more detailed resolution that would have bound Texas to join the new confederacy was tabled, but so was a restrictive motion that would have limited the power of the delegates to forming only a provisional government. Despite the vague, middle-of-the-road nature of the eventual resolution, no major item of business drew more recorded votes in opposition. Secession was easier than building a new nation.[27]

That evening, the convention elected the seven delegates to Montgomery. John Reagan won the highest number of votes. Also elected were Senator Louis T. Wigfall, Senator John Hemphill, John Gregg, W. S. Oldham, Thomas N. Waul, and William B. Ochiltree.[28] With that last major item of business concluded, the convention adjourned on the evening of 4 February to await the public vote on secession. President O. M. Roberts concluded this first session of the Secession Convention by saying, "The ordinance has been submitted to the people for ratification or rejection. Let us go home and appeal to them to sustain our action by their votes; and when we reassemble on the 2nd of March let us bring back with us the voice of a united people, in favor of an immediate action to sustain the rights of the people of Texas and of the South at all hazards, and to the last extremity."[29]

Actually, the convention had already taken steps to sustain the rights of Texans. Having already given the Committee on Public

Safety the power to seize federal property, on 4 February, before electing the delegates to Montgomery, the convention authorized the Committee on Public Safety to stay in session during the convention's recess. Before 23 February, that committee would order Ben McCulloch, a veteran military man who had fought in the Texas Revolution, the Mexican War, and in numerous expeditions against the Indians, to seize the federal arsenal at San Antonio and force the evacuation of the approximately 2,700 federal troops in Texas.[30]

John C. Robertson, a Harvard-educated lawyer who, like O. M. Roberts, lived in Tyler, chaired the Committee on Public Safety, which usually had about twenty members. Besides Robertson, the most prominent members of the committee were Thomas S. Lubbock, brother of F. R. Lubbock, John Henry Brown, one of the leading propagandists for secession, and John S. "Rip" Ford, Texas Ranger, newspaper editor, and politician. Most of the members owned slaves and held substantial amounts of property, but few were extremely wealthy or owned more than twenty slaves. The majority of the group were lawyers, but there were a few physicians and farmers. Ford, of course, had also been a physician and a lawyer at different times in his long career.[31]

Meeting in both Austin and Galveston, the committee oversaw the organization of Texas troops, purchased military stores, arranged the transfer of almost three million dollars' worth of federal stores to Texas, and orchestrated the evacuation of federal troops. The committee was given great power by the convention and used it aggressively. Even before the convention adjourned the committee began negotiating for the surrender of federal stores and troops with General David E. Twiggs, a hero of the Mexican War, who in 1861 at age seventy-one commanded the Department of Texas. When Twiggs, who had been requesting instructions from Washington on how to deal with secession, appeared ready to resign, the committee ordered General Ben McCulloch and his men to enter San Antonio rather than wait and deal with Twiggs's successor, who was less favorably inclined to the South. Twiggs, who only had about 160 men in San Antonio, came to terms with McCulloch and on 18 February agreed to surrender all federal property to the Texans and to evacuate his command. The federal troops kept their sidearms, camp equipment, and horses and wagons. At the time the federal troops in Texas amounted to about 10 percent of the entire U.S. Army, so the Texans regarded themselves as great heroes. Twiggs was later court-martialed for his part in the affair.[32]

In their report to the president of the convention, the committee justified its use of force by saying that a state of emergency had existed. It could not wait upon Twiggs to act without coercion or wait upon the popular referendum. The safety of the public had demanded quick action because the incoming administration of the United States government could not be trusted and because the large number of troops in Texas were a potential threat. The Texans struck first rather than wait for new, more hostile officers to replace Twiggs and his subordinates. In acting before the referendum, however, Robertson's committee diminished the meaning of the popular vote on secession, and made the secessionists vulnerable to charges by the unionists of physical intimidation.[33]

Actually, the use of force and conspiratorial methods had been a factor from the beginning. With news of Lincoln's imminent election, vigilante groups whose ostensible purpose was to prevent slave uprisings formed in some counties. Other Texans turned to already existing paramilitary groups or secret organizations. Early in the secession movement O. M. Roberts and John Reagan both realized the disastrous implications such groups could have on a lawyer's movement. On 1 November 1860, Reagan wrote Roberts:

> Your reference to the Knights of the Golden Circle, and supposition that the organization may have in view some plan of action in behalf of the South, and implied disapproval of any secret movement for such a purpose meets my unqualified approval. A secret movement, for such a purpose, could not but prove disastrous in the extreme to the cause of the South . . . And our very system of government forbids the idea of secret political parties. . . . And our consultation for the common good and safety should be open and free to all. There is no other means by which we can surely aggregate public sentiment, and secure the popular approval of great public measures. . . . For any citizen or member of citizen's groups as such to array themselves against the federal government without the authority and protection of state sovereignty, they would be rebels in law, and might be dealt with as such.

Despite all the efforts of Roberts and Reagan, the vigilantes and other groups outside the law and established procedure, and incidents like the burning of Ferdinand Flake's press in January 1861 cast doubt on the legitimacy of secession. Unionists asked why the public had to be forced to go along with something allegedly in their best interests, and why the secessionists who claimed to be acting under the legal doctrine of state sovereignty used illegal methods to achieve their ends.[34]

In the long run, the group most often cited as clandestine promoters of secession through the use of force was the Knights of the Golden Circle. The secret organization had been founded and promoted in the 1850s by George W. L. Bickley. Bickley, a man given to secret signs and strange titles, dreamed of raising up a southern empire as great as the Roman Empire. The geographic center of this empire was to be Havana, Cuba, and everything within a radius from Texas to Cuba was to fall within the Empire of the Golden Circle. The organization developed in the Lower South, but by 1858 had spread to Texas. By 1859 Texas had become the heart of the group because it hoped to use the state as a springboard for the capture of Mexico.

Bickley oversaw the organization of about thirty castles, the Knights' term for their lodges, in Texas towns. Each of these castles had a paramilitary division that kept itself ready for the Mexican invasion. Several times Bickley attempted to assemble an army in South Texas and at least once tried to interest Sam Houston in his schemes. Houston, while certainly interested in the conquest of Mexico, considered the Knights' filibustering schemes unpractical, and so they were. Nothing ever came of the attempts to take Mexico.[35]

Besides their military organizations, the Knights also had a very secret political group that promoted secession. At least four members of the Secession Convention, Alfred M. Hobby, John A. Wilcox, Thomas S. Lubbock, and John Littleton, were known Knights. Three others, Pryor Lea, Philip N. Luckett, and George W. Chilton, were suspected members. Wilcox, Lea, and Lubbock were very active members of the convention. Wilcox helped write "A Declaration of the Causes which Impel the State of Texas to Secede from the Federal Union." Lea helped write the "Address to the People of Texas," published at the end of the convention. Lubbock served on the Committee on Public Safety. The Knights, then, certainly had opportunity to express their political views.[36]

Obviously, if the Knights were critical in influencing the convention as a group and in serving as propagandists for secession, then the secession of Texas was much more a conspiracy than it has previously appeared to be. The problem with evaluating the Knights has always been lack of evidence. Not a shred of evidence has been found that Wilcox, Lea, and Lubbock conspired together to sway the convention toward the secessionist views of the Knights. Instead, all three seem to have acted spontaneously; while they might have been extremists, they were not conspirators. They did not need to be. Despite the charges of James P. Newcomb and others, secession was a popular movement, almost a spontaneous, unplanned movement. It certainly had leaders and organizers, but with the possible exception of Lea, Wilcox, and Lubbock, none were members of the Knights. None planned secession before the fall of 1860.[37]

If the Knights were instrumental in the secession of Texas, it was as soldiers and policemen, not propagandists and leaders. When Ben McCulloch entered San Antonio on 18 February, his approximately 250 men were joined by 150 armed Knights organized into companies. The Knights also played a role in the takeover of other government posts in the state. Editor Newcomb accused the Knights of the destruction of his press in San Antonio and believed they had policed the voting places during the secession referendum in order to keep unionists away. When war broke out, groups of Knights quickly joined up, but were just as quickly absorbed into the Confederate army and lost their group identity. Because of the lack of hard evidence and the great quantity of exaggerated allegations and boastful claims, not much more can conclusively be said about the Knights than what Anna Irene Sandbo said in 1914: "The most that one can safely say is that probably the order encouraged secession and the extension of slavery, and that it was a factor of some importance at this time." No amount of mathematical wizardry or circumstantial evidence justifies a stronger statement than Sandbo's.[38]

Whatever their level of involvement in secession, the Knights of the Golden Circle had a mixed effect upon the secessionists' drive for legitimacy. Military force, skillfully and successfully used propaganda released under the heading of the work of the representatives of the people of Texas, and the outcome of elections possibly influenced by the KGC all gave the secessionists the appearance of doing the people's will and of being on the winning side. At the same time, hints of the use of force, of conspiracy, and of unfair and biased elections made the secessionists seem undemocratic usurpers of popular rights. Despite their success, secessionists never completely lost their label of radical conspirators and demagogues. Unionists could always say, "Let the system of terrorism and denunciation which some have sought to inaugurate, be indignantly rebuked, as unworthy in a land in which men yet claim to be free. Let respect be preserved for law, and for public and social order." They could point to the real or imagined role of the Knights of the Golden Circle in the secession movement.[39]

Secessionists, however, shed much of their radical label from 7 January to the eve of the secession referendum of 23 February. The election of delegates, while open to question in some counties, created a secession convention sanctioned first by the state legislature and finally even by the recalcitrant Governor Houston. That convention debated the issues, voted for secession, published much propaganda in support of its actions, made moves to remove federal troops and secure federal property in Texas, and initiated efforts to join Texas to the Confederacy. By mid-February, Texas had begun to act independent of the United States, and every independent action made Texans' new situation less frightening and more customary. In fact, by then the unionists, not the secessionists, seemed extremists and threats to social harmony.

One final act in the process of legitimization remained. The public still had to vote yes or no on secession. Despite the hisses of the crowd and the sense that they were out of step with the majority, Throckmorton and other unionists hoped Texans would at last listen to the voice of the Union and reject secession, if not out of reason, then out of love for their nation.

9

Stilling the Voice of Reason

James W. Throckmorton's hopes that the popular referendum on secession would preserve Texas's place in the Union were doomed;
doomed by two potent political forces present before the February
campaign began: consensus and nationalism. Texans, as Sam Houston noted, did not make an entirely rational choice on 23 February
1861. By the time the public voted on secession, a steadily building
consensus in favor of secession halted all debate of the issue in many
areas of the state. Unionists themselves counted on the irrational—
the pull of flag, Constitution, and country—to preserve their nation.
Nationalism, though, cut two ways. By 23 February, secession not
only tore down the old nation, it built up a new America—one that
Texans hoped would be all the things the United States had once
represented.

In his classic study of nineteenth-century America, Alexis de
Tocqueville noted that in many ways democracies were more tyran-
nical than aristocracies or monarchies. On vital issues, on certain
ideas or values crucial to the stability of society, democracies would
brook no dissidence. Clement Eaton has insisted that one of the best
examples of this intolerance happened in the antebellum South. Over
the thirty years prior to the Civil War, as slavery became threatened
by northern agitation, acceptance and belief in the South's peculiar
institution became a basic requirement for living there. As Texas
Germans could testify, only a few dissenters of the best families,
with great status in their communities or immense wealth, were allowed to speak out against slavery. Orthodoxy on the slavery question became not a matter of choice, but of necessity. In much the
same way, over the winter and early spring of 1860–1861 endorsement of secession became a necessity.[1]

Consensus was both a culmination of the forces that had caused
the growth of secession sentiment from November to February and a
new impetus toward the disruption of the Union. As time passed secession gained legitimacy by the exit from the Union of the six
states of the Lower South, and by the continued support of secession
in Texas by such well-known moderate politicians as John H. Rea-

gan. The separate secession of the states of the Lower South also un-
dercut the cooperationist argument that the South should act in concert. By late January 1861, it was apparent to all Texans that a new
nation of southern states was to be formed. Those cautious men
who might have been reluctant to see Texas act independently could
by that time support secession with the assurance that an alliance
between Texas and the other southern states was sure to follow their
state's departure from the Union. Consensus in favor of secession
was formed as well by the unity of purpose of secessionist leaders
and their political effectiveness. Once the proponents of secession
held a simple majority on local levels, the political process aided
consensus. A slim margin of victory in the election of delegates to
the Secession Convention could be translated into an overwhelming
endorsement of secession when the gavel sounded to open the statewide convention. This endorsement of secession in a legally recognized fashion and the seizure of federal property in Texas further enhanced secession's aura of legitimacy and made opposing secession
seem both impossible and dangerous.[2]

Two final aspects of the cumulative nature of the consensus in
favor of secession were Texans' desire for order within their society
and their often irrational fears of the Republican party and a racial
civil war. Conservative men like John Reagan, who had opposed the
radicals' attempts in 1859 to restore the slave trade because it was
illegal and would disrupt the harmony between North and South,
were willing in 1861 to secede because of this desire for order and
these irrational fears. To many Texans, no law or set of laws, from
the Fugitive Slave Law to the Constitution, seemed sacrosanct to
the Republicans. Republican willingness to violate the Fugitive
Slave Law and their appeals to a higher law demonstrated to Texans
that they could not preserve their legal rights in a government dominated by the "Black Republican" party. Moreover, once the Republicans were in power, they would be able to incite slave rebellions in
the South or even elevate the Negro to a position of equality with
the white man. In either case, the end result seemed destined to be a
violent and bloody clash between the two races—a civil war between classes much like the French Revolution or the Roman civil
wars. If secession was the only alternative to violations of legal
rights and social chaos, then to oppose secession threatened the very
life of the community. Those who still supported the Union in early
February 1861 seemed to many Texans suicidal, not simply political
opponents.[3]

Once such a powerful consensus had been formed from its com-
posite parts, it carried with it all Texans whose support for the Union

was wavering. Those who in calmer times might have listened dispassionately to the unionists' rational arguments turned their backs on reason and logic. Consensus then became a new force in the secession crisis; the fear of physical assault, the herd instinct, a need to hold opinions whose legitimacy was well established, an unwillingness to be cast in the role of traitor, a lack of alternative role models, and a fondness for action, not reflection, swayed Texans.[4]

Pressure for consensus often took the form of physical violence. Abolitionists had been hung or ridden out of Texas on a rail throughout the 1850s. In 1861 unionists' property was destroyed, and their families threatened with bodily harm. In Galveston, a mob destroyed editor Ferdinand Flake's press after he published a letter in English which decried the secession of South Carolina. The mysterious Knights of the Golden Circle harassed editor James Newcomb in San Antonio. The crowd in the gallery and even some delegates hissed and booed James Throckmorton when he cast his vote against secession at the Secession Convention. A mob almost attacked Sam Houston, the state's greatest hero, in Galveston. These were only the most notable of incidents involving figures in the public spotlight. No matter how much Judge O. M. Roberts and Representative Reagan pictured secession as a movement led by the best men, the threat of physical violence to those who opposed it was clearly present.[5]

More prevalent and probably more important were less overt forms of pressure for consensus. By 1 February, when the Secession Ordinance passed the convention, secession appeared the will of a large majority of Texans. Cautious men, like William Pitt Ballinger, might in their hearts oppose secession and hope that it could somehow be prevented, but they would not risk the brand of social deviant by going against the majority. Appearances mattered, not realities. If people thought the majority supported secession and were unwilling to alienate their neighbors in a vain attempt to halt the flight of Texas out of the Union, then it mattered little if such a majority actually existed. The desire to be like the herd would move them like lemmings over the cliff and into the sea.[6]

It took real courage to risk social, political, and economic sanctions by opposing secession, particularly for those whose place in society had the least legitimacy or authority. If Ballinger had been outspoken in his criticism of secession, his Anglo-Saxon Protestant background and his long residency in Texas would have given his words legitimacy. His wealth, high social standing, prominence as a lawyer, and history of political leadership would have given his message authority. It was all the more difficult for those without Ballinger's qualifications but who aspired to them to speak out or to be heard. Ferdinand Lindheimer, having experienced the disastrous effect of linking Germans with abolitionists, was especially concerned during the secession crisis that Germans act as other Texans—that they not alienate other citizens of their state by opposing what he considered an inevitable course of events. For him Germans could not speak out because they did not share equal creditability with other Texans, and protesting would have destroyed what creditability they had built up. What was true of the Germans was true of all other minority groups who lived in a Texas dominated by a Lower South culture.[7]

Southerners had displayed little regional solidarity prior to 1860, but by the fall of that year a growing conception that all southerners must stand by the South added to the force of consensus. Democratic editors insisted that Breckinridge deserved their readers' votes because it would be a sign of the South's solid resolve to resist northern aggression. They said the same thing about secession. Secession, they argued, was a necessary act. Even if it were later rescinded and a compromise worked out between North and South, moving toward secession would demonstrate the South's united resolve and highlight the seriousness of their grievances. Once the Confederacy began to emerge as a nation—and the convention that framed the Confederate Constitution and elected the provisional government began to meet well before the February referendum on secession in Texas —then to oppose secession became not only unwise and suicidal but traitorous. The successful birth of this new nation demanded the full support of all citizens or potential citizens, and if they did not give such support willingly, then the desperateness of the situation justified other methods of forcing consensus. Not only was the conversion from regional solidarity to national solidarity a force which created consensus, it made coercion seem more acceptable in a democracy.[8]

Gradually, in the central portion of the state, on the northern frontier, in East Texas, in South Texas, and along the Gulf Coast, defenders of the Union were silenced or muffled. In January, Colonel J. W. Barret, editor of the *Harrison Flag* and one of the most persistent critics of secession in his region, ceased publication of his newspaper because of ill health. By February 1861, few men in East Texas and the lower Brazos and Colorado river areas consistently and openly opposed secession. Flake still published articles and editorials against secession in both English and German. Even after his press was wrecked he continued publication with a second press he had hidden in his house. Most of those who doubted the wisdom of secession, however, followed Ballinger's course and kept their doubts to themselves or set them down in private diaries. This absence of opposition in February, particularly respected opposition, further aided consensus. There were no leaders for those with powerful but unuttered and unfocused feelings for the Union. The result was that citizens of Lower South–dominated counties voted with abnormal unanimity for secession (see Table 2).[9]

Only in regions culturally isolated from Lower South Texas did the pressures for consensus remain weak in February. In North Texas, Charles De Morse, although favoring secession, repeatedly defended the right of the people of his region to work against the disruption of the Union. In Austin and the Travis County area the most prestigious citizens set an example of Unionism and served as alternative role models. Dignified and respected former Governor E. M. Pease, prosperous merchant Swante Palm, lionlike Sam Houston, brilliant A. J. Hamilton, and outspoken George Paschal set an example which others in their region could follow. In frontier German counties Edward Degener and Hermann Speiss served much the same function. Frontiersmen who valued the army and North Texans who worried about Indian incursions from federally controlled Indian Territory had pragmatic reasons for opposing secession. In all these places slavery and the plantation system were of less value than the Union. These were the domains of the freeholding farmer and the merchant capitalist, not of the planter. These were the places in which nature itself prevented the expansion of the cotton culture. These were to be the places in which the secession referendum went down in defeat.[10]

Unionists from these non–Lower South regions still tried in February to resist the pressure to conform to the secessionist point of view—not only in their own regions but around the state. Their most notable effort was a carefully prepared "Address to the People of Texas." It was signed by twenty-four state legislators or delegates to the Secession Convention. Among them were I. A. Paschal, brother of George Paschal, James W. Throckmorton, and Ben H. Epperson. The address began by conceding that there were difficulties between North and South, but its authors insisted these difficulties could be solved by adjustments to the federal Constitution. Lauding the Constitution—citing its flexibility and the wisdom of the founding fathers in forging a document which could be adjusted to suit the times—they presented secession as a revolutionary conspiracy. South Carolina and politicians imbued with the philosophies of South Carolina were the villains of the plot. South Carolina was undemocratic. Its planter-aristocrats ruled the state unfettered

TABLE 2. Texas Counties that Cast at Least 95 Percent of
Their Votes for Secession on 23 February 1861

Dominant Culture and County	Region	For	Against	Percent For
Upper South				
Brown	N. Frontier	0	16	100
Lower South				
Anderson	East	870	15	98
Bowie	East	268	15	95
Brazoria	Coastal	527	2	99
Cherokee	East	1,106	38	97
Comanche	N. Frontier	86	4	96
Fort Bend	Coastal	486	0	100
Freestone	East	585	3	99
Grimes	East	907	9	99
Hamilton	N. Frontier	86	1	99
Harrison	East	866	44	95
Karnes	Central	153	1	99
Liberty	East	422	10	98
Limestone	Central	525	9	98
Madison	East	213	10	96
Marion	East	467	0	100
Matagorda	Coastal	243	8	97
Newton	East	178	3	98
Orange	East	142	3	98
Palo Pinto	N. Frontier	107	0	100
Panola	East	556	5	99
Polk	East	567	22	96
Smith	East	1,149	50	96
Trinity	East	206	8	96
Tyler	East	417	4	99
Washington	Central	1,131	43	96
Wharton	Coastal	249	2	99
German/Lower South				
Galveston	Coastal	765	33	96
Mexican				
El Paso	Far West	871	2	99
Starr	South	180	2	99
Webb	South	70	0	100
Zapata	South	212	0	100
Mexican/Lower South				
San Patricio	Coastal	56	3	95

SOURCE: Timmons, "The Referendum in Texas on the Ordinance of
Secession"; Jordan, "The Imprint of the Upper and Lower South."

by the wishes of the people. These planters sought their own self-interest. They sought an end to tariffs, which they blamed for their economy's stagnation, and the preservation of a slave system that would maintain their economic, political, and social dominance. In reality, unionists argued, secession would only increase the tax burden for the average southerner and result in a long, expensive, and bloody civil war. Secession did not cure the evils of the day. Lincoln's election was not really an affront to southern pride. Kentuckians had not seceded, and they still held up their heads. Besides, secession would only result in the ultimate extinction of slavery, not its preservation. In all likelihood, some border states would remain in the Union, and in these states, lacking the political support of the Deep South slave states, slavery would gradually wither away. Even slavery within a confederacy of the cotton states would be threatened. A southern confederacy would be the only avowed slaveholding country in the civilized world. Being smaller than the current United States, this confederacy could not long resist the pressure for conformity with the rest of the world. In their long and reasoned approach, unionists insisted that secession would be disastrous for all Texans, slaveholder and nonslaveholder alike.[11]

In particular, the unionist authors of the "Address to the People of Texas" focused on the antidemocratic nature of secession and its portent to the nonslaveholder. Just as they forecast that externally a "Cotton State Confederacy" would be isolated in the civilized world, they declared that internally power would gravitate toward a slaveholding aristocracy. South Carolina was the model for secession, and they warned that South Carolina would be the model for the Confederacy. Beyond that, they believed that because the South would be constantly threatened by external invasion a large standing army would be required, and the military establishment would gradually usurp democratic freedoms. They offered the Secession Convention itself as a model of what was to come. They claimed it was gradually taking over the power of the legally elected state legislature and governor. Besides, it was a convention whose members had been elected by a minority of Texas voters. Minority rule was the essential characteristic of the Secession Convention, and the unionists reiterated time and again that this same characteristic would permeate the new Confederacy.

In the end, the authors of the "Address" called for the voters of Texas to be reasonable and conservative. The convention, they argued, acted with unseemly haste. Secession's seriousness demanded careful consideration, not rash action. In giving the voters only twenty-three days to consider the momentous question of secession, the leaders of the Secession Convention had denied the citizens of Texas a chance to make a rational decision. Secessionists, appealing to prejudice and hysteria and taking advantage of the moment to achieve selfish ends, had violated the very process of change outlined by the constitution of the state of Texas. That constitution provided that a majority of eligible voters decide any major constitutional question. The Secession Convention required only that a majority of those who voted on 23 February decide the question. As the unionists put it: "Let respect be preserved for law, and for public and social order. Let it not be forgotten that trial by jury, and by due course of the law of the land is the birthright of every American citizen, and let no Vigilance Committees or irresponsible tribunals have power over the liberties and lives of men." In the minds of the unionists, the actions of the secessionists threatened to tear their beloved state and their country apart. Secession was as great an evil as northern aggression. Texans should resolve their differences, carefully consider their plight, and form a united front to protect their rights.[12]

In this classical model of conservatism, unionists sought a well-considered compromise or a legal and constitutional solution to their problems. They believed in staying within the established form. They showed a special reverence for the makers of the Constitution and exhibited an almost mystical attachment to the nation. They stressed reason but, to most Texans, the times called for action. Years of conflict and dialogue between North and South and between unionists and secessionists within the South now called for resolution by a simple manly act. Only the secessionists promised such an act. Here again role models and perceptions of how Texans ought to act aided the growth of a consensus in favor of secession. Only secessionists were moving toward a solution of the problem of the place of the South in the Union. This was a problem that had been with the American nation almost from its inception. It had been the subject of much dialogue and continual compromise. In 1861, at the end of a decade of tension between North and South, there seemed to be in the minds of many Texans a desire to somehow put the problem behind them—to act instead of talk, to achieve a total instead of a partial cure. American politics have often been explained as reaction to things as they are. This discontent with the status quo in 1861 meant not just discontent with the election of Abraham Lincoln, but discontent with the long and wordy conflict between North and South. Secessionists promised a way out of this conflict. Unionists offered only a continuation of things as they were.[13]

Despite the apathy or indignation that often greeted their efforts in the three weeks between the close of the convention and the secession referendum unionists reiterated again and again the points made in "The Address" and constantly sought new means to prevent secession. One new argument added to their campaign was that for Texas to secede meant deserting the border states. Appealing to the history of good relations between Texas and Tennessee, unionists urged voters not to turn their backs on the state that had befriended them more than any other. In selecting this line of attack, unionists ignored the realities and dreams of Texans in February of 1861. Over the past decade, Texans had increasingly migrated from the Deep South or were absorbed into that region's culture. By 1861 Texans' hopes and habits were not as Tennessean as they once had been. That should have been obvious, but less obvious was that by February, nationalism separated Texans from Tennessee and the rest of the old Union.[14]

American nationalism's intertwined elements made it a shadowy but potent force. As suggested earlier, concepts about an American nation fell into two general categories, internalized values or attitudes and functional purposes or goals. Over time the United States had become important in and of itself. Customarily and ceremonially worshipped, America, like a religion, had its creed and sacred writings: the Constitution, the Bill of Rights, and the Declaration of Independence. It had a special day of worship on the Fourth of July. It had particular saints and heroes: George Washington, Thomas Jefferson, Andrew Jackson, and other founding fathers or protectors and defenders. This religion had its symbol, the flag with one star for each state. It had its moments of epic sacrifice, the Revolution and the War of 1812. Texas unionists did not accidentally speak of stars shooting from the heavenly blue of the flag, or accidentally run their candidates on a platform of the Constitution and the Union and repeatedly invoke the blessing of the patron saints of the nation. When they made 4 July 1860 a day to bind up the nation's wounds or spoke of blood shed in vain in past wars they were expressing perhaps the strongest features of American nationalism.

Added to this religious sense were perceptions of the nation as the ultimate expression of the character of the American people. Europeans asked, who are these Americans? One obvious answer was that they were citizens of the American nation. People and country had the same characteristics and could not exist without each other. If the American people were aggressive, expansive, and legalistic, so was their nation. If Americans believed themselves destined for wealth, greatness, and power, their nation had the same destiny.

Americans had a collective personality. They had a sense of self that depended upon their membership in a larger community. To attack and destroy their nation was to attack and destroy themselves.[15]

Visions of the close ties between the nation and the spirit and character of its people and a worshipful attitude toward that nation were habitual and customary by 1861. Such feelings and beliefs were aided by a romantic view of life which helped make such national-ism common in the western world. Whether they came from a sense of heritage or a view of life, however, these characteristics of nation-alism were internalized by 1861. They did not have to be reasoned or thought out. They surfaced without an examination of self-interest or propriety. Nationalism's creation, sustenance, and potency, how-ever, came not just from what the nation was, but from what the nation should or could do.[16]

For mid-nineteenth-century Americans, northern or southern, the American nation fulfilled, provided, and promoted right atti-tudes and actions, law and stability, growth, and destiny. America promoted Americanism. One of the ongoing political conflicts of the nineteenth century concerned the degree of conformity govern-ments and national institutions should encourage or insist upon. Even the most individualistic of Americans, however, seemed to concede that to some degree the virtues of a free and industrious people should be taught to the next generation and to the new immi-grant. Among the most important of these virtues, so ingrained that it was almost instinctual, was a profound respect for law and a desire for social stability. Even in the roughest of frontier settings, Ameri-cans sought law and order, and they ultimately turned to the na-tional government to arbitrate and create law, and to guarantee sta-bility. Americans prized an orderly and law-abiding society both because that was their customary mode of life, and because it made possible growing material prosperity. Right action, the proper atti-tude, sound law, and a stable climate for business inevitably led to a more prosperous citizenry; so Americans believed. The national government should aid the growth of prosperity as best it could. Americans argued about the role of the national government in the economy, but few would say that it had no role at all. In part this was because most Americans agreed that the individual American as well as the entire nation was meant to become more prosperous, more powerful, more important, even to spread their way of life around the world. Americans optimistically believed they had a mis-sion to fulfill.[17]

This multifaceted sense of destiny and mission pervaded Stephen F. Austin's efforts to colonize Texas, and it caused the annexation of Texas and the Mexican War. In 1861 Texans whose history was so tied up with American destiny had not ceased to feel that destiny's force; nor were they unaffected by any other feature of nationalism. Texans did not cease to be Americans when they ceased to pledge allegiance to the United States. Indeed, their Americanness was one reason they were seceding. Undeniably, the United States was regionalized. As Frederick Law Olmsted and other travelers could testify, Texas and the South were different from New York. Friendship and kinship bonds, barriers to travel and communication, and a widespread semisubsistence lifestyle made Texans think first of their community, then of their state, then their region, and finally of their nation. Slavery and the cotton culture set them apart from other Americans. This localism made secession easier. Yet Americans shared common values, aspirations, religion, and most important for understanding secession—a common nationalism.

Texans' nationalism was perhaps the most interesting variety to be found in the South. In thirty years' time Texans had pledged loyalty to four nations: Mexico, the Republic of Texas, the United States, and the Confederate States of America. Yet they sought essentially the same things in those four nations. They sought a nation that would fulfill the functions that as Americans they were conditioned to expect a nation to fulfill.[18]

Of all these changes in allegiance, the most difficult was the last. Secessionists pointed to the frontier and insisted that the United States had failed to provide stability and protection from Indian attack. Furthermore, as long as the sectionally minded Republicans dominated the federal government such protection would be slow in coming. Secessionists further argued that Republicans were lawbreakers. They did not act as proper Americans should act. Republican-controlled state or local governments had often refused to enforce the Fugitive Slave Law. When Republicans were linked to such frightening creators of social discord as John Brown or the villains behind the Texas Troubles, they became both lawbreakers and fomenters of chaos. How could Texas prosper amidst such chaos, especially if its prosperity depended upon slavery, cotton, and the expansion of the frontier? Since the days of Stephen F. Austin and Mirabeau B. Lamar, Texans had dreamed not only of increasing material prosperity but of spreading their brand of American civilization into the wilderness. How could they achieve their destiny if they were not aided by their nation? Yet no matter how secessionists stressed the functional failings of the United States they could not override Texans' religious and psychological ties to the United States. Hysteria and the force of consensus could suppress these ties to the nation, but could not eliminate them.

Texans, of course, were not identical. They had varying degrees and types of nationalism. As argued in previous chapters, ideological shadings fell into four basic categories. Since Texans in 1861 often thought in terms of symbols and associated political beliefs with individuals it seems appropriate to name these categories after four of the most prominent members of the immediately preceding generation. Daniel Webster symbolized the strongest identification of self with nation and had the most pronounced religious devotion to that nation. Webster certainly saw the nation as pragmatic, but more than any other he articulated the belief that the United States was intrinsically important. Henry Clay shared this devotion, but he was much more concerned with the nation as a promoter of growth and as a means to achieving destiny. Andrew Jackson, too, had an intense devotion to the nation, but he was less willing than Clay to be loyal to that government if he believed it had strayed from the right and proper course of action or if it had ceased to do for the people what it was meant to do. For Webster and Clay it seemed as if the nation and its government came before the people. For Jackson it was clear that the people and their destiny came first. John C. Calhoun did not entirely lack filial devotion to the nation, and even in his last days he was more committed to an ongoing United States than most gave him credit for. But he more than any other represented a protest against national conformity. Over time he became the premier symbol of particular and peculiar individual rights and of the rights of local governments.[19]

Texans' position on the ideological spectrum from Webster to Calhoun does much to explain their attitude toward secession and the emerging Confederacy. Websterians, like James A. Newcomb, never accepted the destruction of the Union. Texans who resembled Clay and who were not swept away by the tide of consensus, like Throckmorton, did not accept secession in February of 1861. Jacksonian nationalists, like Reagan, clung to the Union persistently in the late 1850s, but abandoned it when in their eyes it had entirely ceased to do what it was supposed to do. Followers of Calhoun, like John Marshall, began to desert the Union when the political storms of the early and mid-1850s demonstrated that the Compromise of 1850 would not protect their vision of the South and of America.[20]

Perhaps because they were the least concerned with conserving and protecting traditional society and traditional values, those who had ideologies like Clay and Jackson were by far the most numerous

in the new land of Texas. Growth, prosperity, and destiny preoc-
cupied Clay and Jackson. They and their followers might have different images of the future, but in both cases they looked to the future, not the past. When the Jacksonian nationalists' vision of the
future was threatened by the Union, particularly if that vision was
identical to the Lower South, they accepted secession. They even
openly advocated secession. Notwithstanding the force of consensus, they did so both because the nation had less religious and psychological hold on them and because they had a more pronounced
sense that the nation should fulfill its obligations to the people. Followers of Clay were less willing to accept secession both because the
nation had more religious and psychological significance and because their vision of the future was quite often less threatened. Clay,
after all, had his greatest following in the border states, and his vision of the nation as one of farms and factories united by the free
flow of commerce did not need slavery. Texans who lived in areas
not resembling the Lower South shared this vision of the future.
That different vision, plus the weakness of the force of consensus
and the more internalized commitment to the nation among the
non-Jacksonian nationalists accounts for the persistent Unionism
among members of the Opposition party and in the non–Lower
South regions of the state.[21]

Describing Texans as patterned after Webster, Clay, Jackson, and
Calhoun, however, can oversimplify their attitudes. What makes
these four men effective political symbols is that all Texans to some
degree identified with them all. Some Texans were more Jacksonian
or Websterian in some cases than in others. Sam Houston and Andrew Jackson Hamilton were both closely identified with Andrew
Jackson all their lives. Houston accepted secession only after the
popular referendum and Hamilton never did. Yet nationalism in the
nineteenth century was as it is in the twentieth century: a complex
thing often only understood and articulated through myths and
symbols. Ranging Texans' nationalism on a scale from that of Calhoun to that of Webster makes both the individual Texan's and his
state's attitude to secession more understandable.[22]

Recognizing the limits of the analogy of Webster, Clay, Jackson,
and Calhoun, and remembering that Texans contained a bit of all of
them within themselves, reminds us of the difficulty of secession for
many Texans and introduces one final reason secession and joining
the Confederacy occurred. Texans needed a nation. They needed an
American nation. Their history proved that Texas could not exist as
a sovereign nation. The Republic of Texas never fulfilled the pragmatic functions or achieved the internalized values of an American

nation. If it had done so, annexation to the United States would not have been necessary. The creation of the Confederate States of America gave Texans a place to go, a place that promised to be familiar because the designers of the Confederacy were busily trying to duplicate almost every detail of the United States Constitution and government as it stood in 1861. Those who led the Confederacy, like John Reagan of Texas, did not advocate retreat to a feudal time of slaveholding baronies and all-powerful states. They meant to create a strong modern nation that could do what a nation was meant to do. Yet despite that modernity they sought to ground that nation in its ancestral past, to transfer to the Confederacy the strength of religious and psychological American nationalism.

Secessionists as well as unionists used George Washington and Thomas Jefferson and all the symbols and creeds associated with them to legitimize their course of action. Texans cast Washington as the ultimate revolutionary and secession as the second American Revolution. They insisted they acted to preserve the freedom and rights listed in the Declaration of Independence and the Bill of Rights and they further legitimized their actions by citing Jefferson's and James Madison's Kentucky and Virginia Resolutions. Seldom mentioning slavery except when insisting that the Republicans threatened harmony between the races and the pursuit of happiness made possible by slavery, secessionists tried to insist that they were the true carriers of the American mission to serve as an example to the rest of the world.[23]

At the beginning of their campaign the previous fall, secessionists had stressed the failings of the United States. By February, they stressed the promise of the Confederacy. They argued that frontier defense would be improved because the needs and interests of Texas would be heard. Better frontier defense and an end to the debate about slavery would permit stability and promote prosperity. Indeed, as part of a nation that no longer had to balance the interests of a manufacturing Northeast with a commodities-producing South, Texas would enjoy ever-increasing prosperity. Attention could be given to Texans' need for railroads and Texans could move forward into the wilderness of the West. Thus not only was the torch of Washington and Jefferson passed to the Confederacy, but the Confederacy promised to do for Texas what Mexico had not, the Republic of Texas could not, and the United States now would not.[24]

Gradually, an increasing number of nationalists accepted the end of the old Union, but there were still many problems in the transition of ties from the United States to the Confederacy. Identification of self with nation which had given Unionism great strength could not be created overnight, nor could the religious sense of the old Union be totally transferred. Even the idea that the smaller Confederacy could better handle the pragmatic functions Texans required of a nation received repeated challenge. Nonetheless, nationalism together with a still-growing consensus moved a few middle-of-the-road Texans into the secessionist camp during February. The victory of the secessionists in the popular referendum of 23 February would move most of the rest.

Despite the threat of physical intimidation and other aspects of forced consensus, and despite the growing idea of a Confederate nation, unionists continued to effectively campaign in some areas during the last days before the secession referendum. In the counties of North Texas Throckmorton, Epperson, and other prominent men toured their counties, making speeches and talking with their friends. Letters and editorials in support of the Union were published in local newspapers. Again and again they underscored the points made in the "Address to the Citizens of Texas." To this they added their special argument that secession would remove the protective screen of federal troops from along the Red River and would make their homes and families potential victims of Indian attack. In the Austin–San Antonio area the old Opposition party leaders attempted with some success to galvanize support for the Union. Unionists repeated familiar arguments, and pointed out in San Antonio that the army played a very large part in the city's economy. Sam Houston, E. M. Pease, James Newcomb, and others set an example for unionists to follow by reiterating their devotion to the United States and decrying the stupidity of secession at that point in time. Germans along the western frontier continued to speak of their exposure to Indian attack and of their unwillingness to go to war for slavery. Vigorous and consistent attacks on secession by numerous prominent citizens in all three of these areas gave the unionists a respectability and legitimacy lacking in the rest of the state. Not only did their arguments expose the detrimental qualities of secession, their actions demonstrated that it was still acceptable to take a position different from the majority of the state.[25]

On the fringes of the cotton-growing South some Texas counties proved exceptions to the general rule. Adjacent Fayette and Bastrop counties were two of the most interesting counties in the state. Both had roughly equal numbers of lower southerners, upper southerners, and Germans. Both were near enough to Austin to feel the influence of the unionist rhetoric of the so-called "Austin clique." In both counties, the Opposition party was traditionally strong and had a high degree of personal loyalty to Sam Houston. In La Grange, the largest city in the two counties, secessionists and unionists had rival newspapers. In both counties ardent local unionists, like George Washington Jones of Bastrop, spoke forcefully for their cause. Van Zandt and Angelina counties in East Texas were somewhat similar to Fayette and Bastrop counties. They had a strong Opposition party with a high degree of loyalty to Sam Houston. Their citizens came from both the Lower and Upper South. Most important, there were few slave plantations in these sandy counties. Most of the folk were herdsmen and small farmers with a tradition of economic, political, and social independence. They did not desire to become planters, and they were not economically dependent upon planters. Instead, they were the champions of highly individualistic democracy. In all four counties citizens listened to both sides of the argument and resisted the pressure for consensus.[26]

On 23 February 1861, campaigning in these counties and across the state ended and Texans voted either for or against secession. Secession was heartily endorsed by a count of 46,153 to 14,747, with over 62 percent of the electorate voting. The secession referendum was defeated in only eighteen counties; in only eleven others did as much as 40 percent of the vote go against secession. With the exception of Angelina County, all twenty-nine of these counties were tightly clustered in the northern and western parts of the state—in those portions of the state least like the Lower South and in those counties where the pressure for consensus had not ended all political dialogue. Two German counties, Gillespie and Mason, had the highest percentage against secession in the state. Reflecting both their cultural bias against secession and the importance of the army to their area, both cast over 95 percent of their vote against secession. Throckmorton and his friends had done their work well in Collin County, and there as well as in neighboring Cooke, Grayson, and Fannin counties sizable majorities against secession were rolled up. Travis County and neighboring Williamson County, thanks in part to the work of the Austin unionists, also polled a large vote against secession. These areas of unionist strength seemed to pull other neighboring counties into their orbit. Bastrop County voters, although primarily of Lower South stock, voted narrowly against secession. Secession did worst in those counties where being a unionist remained socially and politically legitimate. Lower South counties voted in favor of secession by overwhelming margins not just because secession meant the protection of the slave plantation system and an end to the continual debate over the role of the South in the Union, or as a reaction to the threat to law and established procedure posed by the Republican party. They also voted for secession

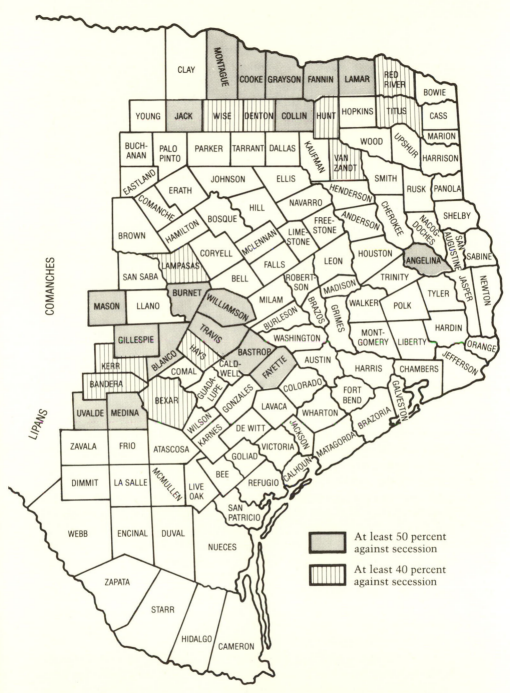

MAP 3.   Popular referendum on secession, February 23, 1861.

Map by Liz Conrad. (County lines from map no. 13 in *Mitchell's School and Family Geography*, 1858. Referendum percentages from Timmons, *The Referendum in Texas on the Ordinance of Secession*.)

because, by 1 February 1861, no one was left in their communities to champion the cause of the Union. It was with some justification that unionists later complained of the disruption of the mails and the closing off of much of Texas to outside information during the month of February. As had never before happened in the state, secessionists silenced political debate in much of Texas during February of 1861. Only in counties whose citizens' mystical or psychological nationalism was strong and where established leaders could not be muffled did the opposition viewpoint continue to be heard.[27]

A few days after the secession referendum, the convention reassembled, declared Texas officially out of the Union, and took steps to join it with the Confederate States of America. Sam Houston decried this last step as an abuse of the convention's legal power. On 16 March 1861 he refused to take the oath of loyalty to the Confederacy required of all state officials by the convention. Acting quickly, the convention deposed him and put the lieutenant governor, Edward Clark, in his place. Although this was seen by many as unlawful—as a despotic act by a convention of limited powers—Houston acquiesced in the actions of the convention. Earlier, unwilling to cause a civil war among his own people, Houston had turned down an offer of President Lincoln to send troops to Texas to maintain him in the governor's office and to prevent secession. Now, for the same reasons, he left Austin with a few parting shots at the demagogues who had brought ruin to Texas. Houston's actions and his words became an inspiration to latter-day Americans, presidents and common citizens alike. The grizzled veteran of many campaigns who sagely resisted secession has become one of the mythic stanchions of the American nation. Look beyond March of 1861, however, and the image of Houston changes. When the war came in earnest he, like most unionists, went with his state and his section. As he said: "All my hopes, my fortunes, are centered in the South. When I see the land in whose defense my blood had been spilt, and the people whose fortunes have been mine through a quarter of a century of toil, threatened with invasion, I can but cast my lot with theirs and await the issue." Sam Houston's Unionism, like that of most Texans, was conditional. Eventually, he, Throckmorton, Flake, and others had to choose between their state and their old nation. They chose their state.[28]

Not only did they choose their state, they chose their new nation. From the end of February to the end of April, unionist after unionist cut his ties to the United States as best he could and began to try to develop ties to the Confederacy. Such ties were needed to make secession palatable, and their development was all the easier under the pressure of war.

This was the last of a three-stage move toward secession. By the late summer of 1860, those most concerned with the place of the plantation South in the Union had already decided upon secession. For them secession seemed long overdue and the imminent election of a Republican president was only one more demonstration that the nation had ceased to be a nation to which the slaveholding South could belong. In the early fall of 1860, the second stage of secession began when more reluctant secessionists became convinced that the predicted election of Lincoln in November posed a dire threat to slavery, social stability, the law, material prosperity, and growth. During this second stage of secession news that Lincoln had indeed been elected president spread throughout Texas and the debate within Texas shifted from the necessity of defending slavery to the nature of the once and future Union. Gradually, especially in the Lower South areas of the state, a powerful consensus in favor of secession forced its tacit acceptance by Texans whose feeling for the nation was based less on pragmatism than on internalized values. Despite appeals by remaining unionists, the Secession Convention passed the Ordinance of Secession and brought to an end the second stage of secession in Texas on 1 February 1861. In the third stage of secession, an ever-building consensus and the knowledge that a new American nation would replace the old Union led to a surprisingly large popular vote in favor of secession. Gradually during the debate about the secession referendum, and especially after it passed and fighting broke out between North and South, nationalism refocused on the Confederacy and brought even those Texans with strong mythical and psychological ties to the United States to acceptance of secession. Thus, the third and final stage of secession ended by 1 May 1861.

Within individual Texans and within the state as a whole, however, Unionism would not die. There remained many Texans still committed to the United States despite consensus, pragmatism, and refocused nationalism. They openly opposed the Confederacy. Within at least a part of the minds of most other Texans remained a seed of commitment to the Union and a seed of doubt about the legitimacy and viability of their new nation, the Confederate States of America. As Sam Houston said, "one's section was his country."[29] But rational doubts about that country still existed and emotional bonds to the Union remained. Texans still wondered if a mere section could ever be an American nation.

Epilogue: Across the River

One by one, the protagonists of the secession era crossed the waters dividing their state from the larger world around them. As they did so, they crossed divisions in their own minds and in the courses of their lives that could not easily be bridged and recrossed. Radical southerners and longtime advocates of secession enjoyed a brief moment of glory in 1861 but soon began to vanish from the scene. The war demanded sacrifice and steadiness of purpose, not fiery courage and unbridled individualism. John Marshall died in his first major battle in June 1862. Louis T. Wigfall, acting on his own, helped engineer the surrender of Fort Sumter, but then receded into long years of futile criticism of Jefferson Davis. On the other hand, moderate Texas secessionists buoyed up the Confederacy throughout the war. John Reagan served as postmaster general of the Confederacy and was one of the few cabinet members whose tenure lasted the entire war. F. R. Lubbock was the most effective wartime governor of Texas and closed out the war as a trusted aide of Jefferson Davis. As they had promised, moderate unionists also contributed greatly to the war effort. James Throckmorton rose to the rank of brigadier general in the Confederate army. Sam Houston openly supported the South and thereby helped preserve unity on the homefront. Militant unionists, however, never accepted secession and the Confederacy. A. J. Hamilton fled the state in 1862 and was appointed provisional governor by President Lincoln. George Paschal went into seclusion in Austin and began working on his plan to prove in the courts that Texas and the United States had an "indissoluble relation."[1]

By as early as the summer of 1862, little remained the same for these champions and the groups they represented. Fire-eaters were dead or discredited. Moderate secessionists faced the rigorous and onerous duty of directing a modern war and building a new nation at the same time. Moderate unionists swallowed their principles and helped in these efforts. Only later would both groups have time to assay the costs of secession and wonder how it had all come about. At least for the war years, though, they were luckier than the militant unionists whose steadfast commitment forced them to abandon their homes or silently remain in seclusion, cut off from their communities.[2]

Gilbert Kingsbury was one of those committed unionists who left a record of his own sense of loss. Kingsbury, a New Englander with a peripatetic past, served as postmaster at Brownsville in the late 1850s. Like many other unconditional unionists, he fell outside of the mainstream in Texas. Neither southern nor totally assimilated into a southern culture, Kingsbury nonetheless loved his state and regarded himself as a Texan. In June 1860, Kingsbury, like many Americans, discounted the talk of secession and wrote: "Mr. Lincoln may be elected. I hope he will not. Still if he should, I apprehend no earthquake or disaster to the country—no abandonment of the government of which we are all proud." In August 1862, the growing Confederate need for manpower brought the full reality of secession home and Kingsbury wrote to a friend: "It may surprise you that I have fled the State to avoid the Conscription. If our countrymen were fighting anything except the flag of our fathers, I should have been in the ranks without waiting for a conscript law. But I will die sooner than assail this 'Land of the free'—the Republic of Washington." Kingsbury crossed the Rio Grande and left his "countrymen" for the sake of the country.[3]

Looking back across a much wider river than the Rio Grande, a river of over a hundred years in time, Kingsbury's tragic situation still captures the imagination. Through no fault of his own, he had been placed in a situation that any choice he made brought pain and loss. Kingsbury had lived in a comfortable world in which belief in slavery, devotion to nation, attachment to community, cultural ties, ideology, and partisanship occupied a stable if obscured universe. In fact, the multifaceted and complex nature of Texans' loyalties, beliefs, ambitions, and dreams fostered stability. If Texans' commitment to slavery became excessive, as it seemed to be doing in 1859 with the move to reopen the African slave trade, then that excess was balanced by fear for the life of the nation or fear of disrupting the local community. It was as if some law of physics guaranteed that the Union would avoid every serious crisis. No wonder that Kingsbury could write in 1860, "I apprehend no earthquake or disaster to the country." He was wrong. As had happened before, disputes over slavery and the fears and hysteria accompanying them let loose Sam Houston's "demons of anarchy." This time, however, the hold of the Union on the minds and hearts of Texans was too weak to balance the drive for secession.[4]

Secession began out of the dispute over slavery and was ignited by the election of Abraham Lincoln, but in the end it became a debate about the past, present, and future roles of Texas in the Union. Although complex, Texans' ties to the Union were real and strong. Texans cherished the Union as a guarantor of rights, as a beacon for the world to follow, and as a means for national greatness. They valued the Union and the Constitution as shrines of their forefathers, and as something to be worshipped. They could not conceive of themselves except as part of this nation. Yet, gradually, other conceptions of the functional value of the Union lost their meaning. The constitutionally guaranteed rights of southerners to hold slaves seemed threatened by Republican control of the government. Republicans, furthermore, were conceived of as a strictly sectional party dedicated to the interests of the North. To southerners it seemed their great nation would be dominated by the partisan interests of one region of the country. When that happened the beacon to the world lost its luster, and the chances for continued national greatness seemed diminished. Besides, Republican agitation of the slave issue might unleash a slave rebellion. Long-term Republican dominance of the national government might elevate Negroes to a place of equality with whites. Finally, for those areas in Texas like the Lower South or in the process of becoming like the Lower South, any threat to slavery, cotton production, and the plantation system threatened prosperity.

This was not a debate in which Texans calmly weighed the merits of their mystical and emotional bonds to the Union against their growing doubts of the utility of continued membership in that Union. Instead, a host of other factors influenced the outcome of the debate over the Union. As Texas became more like the plantation South, Texans came to share the hopes, fears, and needs of that region and to be led by the actions of Lower South states. The desire to conform, the example of the Lower South, and the strong ties of the Democratic party to other state parties in the Lower South did much to expedite secession. These things together with the emotional nature of the slavery issue gave secessionists a sense of unity and energy.

That sense of unity and energy was not present among the natural opponents of secession. Texans from an Upper South, German, or Mexican culture were influenced to support secession by a desire to conform, by an ideology which stressed the functional nature of the Union, and by the Democratic party. When their cultural groups lost their unity, the demand for consensus moved the faint of heart or the undecided into the ranks of the secessionists. A similar story was true of the Opposition party. Ideological differences and a desire to conform to the dominant plantation culture stripped it of what little statewide unity it possessed. Even frontiersmen were convinced by past experience that the pragmatic value of the Union was not what it once had been.

Still, the very variety of interests and perspectives on the Union made Unionism an incredibly resilient force. From the secession of South Carolina to the vote of the Texas Secession Convention and the seizure of military posts, however, secessionists gained credibility and legitimacy while unionists were silenced by forced consensus. As secessionists became more numerous and as secession seemed increasingly necessary for the survival of society, unionists faced ostracism and physical intimidation.

Sam Houston was right: secession depended upon the irrational. He was right but he was wrong. Unionists counted upon the pull of flag and country to prevent secession. Country did not pull as hard as it once had because Texans had examined what the nation did for them in a direct and pragmatic way and found that the Union no longer measured up to their expectations of what an American nation should be. This did not mean the death of emotional, psychological, or spiritual attachments to the nation. Indeed, these attachments sustained the Union even after the nation had been found wanting. Once the Confederacy began to emerge as a new American nation, however, these ties to the Union gradually began to be transferred to that new creation. The process was slow and never complete. For those like Gilbert Kingsbury, loyalties never shifted.

Andrew Jackson Hamilton, famed for his excellence as an orator, captured the spirit of the remaining unionists in Texas on 1 February 1861, when he spoke before the U.S. House of Representatives:

> I might be excused for doubting my own identity. Surely I may
> be pardoned for having involuntarily prayed that this might
> prove a troubled and protracted dream. Yet it is true—too
> many evidences force a conviction of the sad reality. But a few
> days past, Mr. Speaker, the noble temple of American liberty
> stood complete in all its parts—stood in all the majesty of its
> vast proportions, and in the glory of its apparent strength and
> beauty of construction; not a pillar missing or a joint dis-
> severed. And its votaries were gathered about the altar wor-
> shipping, as was their wont, with hopeful hearts. Forebodings
> were felt, and predictions made of the coming storm and the

destruction of the temple. And the storm has come and still rages—the temple still stands but shorn of its fair proportions and marred in its beauty. Pillar after pillar had fallen away.[5]

Pillars of the Union were down, but as Hamilton went on to say, "yet there are worshippers there, about the shrine." Within Texas and Texans in 1861 was the potential both for loyalty and love for the Union and support of secession. The war was to make the decision between these two much clearer. Yet, after the war, Texans moved back into the Union with relative ease because despite all the changes brought by secession and war their old ideas and feelings about an American nation remained.[6] But they remained in suspension with new elements. Belief in the greatness of George Washington, love of the Constitution, and a fondness for things American lived on together with the haunting sense of the Lost Cause and an un-American knowledge of failure and human frailty.

Notes

PROLOGUE: DEMONS OF ANARCHY

1. William M. Baker, "A Pivotal Point," *Lippincott's Magazine* 26 (November 1880): 566.
2. The best biographies of Houston are Llerena Friend, *Sam Houston: The Great Designer*, and Marquis James, *The Raven: A Biography of Sam Houston*. Also see Sam Houston, *The Writings of Sam Houston, 1813–1863*, ed. Amelia W. Williams and Eugene C. Barker (8 vols.) (cited hereafter as *Writings*); Charles A. Culberson, "General Sam Houston and Secession," *Scribner's Magazine* 39 (May 1906): 584–591; George W. Paschal, "The Last Years of Sam Houston," *Harper's Magazine* 32 (April 1866): 630–635; Alexander W. Terrell, "Recollections of General Sam Houston," *Southwestern Historical Quarterly* (hereafter *SWHQ*) 16 (October 1912): 113–136; Edward R. Maher, Jr., "Sam Houston and Secession," *SWHQ* 55 (April 1952): 448–458.
3. Sam Houston to Sam Houston, Jr., 6 November 1860, *Writings* 8: 184–185, 220. On the Secession Convention, see Anna Irene Sandbo, "Beginnings of the Secession Movement in Texas," *SWHQ* 18 (July 1914): 41–73; idem, "The First Session of the Secession Convention of Texas, *SWHQ* 18 (October 1914): 162–194; Ralph A. Wooster, *The Secession Conventions of the South*, pp. 121–135; Ernest William Winkler (ed.), *Journal of the Secession Convention of Texas, 1861*.
4. Extract from Houston letter, 20 February 1861, *Writings* 8: 264. For an analysis of voting returns, see Joe T. Timmons, "The Referendum in Texas on the Ordinance of Secession, February 23, 1861: The Vote," *East Texas Historical Journal* (hereafter *ETHJ*) 11 (Fall 1973): 12–28.
5. Friend, *Houston*, pp. 336–349.
6. Houston, *Writings* 8: 299.
7. Houston, "Speech at Brenham, March 31, 1861," *Writings* 8: 295–299.
8. Houston, "Speech at Independence, May 10, 1861," *Writings* 8: 301–302. Also see Houston, "To the Editors of the *Civilian*, September 12, 1861," *Writings* 8: 310–315. On Fort Sumter, see David M. Potter, *The Impending Crisis, 1841–1861*, pp. 444–483.
9. John H. Reagan, "A Conversation with Governor Houston," *Texas Historical Association Quarterly* (later *SWHQ*) 3 (April 1900): 281.
10. On the sources and variety of cultures within Texas in 1860, the best starting point is the various works by Terry G. Jordan. Most significant of these are *German Seed in Texas Soil: Immigrant Farmers in*

Nineteenth-Century Texas; "The Imprint of the Upper and Lower South on Mid-Nineteenth-Century Texas," *Annals of the Association of American Geographers* 57 (December 1967): 667–690; "The Texan Appalachia," ibid. 60 (September 1970): 409–427; "Population Origins in Texas, 1850," *Geographical Review* 59 (January 1969): 83–103.

11. Sam Houston to Sam Houston, Jr., 6 November 1860, *Writings* 8: 184–185.

1. ANTEBELLUM TEXAS AND THE PLANTATION SOUTH

1. Sam Houston, "Speech at Brenham, March 31, 1861," *Writings* 8: 295–296.

2. For a survey of the secession of Texas see Ralph A. Wooster, *The Secession Conventions of the South*, pp. 121–135; Anna Irene Sandbo, "Beginnings of the Secession Movement in Texas," *SWHQ* 18 (July 1914): 41–73; idem., "The First Session of the Secession Convention of Texas," *SWHQ* 18 (October 1914): 162–194; Oran M. Roberts, "The Political, Legislative, and Judicial History of Texas for Its Fifty Years of Statehood, 1845–1895," *A Comprehensive History of Texas 1685–1897*, ed. Dudley G. Wooten, vol. 2: 7–325; Ernest William Winkler (ed.), *Journal of the Secession Convention of Texas, 1861*; Edward R. Maher, Jr., "Secession in Texas" (Ph.D. dissertation); Nancy Ann Head, "State Rights in Texas, the Growth of an Idea, 1850–1860" (M.A. thesis). Two more recent studies which deal with secession and slavery are C. Alwyn Barr, "The Making of a Secessionist: The Antebellum Career of Roger Q. Mills," *SWHQ* 79 (October 1975): 129–144; Billy D. Ledbetter, "Slavery, Fear, and Disunion in the Lone Star State: Texans' Attitudes toward Secession and the Union, 1846–1861" (Ph.D. dissertation). On the distinctiveness of Texas see Frank E. Vandiver, *The Southwest: South or West?*; D. W. Meinig, *Imperial Texas: An Interpretive Essay in Cultural Geography*; Terry G. Jordan, "The Imprint of the Upper and Lower South on Mid-Nineteenth-Century Texas," *Annals of the Association of American Geographers* 57 (December 1967): 667–690.

3. On Texas geography and its influence on settlement see A. W. Spaight, *The Resources, Soil and Climate of Texas*; Jacob De Cordova, *Texas: Her Resources and Her Public Men*; Elmer H. Johnson, *The Natural Regions of Texas*; W. T. Carter, *The Soils of Texas*; Allan C. Ashcraft, "East Texas in the Election of 1860 and the Secession Crisis," *ETHJ* 1 (July 1963): 7–8; Terry G. Jordan, "Pioneer Evaluation of Vegetation in Frontier Texas," *SWHQ* 76 (January 1973): 233–254. On transportation in antebellum Texas see Andrew F. Muir, "Railroads Come to Houston, 1857–1861," *SWHQ* 67 (July 1960): 42–63; idem., "The Destiny of Buffalo Bayou," *SWHQ* 47 (October 1943): 19–22; Frederick Law Olmsted, *A Journey through Texas; or, a Saddle-Trip on the Southwestern Frontier*, pp. 362–367; "Trinity River and Its Valley," *Texas Alamac for 1861*, ed. Willard Richardson, pp. 122–126; Judy Watson, "The Red River Raft," *Texana* 5 (Spring 1967): 68–76; Carl Newton Tyson, *The*

Red River in Southwestern History; De Cordova, *Texas*, 53; Charles W. Ramsdell, "Internal Improvement Projects in Texas in the Fifties," *Proceedings of the Mississippi Valley Historical Association* 9 (1915–1916): 99–109. For a map showing the areas of Texas clearly dominated by planters see Terry G. Jordan, "Population Origins in Texas, 1850," *Geographical Review* 59 (January 1969): 87.

4. Barnes F. Lathrop, *Migration into East Texas, 1835–1860: A Study from the United States Census*, pp. 34–58.

5. On cluster migration see Jordan, "Population Origins," pp. 89–93.

6. On the Houston–Galveston area see Earl W. Fornell, *The Galveston Era: The Texas Crescent on the Eve of Secession*; Muir, "Railroads Come to Houston"; idem, "Destiny of Buffalo Bayou"; Jordan, "The Imprint of the Upper and Lower South," pp. 672–677; Kenneth W. Wheeler, *To Wear a City's Crown: The Beginnings of Urban Growth in Texas, 1836–1865*.

7. Ralph A. Wooster, "Foreigners in the Principal Towns of Ante-Bellum Texas," *SWHQ* 66 (October 1962): 208–220; Terry G. Jordan, *German Seed in Texas Soil: Immigrant Farmers in Nineteenth-Century Texas*, pp. 192–204; idem., "Population Origins," pp. 97–98; Rudolph Leopold Biesele, *The History of the German Settlements in Texas, 1831–1861*, pp. 42–227.

8. On Harrison County see Randolph B. Campbell, "Planters and Plain Folk: Harrison County, Texas, as a Test Case, 1850–1860," *Journal of Southern History* 40 (August 1974): 369–398; idem., "Human Property: The Negro Slave in Harrison County, 1850–1860," *SWHQ* 76 (April 1973): 384–396; James Curtis Armstrong, "The History of Harrison County, Texas, 1839–1880" (M.A. thesis), pp. 57–64. On wealth, slaveholding, and the agricultural economy see Randolph B. Campbell and Richard G. Lowe, *Wealth and Power in Antebellum Texas*; idem., "Some Economic Aspects of Antebellum Texas Agriculture," *SWHQ* 82 (April 1979): 351–378; idem., "Slave Property and the Distribution of Wealth in Texas, 1860," *Journal of American History* 63 (September 1976): 316–324; Ralph A. Wooster, "Democracy on the Frontier: Statehouse and Courthouse in Ante-Bellum Texas," *ETHJ* 10 (Fall 1972): 83–97; idem., "Notes on Texas' Largest Slaveholders, 1860," *SWHQ* 65 (July 1961): 72–79; idem., "Wealthy Texans, 1860," *SWHQ* 71 (October 1967): 163–180; Karl E. Ashburn, "Slavery and Cotton Production in Texas," *Southwest Social Science Quarterly* 14 (December 1933): 257–271; William R. Johnson, *A Short History of the Sugar Industry in Texas*; Raymond E. White, "Cotton Ginning in Texas to 1861," *SWHQ* 61 (October 1957): 257–269; Jordan, "The Imprint of the Upper and Lower South," pp. 675–677, 682.

9. On the dependence of the entire Texas economy on marketable crops and on the self-sufficiency of Texas plantations see Campbell and Lowe, "Economic Aspects of Antebellum Texas Agriculture," pp. 1–2, n. 1, 369–374, n. 17. The best single work on agriculture in the entire South remains Lewis C. Gray, *History of Agriculture in the Southern United*

States to 1860 (2 vols.). On the importance of livestock see Forrest Mc-
Donald and Grady McWhiney, "The Antebellum Southern Herdsman:
A Reinterpretation," *Journal of Southern History* 41 (May 1975): 147–
166; Terry G. Jordan, "The Origin of Anglo-American Cattle Ranching
in Texas: A Documentation of Diffusion from the Lower South," *Economic Geography* 45 (January 1969): 63–87; Francis Richard Lubbock,
Six Decades in Texas, ed. C. W. Raines, pp. 120–140. For a brief survey
of lumber and other industries in 1860 see Vera Lea Dugas, "Texas Industry, 1860–1880," *SWHQ* 59 (October 1955): 151–157.

10. Walter Prescott Webb in *The Great Plains*, pp. 8–9, used longitude 98°
west as the approximate dividing line between the humid east and arid
west and emphasized the effect of geography on history and culture. In
Texas the region between longitudes 96° west and 98° west was both an
environmental and cultural transition zone. Using the precedent of
Webb, therefore, it seems appropriate to designate longitude 96° west as
the approximate western limit of an homogeneous Lower South. Obviously, some counties to the west of this line such as Brazos and Wharton were very much within the geographic and cultural bounds of the
Lower South, but longitude 96° west remains a recognizable and generally appropriate boundary between a region of great similarities and one
of growing contrasts. See Jordan, "The Imprint of the Upper and Lower
South"; idem, "The Texan Appalachia," *Annals of the Association of
American Geographers* 60 (September 1970): 409–427; idem., "Popula-
tion Origins in Texas." Local histories support the thesis that eastern
Texas was culturally homogeneous. See Armstrong, "The History of
Harrison County"; Effie Boon, "The History of Angelina County" (M.A.
thesis); George L. Crocket, *Two Centuries in East Texas, A History of
San Augustine County and Surrounding Territory*; John B. Dickson,
"History of Gregg County, Texas" (M.A. thesis); Garland Farmer, *The
Realm of Rusk County*; Richard W. Haltom, *History and Description
of Angelina County, Texas*; Pauline Buck Hohes, *A Centennial History
of Anderson County, Texas*; Doyal T. Loyd, *A History of Upshur County,
Texas*; Hattie Joplin Roach, *A History of Cherokee County, Texas*; Dorman H. Winfrey, *A History of Rusk County, Texas*; Robert W. Glover,
ed., *Tyler and Smith County History: An Historical Appraisal*; Clarence R. Wharton, *History of Fort Bend County*.

11. On Lamar see Herbert P. Gambrell, *Mirabeau Buonaparte Lamar:
Troubadour and Crusader*; Dorman H. Winfrey, "Mirabeau B. Lamar
and Texas Nationalism," *SWHQ* 59 (October 1955): 184–205. On Texas
nationalism see Mark W. Nackman, *A Nation within a Nation: The
Rise of Texas Nationalism*; Meinig, *Imperial Texas*.

12. On the most obvious nonmarket-oriented subculture see Jordan, "The
Texan Appalachia." On assimilation see ibid., pp. 414–415; idem, "The
Imprint of the Upper and Lower South"; Milton M. Gordon, *Assimila-
tion in American Life: The Role of Race, Religion, and National Ori-
gins*, pp. 66–83; Egon Richard Tausch, "Southern Sentiment among the
Texas Germans During the Civil War and Reconstruction" (M.A. the-

sis), pp. 1–53; Jordan, *German Seed*, pp. 8–117; Campbell, "Planters and Plain Folk."

13. No complete studies of the economic development of antebellum Texas exist, but for some indication of the nature and prosperity of the Texas economy see Gray, *Agriculture in the Southern United States to 1860* 2: 906–907; Abigail Curlee Holbrook, "Cotton Marketing in Antebellum Texas," *SWHQ* 73 (April 1970): 456–478; *De Bow's Review* 5 (1848): 316–324; 6 (1848): 153, 364–365; 7 (1849): 273–368, 478; 8 (1850): 159, 195–197, 200, 238; 10 (1850): 77–78, 336, 337, 453, 464, 627–645; White, "Cotton Ginning in Texas to 1861," pp. 268–269; *Texas Almanac for 1857*, pp. 69–72; Clarksville *Standard*, 10 May 1856; Galveston *News*, 22 April 1856; Campbell and Lowe, "Economic Aspects of Antebellum Texas Agriculture," pp. 371–378.

14. An example of the public interest in railroads may be found in the letters to the editor of the Houston *Telegraph*, 18 March and 1 July 1857, 7 February and 21 March 1859; Galveston *News*, 20 June and 3 December 1857; Marshall *Texas Republican*, 30 January, 9 September, and 29 October 1858. On government interest in railroads see *Journal of the Senate of the State of Texas, Sixth Legislature*, pp. 27–30; *Journal of the House of Representatives of the State of Texas, Fifth Legislature*, pp. 16–19. On the potential wealth that railroads would bring Texas see *Texas Almanac for 1857*, p. 123; "Address of Governor P. H. Bell to the Legislature," printed in *Journal of the House, Fifth Legislature*, pp. 30–31. During the controversy over the Mississippi Pacific Railroad in the mid-1850s, Thomas J. Green described that railroad as the "great slavery road," and he hoped that when the railroad was built that, "if the people of Texas and the South be true to themselves, they will see that the remaining five hundred miles to the junction of the Gila and Colorado will, under the privileges of the Nebraska Bill, be also a slave state," Austin *Texas State Gazette*, 29 July 1854. Also see Roger A. Griffin, "Governor E. M. Pease and Texas Railroad Development in the 1850s," *ETHJ* 10 (Fall 1972): 103–118.

15. Austin *Texas State Gazette*, 4 April 1857 and 16 April 1859; William Campbell Binkley, *The Expansionist Movement in Texas, 1836–1850*; William H. Bell, "Knights of the Golden Circle, Its Organization and Activities in Texas prior to the Civil War" (M.A. thesis); C. A. Bridges, "The Knights of the Golden Circle: A Filibustering Fantasy," *SWHQ* 44 (January 1941): 287–302; Roy Sylvan Dunn, "The KGC in Texas, 1860–1861," *SWHQ* 70 (April 1967): 543–573.

16. The importance of slavery to young men "on the make" and its influence on secession is described in Barr, "The Making of a Secessionist: The Antebellum Career of Roger Q. Mills."

17. One of the most prominent critics of slavery was Adolph Douai, the German editor of the San Antonio *Zeitung*. The history of his actions in Texas and the storm they invoked can be found in Laura W. Roper, "Frederick Law Olmsted and the Western Texas Free-Soil Movement," *American Historical Review* 56 (October 1950): 58–64; Rudolph Leo-

pold Biesele, "The Texas State Convention of Germans in 1854," *SWHQ* 33 (April 1930): 247–261. Lorenzo Sherwood, a prominent Texas entrepreneur, was forced out of the state legislature because he had expressed some reservations about slavery. See Fornell, *Galveston Era*, pp. 171–178; Zoie Odom Newsome, "Antislavery Sentiment in Texas, 1821–1861," pp. 61–83.

18. John Salmon Ford, *Rip Ford's Texas*, p. 313. Also see Clarksville *Standard*, 19 February 1859; *Almanac for 1858*, p. 133; J. P. Osterhout to Brother Orlando, 1 February 1860, J. P. Osterhout to mother, 12 March 1856, John Patterson Osterhout papers.

19. William Pitt Ballinger, diary, 21 June 1860. For studies of slavery in Texas see James Smallwood, "Blacks in Antebellum Texas: A Reappraisal," *Red River Valley Historical Review* 2 (Winter 1975): 445, 453–466; W. E. Lockhart, "The Slave Code in Texas" (M.A. thesis); A. E. Keir Nash, "The Texas Supreme Court and Trial Rights of Blacks, 1845–1860," *Journal of American History* 58 (December 1971): 622–642; Abigail Curlee Holbrook, "A Glimpse of Life on Antebellum Slave Plantations in Texas," *SWHQ* 76 (April 1973): 361–383; Abigail Curlee, "A Study of Texas Slave Plantations, 1822–1865" (Ph.D. dissertation).

20. Austin *Texas State Gazette*, 27 March 1858 and 12 March 1859.

21. De Cordova, *Texas*, p. 352. Also see Galveston *News*, 27 April 1858.

22. *Neu Braunfelser Zeitung*, 11 March 1869; Benjamin, *The Germans in Texas*, pp. 106–108. For other examples of German attitudes toward slavery see Galveston *Die Union*, 12 January 1861; San Antonio *Herald*, 24 May 1859; San Antonio *Texas Staats-Zeitung*, 4 June 1859. On the slave trade see Earl W. Fornell, "Agitation in Texas for Reopening the Slave Trade," *SWHQ* 60 (October 1956): 145–159; idem., *Galveston Era*, pp. 193–266; Ronald T. Takaki, *A Pro-Slavery Crusade: The Agitation to Reopen the African Slave Trade*; Austin *Texas State Gazette*, 1 January and 12 February 1859; Peter W. Gray, "Address to the Citizens of Houston on the African Slave Trade," Osterhout papers; San Antonio *Herald*, 22 June 1859.

23. Marshall *Texas Republican*, 29 March 1856.

24. On the Texas Troubles of the summer of 1860 see Ollinger Crenshaw, *The Slave States in the Presidential Election of 1860*, pp. 89–111; Wesley Norton, "The Methodist Episcopal Church and the Civil Disturbances in North Texas in 1859 and 1860," *SWHQ* 68 (January 1965): 317–341; Donald E. Reynolds, *Editors Make War: Southern Newspapers in the Secession Crisis*, pp. 97–117.

25. Austin *Texas State Gazette*, 17 November 1860. Also see Ledbetter, "Slavery, Fear, and Disunion in the Lone Star State;" William W. White, "The Texas Slave Insurrection in 1860," *SWHQ* 52 (January 1949): 259–286. On the effect of conceptions of the future on the Lower South see William L. Barney, *The Secessionist Impulse: Alabama and Mississippi in 1860*, pp. 3–49, and Steven A. Channing, *Crisis of Fear: Secession in South Carolina*. On Reagan see his speech delivered in Congress on 15 January 1861 which is reprinted in John H. Reagan,

Memoirs, With Special Reference to Secession and the Civil War, pp. 253–270.

26. Head, "State Rights in Texas," pp. 31–100; Ledbetter, "Slavery, Fear, and Disunion in the Lone Star State," 150–225; Dallas *Herald,* 14 November 1860.

2. PARTISANSHIP AND IDEOLOGY

1. For a brief review of Opposition parties in the South see John V. Mering, "The Slave-State Constitutional Unionists and the Politics of Consensus," *Journal of Southern History* 43 (August 1977): 396–401.
2. On the Whigs in Texas see Ernest William Winkler (ed.), *Platforms of Political Parties in Texas,* pp. 17–54; Randolph B. Campbell, "The Whig Party of Texas in the Elections of 1848 and 1852," *SWHQ* 73 (July 1969): 17–34. Also see Arthur C. Cole, *The Whig Party in the South;* Charles G. Sellers, Jr., "Who Were the Southern Whigs?" *American Historical Review* 59 (January 1954): 335–346; Thomas B. Alexander, "Persistent Whiggery in the Confederate South, 1860–1877," *Journal of Southern History* 27 (August 1961): 305–329. Whigs in East Texas seem to have carried their party ties with them from the South and entered politics in semiorganized fashion at an early date. See, for example, the comments on Harrison County Whigs in Austin *Texas Democrat,* 15 April 1846. Also see Austin *Texas State Gazette,* 8 May 1852; Galveston *Journal,* 7, 28 January 1853.
3. Galveston *Journal,* 7 January 1853. Also see Sellers, "Southern Whigs," pp. 340–343.
4. Politics in the 19th-century South was an all-consuming passion. See Francis Richard Lubbock, *Six Decades in Texas,* edited by C. W. Raines, pp. 179–313. For a comparison with other parts of the South see William L. Barney, *The Secessionist Impulse: Alabama and Mississippi in 1860.*
5. Galveston *Journal,* 24 December 1850. Also see Mering, "Constitutional Unionists," pp. 395–410; Claude Elliott, *Leathercoat: The Life History of a Texas Patriot,* pp. 15–60; Austin *Southern Intelligencer,* 13 February 1861; Marshall *Texas Republican,* 2 July 1859 and 14 February 1860, 15 December 1860.
6. This quote from John Ashe may be found in Austin *Texas State Gazette,* 24 July 1854. Also, see the letter of Ashe to the Whig Central Committee, Austin *Texas State Gazette,* 16 October 1852. For an example of various newspapers' opinion of the Whigs and their leaders see Austin *Texas State Gazette,* 13 September 1851, 8 and 22 May 1852; Galveston *Journal,* 10 December 1852.
7. Austin *Texas State Times,* 30 June 1855. Also see Richard Lee Briggs, "The Democratic Party in Early Texas" (M.A. thesis), pp. 1–72.
8. Briggs, "The Democratic Party in Early Texas," p. 16; Lubbock, *Six Decades in Texas,* pp. 190–208; Oran M. Roberts, "The Political, Legislative, and Judicial History of Texas for Its Fifty Years of Statehood, 1845–1895," *A Comprehensive History of Texas, 1685–1897,* ed. Dud-

ley G. Wooten, vol. 2: 34–36; Marshall *Texas Republican*, 24 February 1855.

9. On the Know-Nothing party in general see Ray Allen Billington, *The Protestant Crusade, 1800–1860: A Study of the Origins of American Nativism*; W. D. Overdyke, *The Know-Nothing Party in the South*; Michael F. Holt, "The Politics of Impatience: The Origins of Know-Nothingism," *Journal of American History* 60 (September 1973): 309–331. On the party in Texas see Litha Crews, "The Know-Nothing Party in Texas" (M.A. thesis); Ralph A. Wooster, "An Analysis of the Texas Know-Nothings," *SWHQ* (January 1967): 414–423; Winkler, *Platforms*, pp. 63–71; Oran Lonnie Sinclair, "Crossroads of Conviction: A Study of the Texas Political Mind, 1856–1861" (Ph.D. dissertation), pp. 26–92; Sister Paul of the Cross McGrath, *Political Nativism in Texas, 1825–1860*; Rudolph Leopold Biesele, "The Texas State Convention of Germans in 1854," *SWHQ* 33 (April 1930): 247–261. Population percentages are based on figures found in Terry G. Jordan, "Population Origins in Texas, 1850," *Geographical Review* 59 (January 1969): 85.

10. La Grange *True Issue*, 13 October 1855.

11. On the condemnation of the Kansas-Nebraska Bill by Know-Nothings see San Antonio *Daily Herald*, 31 July 1857; Austin *Texas State Times*, 11 August 1855. Also see H. H. Simms, *A Decade of Sectional Controversy*, pp. 48–49; Arthur C. Cole, *Whig Party in the South*, pp. 277–309; Allan Nevins, *Ordeal of the Union* 2: 301–346.

12. Houston, "Houston's Opinion Concerning the 'American Order,' July 24, 1855," *Writings* 6: 196, 198.

13. Marshall *Harrison Flag*, 10 July 1858.

14. La Grange *True Issue*, 15 December 1855. Also see "Houston's Opinion Concerning the 'American Order,'" pp. 198–199; La Grange *True Issue*, 1 December 1855.

15. Campbell, "Whig Party of Texas," pp. 17–34; Ralph A. Wooster, "Ben H. Epperson: East Texas Lawyer, Legislator and Civic Leader," *ETHJ* 5 (March 1967): 29–42.

16. For a description of the campaigns of 1855 see Lubbock, *Six Decades in Texas*, pp. 195–208; Waymon L. McClellan, "1855: The Know-Nothing Challenge in East Texas," *ETHJ* 12 (Fall 1974): 32–44; Roger A. Griffin, "Intrastate Sectionalism in the Texas Governor's Race of 1853," *SWHQ* 76 (October 1972), pp. 142–160; Clarksville *Standard*, 11 August 1855; Crews, "Know-Nothing Party in Texas," 79–114; Sinclair, "Crossroads of Conviction," pp. 26–62.

17. La Grange, *True Issue*, 6 October and 1 December 1855; Marshall *Texas Republican*, 11 August and 15 September 1855; Austin *Texas State Gazette*, 15 September 1855.

18. Billington, *Protestant Crusade*, pp. 407–436; Overdyke, *Know-Nothing Party in the South*, pp. 127–155; San Antonio *Weekly Herald*, 6 February 1856; Washington (Texas) *American*, 19 March 1856; La Grange *True Issue*, 19 June 1856; Marshall *Texas Republican*, 7, 21

June and 20 September 1856. Election returns may be found in Walter L. Buenger, "Stilling the Voice of Reason: Texans and the Union, 1854–1861" (Ph.D. dissertation), pp. 266–391.

19. On the withering away of the Know-Nothing party see Crews, "Know-Nothing Party in Texas," pp. 161–170. Also compare the course of the Marshall *Harrison Flag* with that of the La Grange *True Issue* and San Antonio *Herald*. While the *Flag* promoted the principles of the American party through 1860, the *Herald* and *True Issue* claimed to be either neutral or independent. See Marshall *Harrison Flag* 22 September 1860 and San Antonio *Herald*, 22 June 1859. For the statement of a Know-Nothing turned Democrat see Rip Ford's *Texas State Times*, 21 March and 23 May 1857. A few East Texas newspapers remained consistently loyal to the American party. See Marshall *Harrison Flag*, 10 July 1858. For details of Houston's 1857 campaign for governor see Llerena Friend, *Sam Houston: The Great Designer*, pp. 246–253. On the election of Reagan over Evans see Ben H. Procter, *Not without Honor: The Life of John H. Reagan*, pp. 87–98, and Lubbock, *Six Decades in Texas*, pp. 218–219.

20. See, for example, *Neu Braunsfelser Zeitung*, 22 July 1859.

21. The best primary source on Democrats besides Lubbock is the Austin *Texas State Gazette*, edited by the chairman of the state's Democratic party, John Marshall. See 9 May, 22 August, 5 September, and 3 October 1857. One of the best histories of the course of the Democratic party in the 1850s can be found in Nancy Ann Head, "State Rights in Texas: The Growth of an Idea, 1850–1860" (M.A. thesis).

22. For an example of how Jacksonianism had mixed with more modern doctrines see the Democratic State Platform and a description of the convention of 1859 in the Austin *Texas State Gazette*, 14 May 1859. Also see Sinclair, "Crossroads of Conviction," pp. 1–87; Billy D. Ledbetter, "Slavery, Fear, and Disunion in the Lone Star State: Texans' Attitudes toward Secession and the Union, 1846–1861" (Ph.D. dissertation), pp. 92–120.

23. Head, "State Rights in Texas," pp. 31–100; Ledbetter, "Slavery, Fear, and Disunion in the Lone Star State," pp. 121–149; Austin *Texas State Gazette*, 5, 26 December 1857.

24. Austin *Southern Intelligencer*, 20 January, 14 March, and 9 June, 1858; W. P. Ballinger to G. W. Paschal, William Pitt Ballinger papers; Marshall *Harrison Flag*, 10, 17 July 1858. For other Democratic newspapers that opposed Buckley see Dallas *Herald*, 24 July 1858 and Galveston *News*, 20 July 1858. Also see Sinclair, "Crossroads of Conviction," pp. 93–114, and James P. Hart, "George W. Paschal," *Texas Law Review* 28 (November 1949): 23–42. For the views of a Democratic proponent of Buckley see Houston *Weekly Telegraph*, 14 July 1858.

25. Head, "State Rights in Texas," pp. 64–100; Austin *Texas State Gazette*, 23 January, 19 June, 6 August, 25 September, and 5, 18, 26 December 1858.

26. Sinclair, "Crossroads of Conviction," pp. 100–102; Clarksville *Stan-*

dard, 22 January, 4 June, and 13 August 1859. On the controversy between Paschal and Marshall see Sinclair, "Crossroads of Conviction."
For the election returns see Buenger, "Stilling the Voice," pp. 266–391.

27. Much confusion remains about the proper name of the coalition which
challenged the Texas Democrats from 1858 to early 1860. At the time
former Whigs were reluctant to be called anything connected with the
word Democrat. Even the term Union Democrat, which Sam Houston
favored, did not suit men who had so long opposed the party of Andrew
Jackson. All concerned wanted to avoid the label Know-Nothing. It was
a loser's tag, especially in the case of a party that needed the votes of
Union-loving Germans. The name American party had a similar image
problem; also, Democrats had the same reluctance to be called Americans as Whigs had to be called Democrats. Independent or Independent
Democrat did not quite fit either. No one could be sure of from what
they were independent. Democrats seem to have been the first to call
their challengers the Opposition, and in truth the only thing that kept
such an ideologically diverse group together was that for a variety of
reasons they opposed the Democrats and could do so successfully only
if they cooperated. Whether they were a party in the usual sense of that
word also remains open to question. Certainly they fielded a slate of
candidates, their victories in 1859 were group efforts with each candidate adding to the strength of the entire ticket. At any rate, some modern historians have adopted the name Opposition party or simply the
Opposition. That seems the simplest and least confusing course, and
so hereafter that organized antebellum group which the *Texas State
Gazette* once called "the independent Jackson-Sam Houston-Know-
Nothing Paschalian Democrats . . . assisted by the disaffected Teutons"
will be referred to as the Opposition or the Opposition party. Austin
Texas State Gazette, 4 June 1859. Also see ibid., 28 May 1859; Houston, "Speech at Nacogdoches, July 9, 1859," *Writings* 7: 343–367; Marshall *Texas Republican* 3 September 1859; Marshall *Harrison Flag*, 3,
17 June 1859; Mering, "Slave-State Constitutional Unionists," pp.
396–401; John B. Stabler, "A History of the Constitutional Union
Party: A Tragic Failure" (Ph.D. dissertation), pp. 349–384.

28. Lubbock, *Six Decades in Texas*, p. 248; San Antonio *Daily Herald*, 20
August 1859. George W. Paschal is the best example of a disillusioned
Democrat who supported Houston in 1859. See Paschal to Ashbel
Smith, 27 May 1859, Ashbel Smith papers; Austin *Southern Intel-
ligencer*, 1 September 1858 and 27 May 1859.

29. Wooster, "Epperson," pp. 29–42; Elliott, *Leathercoat*, pp. 15–60; Marshall *Harrison Flag*, 17 June 1859; San Antonio *Daily Herald*, 20 July
1859. Also see McKinney *Messenger* quoted in the San Antonio *Daily
Herald*, 15 April 1859.

30. Austin *Southern Intelligencer*, 3 August 1859; *Campaign Intelligencer*,
16 July 1859; Galveston *Die Union*, 21 July 1859.

31. On the division in the party caused by the slave trade see Houston *Telegraph*, 6 May 1859; Earl W. Fornell, "Agitation in Texas for Reopening

the Slave Trade," *SWHQ* 60 (October 1956): 145–159; Sinclair, "Crossroads of Conviction," pp. 124–145. Also see Harvey Wish, "The Revival of the African Slave Trade in the United States in 1855–1860," *Mississippi Valley Historical Review* 27 (March 1941): 569–588.

32. Friend, *Sam Houston*, pp. 321–327; Lubbock, *Six Decades in Texas*, pp. 243–254; Austin *Texas State Gazette*, 9 July 1859; Houston, *Writings* 7: 341–368; San Antonio *Daily Herald*, 20 July 1859; Austin *Southern Intelligencer*, 25 May 1859.

33. Speeches and letters of Waul and Hamilton as well as comments on the candidates were published in the *Neu Braunfelser Zeitung*, 3, 17 June and 1 July 1859; San Antonio *Daily Herald*, 6, 15, 27 July 1859; Austin *Southern Intelligencer*, 25 May 1859; Austin *Texas State Gazette*, 28 May and 2 July 1859.

34. Marshall *Texas Republican*, 22 April, 2, 6, 13, 20 May, and 10, 17 June 1859. Clarksville *Standard*, 23 April, 14, 28 May, and 4 June 1859. Also see James H. Bell to W. P. Ballinger, 1 May 1859, William P. Ballinger and Thomas M. Jack papers.

35. Clarksville *Standard*, 13 August 1859. Also see Austin *Southern Intelligencer*, 8 June and 27 July 1859; Paschal to F. M. White, 28 May 1859, Francis M. White papers; Paschal to John H. Reagan, 10 June 1859, and John H. Reagan to Paschal, 26 June 1859, John H. Reagan papers. Many former Democrats in San Antonio switched to the side of the Union Democrats. See San Antonio *Daily Herald*, 15, 20 July 1859.

36. J. W. Throckmorton to B. H. Epperson, 18 August 1859 and 13 September 1859, Benjamin H. Epperson papers.

37. Procter, *Not without Honor*, pp. 107–108; H. R. Runnels to Guy M. Bryan, Guy M. Bryan papers; Marshall *Texas Republican*, 5 September 1859; Reagan to Paschal, 26 June 1859; Throckmorton to Epperson, 18 August 1859.

38. Throckmorton to Reagan, 17 August 1859 and 9 September 1859, John H. Reagan papers; Throckmorton to Epperson, 13 September 1859.

39. Reagan to Paschal, 26 June 1859.

40. On Wigfall's esteem within the Democratic party see Clarksville *Standard*, 15 October 1859; Marshall *Texas Republican*, 5 November 1859; Austin *Texas State Gazette*, 17 September and 2 December 1859. On opposition to Reagan as senator see Marshall *Texas Republican*, 12 November 1859; Reagan to William Alexander, 3 October 1859, John H. Reagan papers. The attempts of the Opposition to find a suitable candidate can be followed in the pages of the Marshall *Harrison Flag*. See 12, 19 August, 9, 23, 30 September, 15 October, and 11 November 1859. For a vote of each member of the legislature see Marshall *Harrison Flag*, 27 January 1860. The best secondary source on the election is Billy D. Ledbetter, "The Election of Louis T. Wigfall to the United States Senate, 1859: A Reevaluation," *SWHQ* 77 (October 1973): 241–254.

41. For expressions of Unionism and nationalism of the heart see Clarksville *Standard*, 28 June 1859; Marshall *Harrison Flag*, 15 September

1860; San Antonio *Alamo Express,* 5 November 1860; Throckmorton to Epperson, 18 August and 13 September 1859. On pragmatic Unionism see Clarksville *Standard,* 13, 20 August 1859 and 22 December 1860; Dallas *Herald,* 31 October 1860; Austin *Southern Intelligencer,* 10 October 1860. Also of interest is Paul C. Nagel, *One Nation Indivisible: The Union in American Thought, 1776–1861;* Major L. Wilson, *Space, Time and Freedom: The Quest for Nationality and the Irrepressible Conflict, 1815–1861;* John McCardell, *The Idea of a Southern Nation: Southern Nationalists and Southern Nationalism, 1830–1860;* Kenneth M. Stampp, *The Imperiled Union: Essays on the Background of the Civil War.* For examples of Opposition ideology see Marshall *Harrison Flag,* 22 September 1860; Galveston *Die Union,* 6 November 1860; San Antonio *Alamo Express,* 10, 17 September 1860; La Grange *True Issue,* 24 January 1861. On the Democrats see Austin *Texas State Gazette,* 16 April, 28 May, 6, 13 August 1859, 4, 25 August and 1 September 1860; Marshall *Texas Republican,* 27 October and 3, 10 November 1860.

3. PUBLIC PREJUDICE

1. Sam Houston, "Speech at Brenham, March 31, 1861," *Writings* 8: 295.
2. Austin *Texas State Gazette,* 26 November and 3 December 1859, 4 February 1860; Clarksville *Standard,* 29 October and 19 November 1869; Marshall *Texas Republican,* 19 November and 10 December 1859; Galveston *Die Union,* 10 November 1859; *Neu Braunfelser Zeitung,* 25 November 1869.
3. Charles W. Goldfinch and Jose T. Canales, *Juan Cortina: Two Interpretations;* John Salmon Ford, *Rip Ford's Texas,* ed. Stephen B. Oates, pp. 260–309; "Report of the Mexican Commission on the Northern Frontier Question," reprinted in Carlos E. Cortés (ed.), *The Mexican Experience in Texas,* pp. 126–163; Paul Schuster Taylor, *An American-Mexican Frontier: Nueces County, Texas,* pp. 40–43.
4. "Letter of Hon. Geo. B. Erath," Austin *Texas State Gazette,* 11 June 1859; Charles W. Ramsdell, "The Frontier and Secession," *Studies in Southern History and Politics,* pp. 63–68. Most Texans considered the army inefficient. See, for example, Sam Houston to A. J. Hamilton, 17 March 1860, *Writings* 7: 526–527.
5. Ollinger Crenshaw, "The Speakership Contest of 1859–1860," *Mississippi Valley Historical Review* 29 (December 1942): 323–338; Ben H. Proctor, *Not without Honor: The Life of John H. Reagan,* pp. 114–118; Oran M. Roberts, "The Political, Legislative, and Judicial History of Texas for Its Fifty Years of Statehood, 1845–1895," *A Comprehensive History of Texas, 1685–1897,* ed. Dudley G. Wooten, pp. 21, 75.
6. Francis Richard Lubbock, *Six Decades in Texas,* ed. by C. W. Raines, pp. 259–266; Roberts, "Political, Legislative, and Judicial History of Texas," pp. 73–76; Billy D. Ledbetter, "The Election of Louis T. Wigfall to the United States Senate, 1859: A Reevaluation," *SWHQ* 77 (October 1973): 241–242; Proctor, *Not without Honor,* pp. 116–119.

7. Austin *Southern Intelligencer*, 28 September 1859. Also see Oran Lonnie Sinclair, "Crossroads of Conviction: A Study of the Texas Political Mind, 1856–1861" (Ph.D. dissertation), pp. 124–160.

8. Sinclair, "Crossroads of Conviction," pp. 161–180; Larry Jay Gage, "The Texas Road to Secession and War: John Marshall and the *Texas State Gazette*," *SWHQ* 62 (October 1958): 198–201.

9. George W. Paschal to A. J. Hamilton, 15 February 1860, Andrew Jackson Hamilton papers.

10. Lubbock, *Six Decades in Texas*, pp. 259–266; Roberts, "Political, Legislative, and Judicial History of Texas," pp. 76–86; Ernest William Winkler (ed.), *Platforms of Political Parties in Texas*.

11. Lubbock, *Six Decades in Texas*, pp. 267–280; Ollinger Crenshaw, *The Slave States in the Presidential Election of 1860*, pp. 11–35; Austin L. Venable, "The Conflict Between the Douglas and Yancey Forces in the Charleston Convention," *Journal of Southern History* 8 (May 1942): 226–241.

12. Lubbock, *Six Decades in Texas*, p. 283; Clarksville *Standard*, 16 June 1860.

13. Lubbock, *Six Decades in Texas*, pp. 295–298; Llerena Friend, *Sam Houston: The Great Designer*, pp. 315–320; Murat Halstead, *Three against Lincoln: Murat Halstead Reports the Caucuses of 1860*, ed. William B. Hesseltine, pp. 118–140. James Alex Baggett, "The Constitutional Union Party in Texas," *SWHQ* 82 (January 1979): 237–244.

14. Lubbock, *Six Decades in Texas*, pp. 280–294; Halstead, *Three against Lincoln*, pp. 185–278.

15. Halstead, *Three against Lincoln*, pp. 141–177.

16. Austin *Texas State Gazette*, 8 September 1860.

17. Baggett, "Constitutional Union Party in Texas," pp. 249–251; Clarksville *Standard*, 20, 27 October 1860; Roberts, "Political, Legislative, and Judicial History of Texas," pp. 81–84; Friend, *Sam Houston*, pp. 318–320; Marshall *Harrison Flag*, 29 June and 6 July 1860; Galveston *Die Union*, 6 November 1860.

18. Ernest Wallace, *Charles De Morse: Pioneer Editor and Statesman*, pp. 1–192; Clarksville *Standard*, 16, 23 June, 14 July and 4 August 1860. For the views of another moderate Democrat who also feared the influence of Yancey see E. L. Dohoney, *An Average American*, pp. 47–59.

19. Roberts, "The Political, Legislative, and Judicial History of Texas," pp. 81–84; Sinclair, "Crossroads of Conviction," pp. 161–180; Austin *Texas State Gazette*, 7 July and 6 October 1860; Clarksville *Standard*, 20 October 1860. On antebellum political parties see Richard P. McCormack, *The Second American Party System: Party Formation in the Jacksonian Era*; Charles G. Seller, Jr., "Who Were the Southern Whigs?," *American Historical Review* 59 (January 1954): 335–337; Fletcher M. Green, "Democracy in the Old South," *Journal of Southern History* 12 (February 1946): 3–23.

20. Austin *Texas State Gazette*, 14 July, 13, 20 October 1860; Clarksville *Standard*, 14 July 1860; San Antonio *Herald*, 21 July 1860.

21. Austin *Southern Intelligencer*, 5 September 1860; San Antonio *Alamo Express*, 18 August 1860.

22. Baggett, "Constitutional Union Party in Texas," pp. 243–251; San Antonio *Alamo Express*, 10 September and 15 October 1860; Marshall *Harrison Flag*, 1, 22 September 1860; Marshall *Harrison Flag*, 22 September 1860.

23. San Antonio *Alamo Express*, 18 August and 10 September 1860; Marshall *Harrison Flag*, 22 September 1860.

24. San Antonio *Alamo Express*, 3, 17 September 1860; William Pitt Ballinger, diary (typescript), 18, 23, 31 August 1860.

25. Quoted from the Marshall *Harrison Flag* in Marshall *Texas Republican*, 29 September 1860. Also see *Harrison Flag*, 29 September and 6 October 1860; La Grange *True Issue*, 1, 8, 15 October 1860; San Antonio *Alamo Express*, 8 October 1860.

26. Austin *Southern Intelligencer*, 10 October 1860; San Antonio *Alamo Express*, 8 October 1860; Friend, *Sam Houston*, pp. 329–330.

27. San Antonio *Alamo Express*, 15 October 1860; Marshall *Harrison Flag*, 20 October 1860; La Grange *True Issue*, 3 November 1860.

28. On the Texas Troubles see Ollinger Crenshaw, *The Slave States in the Presidential Election of 1860*, pp. 89–111; Donald E. Reynolds, *Editors Make War: Southern Newspapers in the Secession Crisis*, pp. 97–117; William W. White, "The Texas Slave Insurrection in 1860," *SWHQ* 52 (January 1949): 259–286; Wendell G. Addington, "Slave Insurrection in Texas," *Journal of Negro History* 35 (October 1950): 408–434.

29. Clarksville *Standard*, 14 July 1860; Houston *Telegraph*, 21 July 1860; Dallas *Herald*, "Extra," 11 July 1860.

30. Marshall *Texas Republican*, 11 August 1860; Corsicana *Navarro Express*, 14 July and 11 August 1860; Reynolds, *Editors Make War*, pp. 100–110.

31. Austin *Texas State Gazette*, 14 July 1860. For other Pryor letters see Bonham *Era*, 17 July 1860; Houston *Telegraph*, 21 July 1860. On the spread of the news of the Texas Troubles across the south see Reynolds, *Editors Make War*, p. 101; Crenshaw, *The Slave States*, pp. 92–100. For background information on Pryor see Thomas N. Wood, "Attitudes of Certain Texas Editors toward Secession" (M.A. thesis), pp. 82–103.

32. For the views of the Opposition party see Austin *Southern Intelligencer*, 15 August and 5 September 1860. For the views of a Breckinridge advocate who doubted the authenticity of the conspiracy see Marshall *Texas Republican*, 28 July 1860. Also see Reynolds, *Editors Make War*, pp. 115–117.

33. Austin *Texas State Gazette*, 8 September 1860. Also see Marshall *Texas Republican*, 8 September 1860; Galveston *News*, 15 September 1860; *Neu Braunfelser Zeitung*, 31 August 1860.

34. San Antonio *Alamo Express*, 17, 24 September and 1, 8 October 1860; Marshall *Harrison Flag*, 29 September and 8 October 1860; Austin *Texas State Gazette*, 29 September and 20 October 1860; Austin *Southern Intelligencer*, 10 October 1860.

35. San Antonio *Alamo Express*, 24 September and 22 October 1860; Clarksville *Standard*, 14 July 1860; Marshall *Harrison Flag*, 15, 29 September and 20 October 1860; Marshall *Texas Republican*, 29 September 1860.

36. Clarksville *Standard*, 27 October 1860; Austin *Texas State Gazette*, 27 October and 3 November 1860; Marshall *Texas Republican*, 27 October 1860. Even the Opposition press was disheartened by the state elections. See San Antonio *Alamo Express*, 22 October 1860; Marshall *Harrison Flag*, 27 October 1860; Galveston *Die Union*, 6 November 1860.

37. Austin *Texas State Gazette*, 16 June 1860. John H. Reagan, an extremely popular congressman, was a good barometer of public opinion. See his speech when he left Congress, U.S., Congress, *Congressional Globe*, 36th Congress, 2nd Session, pp. 389–393. Also see J. H. Reagan to O. M. Roberts, 1 November 1860, Oran Milo Roberts papers.

38. San Antonio *Alamo Express*, 5 November 1860. Also see Marshall *Harrison Flag*, 27 October and 3 November 1860; San Antonio *Alamo Express*, 22 October 1860. Election returns may be found in W. Dean Burnham, *Presidential Ballots: 1836–1892*, pp. 764–813.

39. Roberts, "Political, Legislative, and Judicial History of Texas," pp. 85–99.

40. For a history of attempts to build a southern nation as well as an understanding of the public mood in the South see John McCardell, *The Idea of a Southern Nation: Southern Nationalists and Southern Nationalism, 1830–1860*. O. M. Roberts not only wrote his "Political, Legislative, and Judicial History of Texas," he kept a journal during the secession crisis. Parts of that journal can be found in John Salmon Ford, "The Memoirs of John Salmon Ford" (typescript) 5: 942–966.

41. Ford, "Memoirs," pp. 942–966; Lubbock, *Six Decades in Texas*, pp. 304–305.

4. THE OTHER TEXAS

1. James W. Throckmorton to Louis T. Wigfall, 30 December 1866, James Webb Throckmorton papers. Among the works on Texas unionists are Frank H. Smyrl, "Unionism in Texas, 1856–1861," *SWHQ* 68 (October 1964): 172–195; Claude Elliott, "Union Sentiment in Texas, 1861–1865," *SWHQ* 50 (April 1947): 448–477; Floyd F. Ewing, "Origins of Unionist Sentiment on the West Texas Frontier," *West Texas Historical Association Year Book* 32 (October 1956): 21–29; idem, "Unionist Sentiment on the North West Texas Frontier," ibid. 33 (October 1957): 58–70; Walter L. Buenger, "Secession and the Texas German Community: Editor Lindheimer vs. Editor Flake," *SWHQ* 82 (April 1979): 379–402; idem, "Unionism on the Texas Frontier, 1859–1861," *Arizona and the West* 22 (Autumn 1980): 237–254. Dealing in part with Unionism are Robert W. Shook, "The Battle of the Nueces, August 10, 1862," *SWHQ* 66 (July 1962): 31–42; Terry G. Jordan, *German Seed in Texas Soil: Immigrant Farmers in Nineteenth-Century Texas*, pp. 182–185; idem, "The Imprint of the Upper and Lower South on Mid-Nineteenth Century Texas," *Annals of the Association of American*

Geographers 57 (December 1967): 685–688; Charles W. Ramsdell, "The Frontier and Secession," *Studies in Southern History and Politics*, pp. 63–82; Thomas Barrett, *The Great Hanging at Gainesville, Cooke County, Texas, October A.D. 1862*; Sam Acheson and Julie Ann Hudson O'Connell (eds.), *George Washington Diamond's Account of the Great Hanging at Gainesville, 1862*.

2. For the vote in the twenty-nine counties which cast over 40 percent of their ballots against secession and their location see Smyrl, "Unionism in Texas," 191–192. For more information on these counties' locations and population makeup see Jordan, "Imprint of the Upper and Lower South," pp. 671, 685–688.

3. Claude Elliott, *Leathercoat: The Life History of a Texas Patriot*, pp. 56 and 59. On Throckmorton also see Texas, *Journal of the Senate, 8th Legislature*, pp. 49–50; Elliott, *Leathercoat*, pp. 3–60; J. W. Throckmorton to John H. Reagan, 9 September 1859, John H. Reagan papers.

4. For discussions of Whig nationalism see Robert Dalzell, *Daniel Webster and the Trial of American Nationalism*, and Irving H. H. Bartlett, *Daniel Webster*, pp. 108–121. On Throckmorton's opinion of secession see the following (which he signed and probably helped write) "Address to the People of Texas," 6 February 1861, in John L. Haynes papers.

5. Jordan, "Imprint of the Upper and Lower South"; Jordan, "The Texan Appalachia," *Annals of the Association of American Geographers* 60 (September 1970): 409–427; idem., "Population Origins in Texas, 1850," *Geographical Review* 59 (January 1969): 89–100.

6. Throckmorton to Wigfall, 30 December 1856. On the secession referendum and cultural divisions in Texas see Smyrl, "Unionism in Texas," pp. 191–192; Jordan, "Imprint of the Upper and Lower South," pp. 671, 689; Jordan, "Population Origins," p. 87; Joe T. Timmons, "The Referendum in Texas on the Ordinance of Secession, February 23, 1861: The Vote," *ETHJ* 11 (Fall 1973): 15–19. Jordan lists Titus and Van Zandt counties as Upper South in 1850 but Lower South in 1880.

7. James W. Throckmorton to David G. Burnet, 26 July 1857, David G. Burnet papers; Frederick Law Olmsted, *A Journey through Texas: Or, A Saddle-Trip on the Southwestern Frontier*, p. 421; Jacob De Cordova, *Texas: Her Resources and Her Public Men*, pp. 189–190.

8. J. W. Latimer, "The Wheat Region and Wheat Culture in Texas," *Texas Almanac for 1859*, p. 69n; J. H. S., "The Wheat Region in Texas," *Texas Almanac for 1867*, p. 224n; Clarksville *Standard*, 31 May 1856; Ramsdell, "The Frontier and Secession," pp. 78–80.

9. Jordan, "Imprint of the Upper and Lower South," p. 688.

10. Clarksville *Standard*, 10, 31 May 1856 and 9 June 1860; Dallas *Herald*, 5 April, 24 May, and 5 July 1856, 15 December 1858, 19 January 1859, and 29 February 1860; Donald E. Reynolds, *Editors Make War: Southern Newspapers in the Secession Crisis*, pp. 98–100; Dallas *Herald*, "Extra," 11 July 1860.

11. On Jackson, Polk, Houston, and Clay see Marvin Meyers, *The Jack-*

sonian Persuasion: Politics and Belief; John William Ward, *Andrew Jackson: Symbol for an Age*; Charles G. Sellers, Jr., *James K. Polk* (2 vols.); Clement Eaton, *Henry Clay and the Art of American Politics*; Glyndon G. Van Deusen, *The Life of Henry Clay*; Llerena Friend, *Sam Houston: The Great Designer*; Marquis James, *The Raven: A Biography of Sam Houston*. Two Texas transplants from Tennessee who were also prominent unionists from 1856 to 1859 were James W. Throckmorton and John H. Reagan. See Claude Elliott, *Leathercoat*, pp. 3–60, and Ben H. Proctor, *Not without Honor: The Life of John H. Reagan*, pp. 3–121.

12. John V. Mering has recently argued that the Opposition parties dissolved in the southern states during the secession crisis and that their reason for being was competition for place, not the issue of union or disunion. This was true of East Texas to an extent, but not North Texas or the western counties. See Mering, "The Slave-State Constitutional Unionists and the Politics of Consensus," *Journal of Southern History* 43 (August 1977): 395–410; San Antonio Weekly *Alamo Express*, 9, 16, 23 February 1861; Austin *Southern Intelligencer*, 30 January 1861. Frontier counties, whose population usually came from the Upper South, but whose Unionism was shaped by pragmatism, are treated as distinct from the Upper South region of Texas and will be discussed in later chapters.

13. For an analysis of the reasons for the Opposition's success see Dallas *Herald*, 10 August 1859; Clarksville *Standard*, 6, 13 August 1859.

14. Clarksville *Standard*, 26 March 1859.

15. Dallas *Herald*, 26 January 1859; Clarksville *Standard*, 13, 20 August 1859.

16. Marshall *Texas Republican*, 22 April and 2, 6, 13, 20 May 1859.

17. Austin *Texas State Gazette*, 16 April, 28 May, and 4 June 1859.

18. John L. Waller, *Colossal Hamilton of Texas: A Biography of Andrew Jackson Hamilton, Militant Unionist and Reconstruction Governor*, pp. 1–20; Austin *Southern Intelligencer*, 4 August 1858, 11, 25 May, 11, 18 June, and 27 July 1859.

19. Austin *Southern Intelligencer*, 3 August 1859. For further examples of the rhetoric of Hamilton and Paschal, see Austin *Southern Intelligencer*, 4 August 1858, and Jane L. Scarborough, "George W. Paschal, Texas Unionist and Scalawag Jurisprudent" (Ph.D. dissertation).

20. Dallas *Herald*, 21 September, 19 October, 9 November, and 7, 11 December 1859; Clarksville *Standard*, 15, 29 October and 18 December 1859. Also see Billy D. Ledbetter, "The Election of Louis T. Wigfall to the United States Senate, 1859: A Reevaluation," *SWHQ* 77 (October 1973): 241–254.

21. Austin *Texas State Gazette*, 5, 12 November and 12 December 1859. The vote of each member of the legislature may be found in the Marshall *Harrison Flag*, 27 January 1860. A description of Austin may be found in Larry Jay Gage, "The City of Austin on the Eve of the Civil

War," *SWHQ* 63 (January 1960): 428–438, and Alexander W. Terrell, "The City of Austin from 1839–1865," *Texas Historical Association Quarterly* 14 (October 1910): 113–128.

22. Dallas *Herald*, 30 March and 9 November 1859, 5 January and 8 February 1860. The tie between frontier defense and secession was first discussed in Ramsdell, "The Frontier and Secession," pp. 63–82. The tumult in Congress is described in Ollinger Crenshaw, "The Speakership Contest of 1859–1860," *Mississippi Valley Historical Review* 29 (December 1942): 323–338. Representative John H. Reagan's first severe doubts about the Union came as a result of the discord in the House and the failure of Congress to aid Texas. See J. H. Reagan to O. M. Roberts, 1 November 1860, Oran Milo Roberts papers, and Proctor, *Not without Honor*, pp. 115–128. Even moderates like Throckmorton and Houston were infuriated by the failure of Congress to deal with the Indians. See Sam Houston to Hon. John B. Floyd, secretary of war, *Writings* 7: 519–522; Throckmorton to Reagan, 17 March 1860, John H. Reagan papers.

23. Friend, *Sam Houston*, pp. 301–320; Marshall *Harrison Flag*, 18 May and 29 June 1860.

24. Dallas *Herald*, 11 January, 7 March, and 25 April 1860; Clarksville *Standard*, 10 March and 14, 28 April 1860.

25. Clarksville *Standard*, 16 June 1860; Dallas *Herald*, 16, 23 May 1860; Austin *Texas State Gazette*, 9 June 1860.

26. On East Texas see Marshall *Harrison Flag*, 15, 29 June and 6 July 1860. On North Texas see Dallas *Herald*, 25 April and 20 June 1860; Clarksville *Standard*, 16 June and 14 July 1860. On the Austin area see Austin *Texas State Gazette*, 14–28 July 1860; San Antonio *Herald*, 21 July 1860; La Grange *True Issue*, 4 October 1860.

27. On the Texas Troubles see Ollinger Crenshaw, *The Slave States in the Presidential Election of 1860*, pp. 89–111; Donald E. Reynolds, *Editors Make War, Southern Newspapers in the Secession Crisis*, pp. 97–117; William W. White, "The Texas Slave Insurrection in 1860," *SWHQ* 52 (January 1949): 259–286; Wendell G. Addington, "Slave Insurrections in Texas," *The Journal of Negro History* 35 (October 1950): 408–434. Also see Clarksville *Standard*, 14 July 1860; Houston *Telegraph*, 21 July 1860; Dallas *Herald*, "Extra," 11 July 1860; Marshall *Texas Republican*, 11 August 1860; Corsicana *Navarro Express*, 14 July and 11 August 1860; Austin *Texas State Gazette*, 14 July 1860; Bonham *Era*, 17 July 1860.

28. Jordan, "Imprint of the Upper and Lower South," pp. 685–688, notes the two distinct attitudes toward the Union in Upper South counties of Texas. For a good discussion of the Unionism of southern Whigs see Carl N. Degler, *The Other South: Southern Dissenters in the Nineteenth Century*, pp. 105–190.

29. For an articulate statement of the link between John Brown, the Texas Troubles, and secession see Bellville *Countryman*, 13 December 1860.

30. On the Fusion party see San Antonio *Alamo Express*, 18 August and 10

September 1860; Austin *Southern Intelligencer,* 5 September 1860; Marshall *Harrison Flag,* 22 September 1860.

31. San Antonio *Alamo Express,* 18 August 1860. For coverage of the campaign see San Antonio *Alamo Express,* 2, 10, 17 September, 8, 15 October, and 5 November 1860; Austin *Southern Intelligencer,* 10 October 1860; Clarksville *Standard,* 13, 20, 28 October 1860. For an example of Sam Houston's public rhetoric in support of the Union see Houston, *Writings* 8: 121–122, 173.

32. Compare the Austin *Southern Intelligencer,* 10 October 1860, with the Marshall *Harrison Flag,* 22 September 1860. On Flake and Schleicher see Galveston *Die Union,* 6 November 1860; San Antonio *Alamo Express,* 10, 17 September 1860.

33. Clarksville *Standard,* 13, 27, 29 October 1860.

34. For selected voting returns from Texas see Walter L. Buenger, "Stilling the Voice of Reason: Texans and the Union, 1854–1861" (Ph.D. dissertation), pp. 266–391.

35. Clarksville *Standard,* 27 October and 22 December 1860; Dallas *Herald,* 31 October 1860. For an account of Webster's influence on Americans' attachment to the Union see Dalzell, *Daniel Webster;* Bartlett, *Daniel Webster,* pp. 108–296.

36. Clarksville *Standard,* 20 October and 22 December 1860, 19 January 1861. On the influence of Jackson see Ward, *Andrew Jackson.*

37. On the lives of De Morse and Epperson see Ernest Wallace, *Charles De Morse, Pioneer Editor and Statesman,* and Ralph A. Wooster, "Ben H. Epperson: East Texas Lawyer, Legislator, and Civic Leader," *ETHJ* 5 (March 1967): 29–42. For their views on the Union see B. H. Epperson papers; Clarksville *Standard,* 13, 20 August 1859, 10 March, 14, 28 April, 23 June, 13, 20 October, and 22 December 1860.

38. Ernest William Winkler (ed.), *Journal of the Secession Convention of Texas, 1861,* pp. 26–28, 49–50; Sinclair, "Crossroads of Conviction," p. 186; Dallas *Herald,* 16 January 1861; Jordan, "Imprint of the Upper and Lower South," p. 689.

5. ORTHODOXY AND ETHNICITY

1. Germans, in particular, have long been labeled totally loyal to the Union throughout the Civil War period. This was not true. For a fuller discussion see Walter L. Buenger, "Secession and the Texas German Community: Editor Lindheimer vs. Editor Flake," *SWHQ* 82 (April 1979): 379–402.

2. Moritz Tilling, *History of the German Element in Texas from 1820–1850 and Historical Sketches of the German Texas Singers' League and Houston Turnverein from 1853–1913,* pp. 17–18; Detlef Dunt, *Reise Nach Texas,* p. 52. Rudolph Leopold Biesele, *The History of the German Settlements in Texas 1831–1861,* pp. 42–47, 66–177; Terry G. Jordan, "Population Origins in Texas, 1850," *Geographical Review* 59 (January 1969): 89–101; Julia Nott Waugh, *Castro-Ville and Henry*

Castro, *Empresario*; Lorenzo Castro, *Immigration from Alsace and Lorraine: A Brief Sketch of the History of Castro's Colony*; Julius Fröbel, *Aus Amerika: Erfahrungen, Reisen, und Studien* 2: 320; Ralph A. Wooster, "Foreigners in the Principal Towns of Ante-Bellum Texas," *SWHQ* 66 (October 1962): 208–220; Ferdinand Flake, "Register of 1864 of the Male and Female Inhabitants of Galveston City," (typescript), pp. 34–44.

3. Ada Marie Hall, "Texas Germans in State and National Politics, 1850– 1865"; Sister Paul of the Cross McGrath, *Political Nativism in Texas, 1825–1860*; Earl W. Fornell, *Galveston Era: The Texas Crescent on the Eve of Secession*, pp. 134–135.

4. Terry G. Jordan, *German Seed in Texas Soil: Immigrant Farmers in Nineteenth-Century Texas*, pp. 192–204; Biesele, *German Settlements*, pp. 208–227; Carland Elaine Crook, "San Antonio, Texas, 1846–1861" (M.A. thesis), pp. 46–49; Fornell, *Galveston Era*, pp. 125–139; Crook, "San Antonio," pp. 50–51; *Neu Braunfelser Zeitung* (hereafter *N.B. Zeitung*), 10 December 1852. Also see the San Antonio *Herald*, 19 January and 24 May 1859; Galveston *Civilian*, 13 January, 27 April, and 18 July 1857; Houston *Telegraph*, 30 September 1857; Galveston *News*, 17 December 1856; Austin *Texas State Gazette*, 28 March 1857; Jordan, *German Seed*, pp. 192–203.

5. "Letter from a German," Houston *Telegraph*, 13 July 1859, also quoted in Fornell, *Galveston Era*, p. 139. On the relative ease with which Western Europeans blended with Americans see John Higham, *Strangers in the Land: Patterns of American Nativism, 1860–1925*, pp. 23–27. Also see Houston *Telegraph*, 30 September 1857; San Antonio *Herald*, 24 May 1859; San Antonio *Texas Staats-Zeitung*, 4 June 1859; Galveston *Die Union*, 28 February 1861; *N. B. Zeitung*, 11 February 1858.

6. Willard Richardson, *Galveston Directory for 1859–60, with a Brief History of the Island*, p. 36; Galveston *Die Union*, 23 February 1861; *N. B. Zeitung*, 30 November 1860; Ferdinand J. Lindheimer, *Aufsätze und Abhandlungen*.

7. Olmsted reflected upon the conservative nature of the Germans and their habits of patience and deference. See Frederick Law Olmsted, *A Journey through Texas: Or, A Saddle-Trip on the Southwestern Frontier*, pp. 428–441. Also see *N. B. Zeitung*, 9 December 1853 and 10 February 1854.

8. *N. B. Zeitung*, 11 March 1859. All quotes from the *N. B. Zeitung* and *Die Union* are translated by the author with the assistance of Frederick R. Zuber. For a lengthy translation of the Lindheimer editorial on slavery see Gilbert Giddings Benjamin, *The Germans in Texas: A Study in Immigration*, pp. 106–108. Also see Galveston *Die Union*, 2 April 1859 and 12 January 1861; Houston *Tri-Weekly Telegraph*, 6 May 1859; Olmsted, *A Journey through Texas*, pp. 432–433; Zoie Odom Newsome, "Antislavery Sentiment in Texas, 1821–1861" (M.A. thesis), pp. 47–64; Gilbert Giddings Benjamin, *Germans in Texas: A Study in Immigration*, pp. 98–108.

9. Austin *Texas State Gazette*, 5 March 1859; Clarksville *Standard*, 20 August 1859; Houston *Telegraph*, 30 September 1857; Galveston *Civilian*, 18 July 1857; Galveston *News*, 18 December 1856.

10. The best sources on Spanish and Mexican Texas are Samuel Harman Lowrie, *Culture Conflict in Texas, 1821–1835*, pp. 82–83; Odie B. Faulk, *The Last Years of Spanish Texas, 1778–1821*; Herbert Eugene Bolton, *Texas in the Middle Eighteenth Century: Studies in Spanish Colonial History and Administration*; José Maria Sanchez, "A Trip to Texas in 1828," trans. Carlos E. Castañeda, *SWHQ* 29 (April 1926): 149–188; Juan N. Almonte, "Statistical Report on Texas," trans. Carlos E. Castañeda, *SWHQ* 28 (January 1925): 117–222; Alleine Howren, "Causes and Origin of the Decree of April 6, 1830," *SWHQ* 16 (April 1913): 378–422; Mattie Austin Hatcher, *The Opening of Texas to Foreign Settlement, 1801–1821*; Eugene C. Barker, *The Life of Stephen F. Austin*. Also see Joseph C. G. Kennedy, *Population of the United States in 1860; Compiled from the Original Returns of the Eighth Census*, pp. 487–490; Carey McWilliams, *North from Mexico: The Spanish Speaking People of the United States*; Paul Horgan, *Great River: The Rio Grande in North American History* 1: 298–345; Jordan, "Population Origins in Texas," p. 97.

11. Juan N. Seguín, *Personal Memoirs of Juan N. Seguín: From the Year 1834 to the Retreat of General Woll from the City of San Antonio in 1842*; Joseph Milton Nance, *Attack and Counterattack: The Texas-Mexican Frontier, 1842*; McWilliams, *North from Mexico*, pp. 100–102; Paul Schuster Taylor, *An American-Mexican Frontier: Nueces County, Texas*, pp. 3–40; José Maria Rodríguez, *Rodríguez Memoirs of Early Texas*, pp. 37–39.

12. Quoted in Howren, "Causes and Origin of Decree," p. 395; Contemporary descriptions of the class system may be found in W. Eugene Hollon and Ruth Lapham Butler (eds.), *William Bollaert's Texas*, pp. 216–218; Olmsted, *A Journey through Texas*, pp. 147–165; Rodríguez, *Memoirs*, pp. 18–19; Mary Austin Holley, *Texas*, pp. 127–129; Benjamin F. McIntyre, *Federals on the Frontier: The Diary of Benjamin F. McIntyre*, ed. Nannie M. Tilley, p. 262. Also see Lowrie, *Culture Conflict*, pp. 210–274; McWilliams, *North from Mexico*, pp. 84–88; Betty Gay Hunter Ash, "The Mexican Texans in the Civil War" (M.S. thesis), pp. 17–21.

13. Lowrie, *Culture Conflict*, pp. 120–181; William Ransom Hogan, *The Texas Republic: A Social and Economic History*; Llerena Friend, "The Texan of 1860," *SWHQ* 62 (July 1958): 1–17.

14. Herman Ehrenberg, *With Milam and Fannin: Adventures of a German Boy in Texas' Revolution*, p. 105; Olmsted, *A Journey through Texas*, pp. 151–152, 162; Austin *Texas State Gazette*, 27 August 1859.

15. Olmsted, *A Journey through Texas*, p. 163. Also see Galveston *Weekly News*, 5 September 1854; Austin *Texas State Gazette*, 24 February 1855; Arnoldo De Leon, "White Racial Attitudes toward Mexicanos in Texas, 1821–1900" (Ph.D. dissertation), pp. 70–71, 133–191; L. G. Bugbee, "Slavery in Early Texas," *Political Science Quarterly* 13 (Sep-

tember 1898): 389–412; Eugene C. Barker, The Influence of Slavery in the Colonization of Texas," *SWHQ* 28 (July 1924): 1–33; Ash, "Mexican Texans in the Civil War," pp. 23–27; John Salmon Ford, *Rip Ford's Texas,* ed. Stephen B. Oates, pp. 196, 214–215.

16. De Leon, "White Racial Attitudes," pp. 1–57; Ferdinand Roemer, *Texas: With Particular Reference to German Immigration and the Physical Appearance of the Country,* trans. Oswald Mueller, p. 11; Prince Carl von Solms-Braunfels, *Texas, 1844–1845,* trans. Oswald Mueller, pp. 46–47; Frederic L. Paxson, "The Constitution of Texas, 1845," *SWHQ* 18 (April 1915): 392; William F. Weeks (reporter), *Debates of the Texas Convention,* pp. 53, 157–159; McGrath, *Political Nativism in Texas,* pp. 45–61.

17. San Antonio *El Bejareno,* 2 February 1855. San Antonio *El Ranchero,* 28 July 1856. Also see Frank H. Dugan, "The 1850 Affair of the Brownsville Separatists," *SWHQ* 61 (October 1957): 278–280; Ash, "Mexican Texans in the Civil War," pp. 21–23.

18. James H. Thompson, "A Nineteenth-Century History of Cameron County, Texas" (M.A. thesis), p. 87; "History of Laredo," Laredo Archives; *Handbook of Texas* 1: 416–418, 2: 590–591. For an example of the familial ties that bound Texans to other parts of the Union see the John P. Osterhout collection. Also see Lowrie, *Culture Conflict,* pp. 120–181.

19. The best social history of 19th-century Mexican communities in Texas can be found in Taylor, *American-Mexican Frontier,* pp. 7–67.

20. Ford, *Rip Ford's Texas,* p. 322. Also see *Handbook of Texas* 1: 146, 2: 262–263; Jacob De Cordova, *Texas: Her Resources and Her Public Men,* pp. 145–153; Frederick C. Chabot, *With the Makers of San Antonio,* pp. 202–206; L. E. Daniell, *Types of Successful Men of Texas,* pp. 328, 324–330; Frank W. Johnson, *A History of Texas and Texans,* ed. Eugene C. Barker, pp. 1396–1398; *A Legislative Manual for the State of Texas,* p. 267; Harry McCorry Henderson, *Texas in the Confederacy,* pp. 90, 132; Walter Prescott Webb, *The Texas Rangers: A Century of Frontier Defense,* pp. 175–193; Ford, *Rip Ford's Texas,* pp. 266–307; Charles W. Goldfinch and Jose T. Canales, *Juan Cortina: Two Interpretations*; John C. Rayburn and Virginia Kemp (eds.), *Century of Conflict, 1821–1913: Incidents in the Lives of William Neal and William A. Neale, Early Settlers in South Texas,* pp. 64–68.

21. De Cordova, *Texas,* pp. 145–154; Corpus Christi *Ranchero,* 17 March 1860; Webb, *Texas Rangers,* pp. 176–177.

22. For background information on the Know-Nothing party and its effect on Texas politics see Litha Crews, "The Know-Nothing Party in Texas" (M.A. thesis); Ernest W. Winkler (ed.), *Platforms of Political Parties in Texas,* pp. 63–71; Ralph A. Wooster, "An Analysis of the Texas Know Nothings," *SWHQ* 70 (January 1967): 414–423; Oran Lonnie Sinclair, "Crossroads of Conviction: A Study of the Texas Political Mind, 1856–1861" (Ph.D. dissertation), pp. 26–92.

23. San Antonio *El Bejareno,* 23 June 1855; San Antonio *El Ranchero,* 28

July 1856; McGrath, *Political Nativism in Texas*, pp. 79–182; *N. B. Zeitung*, 23 June and 7 July 1854.

24. Rudolph Leopold Biesele, "The Texas State Convention of Germans in 1854," *SWHQ* 33 (April 1930): 247–261; McGrath, *Political Nativism in Texas*, pp. 92–97; Olmsted, *A Journey through Texas*, pp. 434–439; Laura W. Roper, "Frederick Law Olmsted and the Western Texas Free-Soil Movement," *American Historical Review* 56 (October 1950): 58–64; *N. B. Zeitung*, 7 July 1854 and 11 March 1859; Austin *Texas State Gazette*, 11, 25 July 1855.

25. Galveston *Zeitung*, 19 August 1855; Fornell, *Galveston Era*, pp. 136–137; La Grange *True Issue*, 13 October 1855.

26. La Grange *Paper*, 16 June 1855. Also see Austin *Texas State Gazette*, 1, 18 August 1855 and 28 March 1857; San Antonio *El Bejareno*, 3 July 1855; Austin *Texas State Times*, 11 August 1855; Crews, "Know-Nothing Party," p. 104.

27. La Grange *True Issue*, 20 October 1855.

28. San Antonio *El Ranchero*, 4 July 1856. Also see Fornell, *Galveston Era*, pp. 125–139; Texas, *Journal of the Senate, 1857*, pp. 82–83; McGrath, *Political Nativism in Texas*, pp. 166–169.

29. Galveston *Die Union*, 2 June and 21 July 1859, 28 July 1860, and 12 January 1861; Houston, *Writings* 7:34; Hermann Speiss to Marie, 4 June 1859 and 18 November 1860, Clyde H. Porter collection; San Antonio *Daily Herald*, 15 July 1859; *N. B. Zeitung*, 22 July 1859 and 13 April 1860.

30. Texas, *Journal of the Senate, 1859*, pp. 44–46; Lubbock, *Six Decades in Texas*, p. 251. Frontier German counties will be more fully discussed in the next chapter.

31. San Antonio *Daily Herald*, 8, 22 June, 20 July, and 20 August 1859.

32. Texas, *Journal of the Senate, 1859*, pp. 44–46; Antonio Menchaca, *Memoirs*, pp. 11–12; Rodríguez, *Memoirs*, pp. 21–22; Dugan, "The 1850 Affair of the Brownsville Separatists," pp. 278–280.

33. Galveston *Die Union*, 10 November 1859.

34. F. F. Fenn to Chief Clerk Post Office Department, 3 October and 21 November 1859, Gilbert D. Kingsbury collection; Ford, *Rip Ford's Texas*, pp. 266–307; "Report of the Mexican Commission on the Northern Frontier Question," pp. 126–163; reprinted in Carlos E. Cortés (ed.), *The Mexican Experience in Texas*, pp. 126–163; Leroy P. Graf, "The Economic History of the Lower Rio Grande Valley, 1820–1875," (Ph.D. dissertation), pp. 369–393.

35. *N. B. Zeitung*, December 1859; 36th Congress, 1st Session (Serial 1056), House Executive Document No. 81, pp. 6–7; "Report of the Mexican Commission," pp. 132–133.

36. Taylor, *American-Mexican Frontier*, pp. 40–43; Ash, "Mexican Texans in the Civil War," p. 33.

37. *N. B. Zeitung*, 27 July 1860; Galveston *Die Union*, 20 July and 2 August 1860.

38. *N. B. Zeitung*, 25 May 1860.

39. On the Fusion ticket see Ballinger, diary, 15 August 1860; Galveston *Die Union*, 6 November 1860; Sinclair, "Crossroads of Conviction," pp. 161–183. On Schleicher see Galveston *Die Union*, 2 August 1860; *N. B. Zeitung*, 17 January 1861; Christine Schott, "Gustavus Schleicher: A Representative of Early Emigration in Texas," *West Texas Historical Association Year Book* 28 (October 1952): 50–70.
40. *N. B. Zeitung*, 7 September and 19 October 1860.
41. San Antonio *Daily Herald*, 24 May 1859.
42. Galveston *Die Union*, 28 July 1860.
43. Ollinger Crenshaw, *The Slave States in the Presidential Election of 1860*, pp. 91–100; Donald E. Reynolds, *Editors Make War: Southern Newspapers in the Secession Crisis*, pp. 97–117; Galveston *Die Union*, 26, 30 July 1860; *N. B. Zeitung*, 20, 27 July and 31 August 1860; Marshall *Texas Republican*, 28 July, 4 August, and 8 September 1860; Bellville *Countryman*, 25 August and 12 December 1860.
44. Hermann Speiss to Marie, 17 November 1860, Porter collection. Also see *N. B. Zeitung*, 11 March 1853, 25 May 1855, and 10 October 1856; Olmsted, *A Journey through Texas*, pp. 431–433; Guido E. Ransleben, *A Hundred Years of Comfort in Texas: A Centennial History*, pp. 79–126.
45. Galveston *Die Union*, 6 November 1860. On Flake's attitude toward Fusion and Douglas see Austin *Texas State Gazette*, 20 October 1860; Galveston *Die Union*, 16 October 1860. For details on the Fusion ticket see San Antonio *Alamo Express*, 18 August and 10 September 1860; Austin *Southern Intelligencer*, 5 September 1860.
46. Galveston *Die Union*, 8 November 1860. Also see *N.B. Zeitung*, 9 November 1860; W. Dean Burnham, *Presidential Ballots, 1836–1892*, pp. 764–813.
47. San Antonio *Herald*, 21 July and 27 October 1860, 24 January 1861; San Antonio *Alamo Express*, 17, 24 September and 5 November 1860.
48. Corpus Christi *Ranchero*, 13 October and 10 November 1860; San Antonio *Alamo Express*, 8 October 1860; Burnham, *Presidential Ballots*, pp. 764–813.
49. *N.B. Zeitung*, 27 July, 7 September, and 19 October 1860; Galveston *Die Union*, 20, 28 July, 2, 30 August, and 6 November 1860.

6. THE FRONTIER

1. For conceptions of the Union in the antebellum United States, see Paul C. Nagel, *One Nation Indivisible: The Union in American Thought, 1776–1861*; Major L. Wilson, *Space, Time and Freedom: The Quest for Nationality and the Irrepressible Conflict, 1815–1861*; Kenneth M. Stampp, *The Imperiled Union: Essays on the Background of the Civil War*, pp. 3–38.
2. For a description of the western frontier of Texas see Ernest Wallace, *Texas in Turmoil, 1849–1875*, pp. 1–28. The frontier line is based on those counties that were organized and that voted. Also taken into con-

sideration were letters from these counties to the governor or to the press in which frontier citizens expressed their need for protection from the Indian. See election returns, records of the secretary of state (manuscript); Governor's correspondence; Weatherford *Whiteman*, 13 September 1860; Austin *Texas State Gazette*, 15 April, 7, 21, 28 May, and 11 June 1859, 4, 18 February, 10 March, and 17 November 1860.

3. William W. White, "Migration into West Texas, 1845–1860" (M.A. thesis), pp. 22–23. Terry G. Jordan, "The Imprint of the Upper and Lower South on Mid-Nineteenth-Century Texas," *Annals of the Association of American Geographers* 57 (December 1967): 671, 677; idem., "Population Origins in Texas, 1850," *Geographical Review* 59 (January 1969): 86–87.

4. Walter Prescott Webb, *The Great Plains*, p. 9.

5. Ibid., pp. 8–84. See also Terry G. Jordan, *German Seed in Texas Soil: Immigrant Farmers in Nineteenth-Century Texas*, pp. 8–120; Rupert Norval Richardson, *The Comanche Barrier to South Plains Settlement: A Century and a Half of Savage Resistance to the Advancing White Frontier*, pp. 15–266.

6. Richardson, *Comanche Barrier*, pp. 117–398; H. R. Runnels to James Buchanan, 17 September 1858, in Dorman H. Winfrey and James M. Day (eds.), *The Indian Papers of Texas and the Southwest, 1825–1916* 5: 269–273; Sam Houston to John B. Floyd, 12 March 1860, *Writings* 7: 519–522; Webb, *The Great Plains*, pp. 167–179.

7. Charles W. Ramsdell, "Internal Improvement Projects in Texas in the Fifties," *Proceedings of the Mississippi Valley Historical Association* 9 (1915–1916): 99–109; Ray Allen Billington, *The Far Western Frontier, 1830–1860*; Jacob De Cordova, *Texas: Her Resources and Her Public Men*, pp. 187–190; Robert Penniger, *Fest-Ausgabe zum fünfzigjahrigen Jubiläum der Grundung der Stadt Friedrichburg*.

8. De Cordova, *Texas*, p. 352; Andrew Jackson Hamilton, "Speech of Andrew J. Hamilton, of Texas, on the State of the Union, February 1, 1861," p. 12; Charles W. Ramsdell, "The Natural Limits of Slavery Expansion," *Mississippi Valley Historical Review* 16 (September 1929): 151–171.

9. J. W. Latimer, "The Wheat Region and Wheat Culture in Texas," *Texas Almanac for 1859*, pp. 65–69; Jordan, "Imprint of the Upper and Lower South," pp. 684–685; idem., *German Seed*, pp. 170–171. *N. B. Zeitung*, 11 March 1853, 25 May and 10 October 1856.

10. For examples of frontier complaints see W. Jones to Runnels, 17 October 1858, B. S. Whitaker to Runnels, 25 October 1858, Runnels to Floyd, 2 November 1858, H. Allen to Runnels, 21 November 1858, Winfrey and Day, *Indian Papers* 3: 297, 299–300, 302–303, 308–310. See also Austin *Gazette*, 11 June 1859 and 10 March 1860. Also see Runnels to Guy M. Bryan, 20 September 1859, Guy M. Bryan papers.

11. On the fiscal policy of the state government see Runnels to Floyd, 9 August 1858, Winfrey and Day, *Indian Papers* 3: 258–259; Texas, *Journal*

of the Senate, 1859, pp. 120–121; George Bernard Erath, "Memoirs of George Bernard Erath," edited by Lucy A. Erath, *SWHQ* 27 (October 1923): 154–155.

12. David G. Burner to Henry R. Schoolcraft, 29 September 1857, Winfrey and Day, *Indian Papers* 3: 84–99; Richardson, *Comanche Barrier*, pp. 149–282; Ernest Wallace and E. Adamson Hoebel, *The Comanches: Lords of the South Plains*, pp. 301–302; J. W. Wilbarger, *Indian Depredations in Texas*, pp. 439–464.

13. For an explanation of the role of the federal government in Indian affairs in a state which owned its public lands and therefore reservation lands, see Lena Clara Koch, "The Federal Indian Policy in Texas, 1845–1860," *SWHQ* 29 (July 1925): 19–25. G. R. Paul to J. Withers, 18 December 1857; E. M. Pease to Jefferson Davis, 23 September 1854; Runnels to D. E. Twiggs, 22 December 1857; John S. Ford to Runnels, 2 June 1858; Runnels to Buchanan, 17 September 1858, Winfrey and Day, *Indian Papers* 3: 267–269; 5: 185–187, 205–206, 241–244, 269–273.

14. Dallas *Herald*, 18 May 1859; Austin *Gazette*, 7, 21 May 1859. Anonymous letter to Runnels, 24 May 1859; Withers to G. H. Thomas, 2 June 1859; Twiggs to Runnels, 6 June 1859; Runnels, Appointment of Peace Commission, 6 June 1859, Winfrey and Day, *Indian Papers* 3: 328–333. On the Indian reservations in Texas see Richardson, *Comanche Barrier*, pp. 211–233; Koch, "Federal Indian Policy in Texas," pp. 98–119.

15. Charles W. Ramsdell, "The Frontier and Secession," *Studies in Southern History and Politics*, pp. 71–72; Koch, "Federal Indian Policy in Texas," pp. 118–123; Austin *Gazette*, 11 June 1859 and 17 November 1860; Clarksville *Standard*, 10 March 1860.

16. Pease to G. M. Bryan and John H. Reagan, 3 November 1857; Runnels to the Senate, 22 January 1858; Runnels, Congressional Message, 22 December 1857, Winfrey and Day, *Indian Papers* 3: 265–266, 269–271; Thomas Harrison to George B. Erath, 2 January 1858; A. Nelson to Erath, 4 January 1858; Thomas R. Carmack to governor, 7 January 1858; A. Bishop to Runnels, 26 September 1858; Petition from the Citizens of San Saba County, 29 September 1858, ibid. 5: 207–209, 274–280.

17. For election returns see Walter L. Buenger, "Stilling the Voice of Reason: Texas and the Union, 1854–1861," (Ph.D. dissertation), pp. 266–391. Also see Francis Richard Lubbock, *Six Decades in Texas*, ed. C. W. Raines, pp. 243–266, and Llerena Friend, *Sam Houston: The Great Designer*, p. 325.

18. Forbes Britton to Houston, 3 March 1860, Governor's letters. Houston to Floyd, 12 March 1860, *Writings* 7: 519–522; James W. Throckmorton to Reagan, 9 September 1839, John H. Reagan papers; Koch, "Federal Indian Policy in Texas," pp. 20–23. On the difficulties in Congress see Ollinger Crenshaw, "The Speakership Contest of 1859–1860," *Mississippi Valley Historical Review* 29 (December 1942): 323–338; Ben H. Procter, *Not without Honor: The Life of John H. Reagan*, pp. 113–118.

See also the letters from Clay and Montague counties criticizing Houston in Clarksville *Standard*, 30 June 1860.

19. Austin *Gazette*, 17 November 1860; Ramsdell, "The Frontier and Secession," pp. 74–75; Weatherford *Whiteman*, 13 September 1860; J. H. Crisman to Houston, 11 February 1860; A. Walters to Houston, 12 February 1860, Winfrey and Day, *Indian Papers* 8: 2–6.

20. Ford to Runnels, 2 June 1858, Winfrey and Day, *Indian Papers* 5: 242–243; Erath letter in Austin *Gazette*, 11 June 1859.

21. Austin *Gazette*, 17 November 1860; Ramsdell, "The Frontier and Secession," pp. 74–84.

22. Marshall's attempts to proselytize the state to the southern cause are described in Larry Jay Gage, "The Texas Road to Secession and War: John Marshall and the *Texas State Gazette*," *SWHQ* 62 (October 1958): 191–226. Also see Austin *Gazette*, 11, 18 December 1858, 16 April, 7, 21, 28 May, 11 June, and 30 July 1859, 11, 18, 25 February, 3, 10 March, 9, 23 July, 4, 11, 25 August, 8, 22 September, 3, 17 November, 1 December 1860, and 2 January 1861.

23. Voting returns are in Buenger, "Stilling the Voice," pp. 266–391.

24. Clarksville *Standard*, 20, 27 October 1860; San Antonio *Herald*, 18 September and 27 October 1860; Weatherford *Whiteman*, 13 September 1860.

25. Weatherford *Whiteman*, 13 September 1860; *Handbook of Texas* 2: 124; John Salmon Ford, "Memoirs of John Salmon Ford," (typescript) 5: 942–983; Clarksville *Standard*, 19 May 1860; Austin *Gazette*, 22 September 1860.

26. "A Declaration of the Causes which Impel the State of Texas to Secede from the Federal Union," in Ernest William Winkler (ed.), *Journal of the Secession Convention of Texas, 1861*, pp. 61–66. For information on Baylor's attitude toward the federal government see Austin *Gazette*, 22 September, 17 November, and 1 December 1860; Clarksville *Standard*, 19 May 1860; Ford, "Memoirs" 5: 942–945. See also Richardson, *Comanche Barrier*, pp. 248–249; Clarksville *Standard*, 28 May, 12, 19 June 1858.

27. Erath, "Memoirs of George Bernard Erath," p. 156.

28. Ike Moore, *The Life and Diary of Reading W. Black: A History of Early Uvalde*. For Degener see *Handbook of Texas* 2: 482; Carl Wittke, *Refugees of Revolution: The German Forty-Eighters in America*, p. 119. Information on Speiss is in Hermann Speiss to Marie, 4 June 1859 and 17 November 1860, Clyde H. Porter collection.

29. Austin *Gazette*, 11 August and 17 November 1860; Weatherford *Whiteman*, 13 September 1860; Clarksville *Standard*, 19 May 1860; *N. B. Zeitung*, 1 March 1861.

30. Austin *Gazette*, 17 November 1860; "A Declaration of the Causes which Impel the State of Texas to Secede from the Federal Union"; Dallas *Herald*, 6 December 1860; San Antonio *Herald*, 27 November 1860.

7. THE DEBATE OVER THE UNION

1. For other examples of this debate see David M. Potter, *The Impending Crisis, 1848–1861*, pp. 448–554. For evidence on Texas see Ernest William Winkler (ed.), *Journal of the Secession Convention of Texas, 1861;* Oran Milo Roberts, "Journal" in John Salmon Ford, "The Memoirs of John Salmon Ford" (typescript) 5: 943–966.

2. On the arguments and tactics of secessionists and unionists see Edward R. Maher, Jr., "Sam Houston and Secession," *SWHQ* 60 (April 1952): 448–458; James P. Newcomb, *Sketch of Secession Times in Texas and Journal of Travel from Texas through Mexico to California*, pp. 6–12; James W. Throckmorton to Louis T. Wigfall, 30 December 1866, James Webb Throckmorton papers; John H. Reagan to O. M. Roberts, 1, 20 November, and 7 December 1860, Oran Milo Roberts papers; Billy D. Ledbetter, "Slavery, Fear, and Disunion in the Lone Star State: Texans' Attitudes toward Secession and the Union, 1846–1861" (Ph.D. dissertation); Donald E. Reynolds, *Editors Make War: Southern Newspapers in the Secession Crisis*, pp. 97–117; Ralph A. Wooster, *The Secession Conventions of the South*, pp. 121–135.

3. A general history of the secession movement can be found in Anna Irene Sandbo, "Beginnings of the Secession Movement in Texas," *SWHQ* 18 (July 1914): 41–73; idem., "The First Session of the Secession Convention of Texas," *SWHQ* 18 (October 1914): 162–194; Edward R. Maher, Jr., "Secession in Texas" (Ph.D. dissertation). Also see Reagan to Roberts, 1 November 1860; Sandbo, "First Session," pp. 178–185; Maher, "Secession in Texas," pp. 104–110.

4. Ford, "Memoirs" 5: 944. Also see F. B. Sexton to O. M. Roberts, 2 December 1860, Oran Milo Roberts papers; William Pitt Ballinger, diary (typescript), 14, 15, 16, 17 November 1860; Austin *Texas State Gazette*, 17 November 1860.

5. Ford, "Memoirs" 5: 942–944; Reagan to Roberts, 20 November 1860; Austin *Texas State Gazette*, 24 November 1860.

6. Thomas F. McKinney to Thomas Jack, W. P. Ballinger, and Guy M. Bryan, 22 November 1860, Guy M. Bryan papers.

7. Maher, "Sam Houston and Secession," pp. 448–458; Llerena Friend, *Sam Houston: The Great Designer*, pp. 330–334; Claude Elliott, *Leathercoat: The Life History of a Texas Patriot*, pp. 46–49; Jane L. Scarborough, "George W. Paschal, Texas Unionist and Scalawag Jurisprudent" (Ph.D. dissertation), pp. 58–60; Oran Lonnie Sinclair, "Crossroads of Conviction: A Study of the Texas Political Mind, 1856–1861" (Ph.D. dissertation), pp. 181–204.

8. Oran M. Roberts, "The Political, Legislative, and Judicial History of Texas for Its Fifty Years of Statehood, 1845–1895," *A Comprehensive History of Texas 1685–1897*, ed. Dudley G. Wooten, vol. 2: 85–87; Ford, "Memoirs" 5: 943–944; Sandbo, "First Session," pp. 179–185.

9. Houston to H. M. Watkins and others, 20 November 1860, *Writings* 8: 197. Also see Houston to the governors of the various southern states,

28 November 1860, *Writings* 8: 197–198; Maher, "Sam Houston and Secession," pp. 448–458.

10. D. M. Prendergast et al., "To Our Fellow-Citizens of the State of Texas," Secession broadsides, William Harrison Hamman papers. Also see Ford, "Memoirs" 5: 945–951.

11. Sandbo, "First Session," pp. 179–180.

12. Houston, "Proclamation Calling an Extra Session of the Legislature, December 17, 1860," *Writings* 8: 220–221; Marshall *Texas Republican*, 5 January 1851; Maher, "Sam Houston and Secession," pp. 448–458.

13. Scarborough, "Paschal," pp. 39–136; Elliott, *Leathercoat*, pp. 46–51; J. W. Throckmorton to R. S. Guy, published in the Dallas *Herald*, 22 July 1865; Marshall *Harrison Flag*, 1, 8, 15 December 1860; San Antonio *Alamo Express*, 16 February 1861.

14. Marshall *Texas Republican*, 5, 12, 19, 26 January 1861; Austin *Texas State Gazette*, 29 December 1860, 5, 12, 19, 26 January and 9 February 1861; Winkler (ed.), *Journal of the Secession Convention*, p. 65; Lubbock, *Six Decades in Texas*, pp. 305–306; Potter, *Impending Crisis*, pp. 485–513.

15. Sexton to Roberts, 2 December 1860. R. L. Loughery expressed similar concern that the secession movement be seen as being led by the best people. See Marshall *Texas Republican*, 5, 12 January 1861. Also see Reagan to Roberts, 1 November 1860; Lubbock, *Six Decades in Texas*, pp. 310–311. On the concept that the African slave trade and filibustering were a threat to established order see J. H. Reagan, "To the Voters of the First Congressional District," 12 April 1859, John H. Reagan papers. Reagan and his circular were overwhelmingly endorsed by the voters. On the Texas Troubles and law and order see Donald E. Reynolds, "Vigilante Law During the Texas Slave Panic of 1860," paper given before the Southwest Social Sciences Convention, 1978.

16. For a summation of the complaints Texans bore toward the North and the federal government see "A Declaration of the Causes which Impel the State of Texas to Secede from the Federal Union," *Journal of the Secession Convention, 1861*, ed. Ernest William Winkler, pp. 61–66. Also see J. H. Reagan to Dr. Joseph Tyler, 23 December 1860, published in Marshall *Texas Republican*, 12 January 1861; "Speech of Judge P. W. Gray," reported in Austin *Texas State Gazette*, 1 December 1860.

17. Marshall *Texas Republican*, 19 January 1861. Also see Ford, *Rip Ford's Texas*, pp. 316–317; Houston, "Message to the Legislature of Texas, January 21, 1861," *Writings* 8: 247–252; Clarksville *Standard*, 23 March 1861.

18. J. H. Reagan to the Nacogdoches *Chronicle* reprinted in the Marshall *Texas Republican*, 9 February 1861. For an extensive treatment of the fear of race war and opposition to the elevation of the Negro to a position of equality as a cause of secession see Ledbetter, "Slavery, Fear, and Disunion in the Lone Star State," pp. 150–276.

19. Marshall *Texas Republican*, 1 December 1860. Also see Lubbock, *Six Decades in Texas*, p. 311.

20. For some light on the process of changing attitudes toward secession and the Union see Nancy Ann Head, "State Rights in Texas, the Growth of an Idea, 1850–1860" (M.A. thesis), and Sinclair, "Crossroads of Conviction."

21. For a description of the Reagan-Ochiltree campaign see Lubbock, *Six Decades in Texas*, pp. 245–254; Ben H. Procter, *Not without Honor: The Life of John H. Reagan*, pp. 108–113; Marshall *Texas Republican*, 9 July 1859. Also see Roberts, "Political, Legislative, and Judicial History of Texas," pp. 77–84; Austin *Texas State Gazette*, 15 September 1860.

22. Marshall *Texas Republican*, 24 November 1860. Also see Austin *Texas State Gazette*, 1 December 1860; Marshall *Harrison Flag*, 3, 10, 17, 24 November, 1, 8, 15, 22 December 1860, and 5, 12 January 1861; Sexton to Roberts, 2 December 1860; Marshall *Texas Republican*, 24 November 1860, and 26 January 1861; Texas, *Journal of the Senate, Special Session, 1861*.

23. Collin County is a good example of the continuity of party opposition to threats to the Union. See Elliott, *Leathercoat*, pp. 47–51; Clarksville *Standard*, 9 March 1861.

24. Austin *Southern Intelligencer*, 30 January 1861; Claude Elliott, "Union Sentiment in Texas, 1861–1865," *SWHQ* 50 (April 1947): 449–477.

25. Clarksville *Standard*, 19 January, 9, 23 February, and 9 March 1861; Dallas *Herald*, 6, 12, 19 December 1860, 2, 16 January and 20 February 1861; Reagan to Roberts, 1 November 1860; Ledbetter, "Slavery, Fear, and Disunion in the Lone Star State," pp. 150–224.

26. Larry J. Gage, "The Texas Road to Secession and War, John Marshall and the *Texas State Gazette*, 1860–1861," *SWHQ* 62 (October 1958): 191–226; W. S. Oldham, "Colonel John Marshall," *SWHQ* 20 (October 1916): 132–138; Sinclair, "Crossroads of Conviction," pp. 63–204; Alexander W. Terrell, "The City of Austin from 1839–1865," *Texas Historical Association Quarterly* 14 (October 1910): 113–128; Frank Brown, "Annals of Travis County and the City of Austin from the Earliest Times to the Close of 1875" (typescript, 12 vols.).

27. Brown, "Annals of Travis County" 12: 7–19; Roberts, "Political, Legislative, and Judicial History of Texas," pp. 83–99; Ford, "Memoirs" 5: 942–952; Austin *Texas State Gazette*, 1 December 1860, and 5, 12, 19 January 1861.

28. *N. B. Zeitung*, 11 January and 1, 22 February 1861; Galveston *Die Union*, 5, 8, 12, 19, 22, 31 January and 5, 7, 19, 23 February 1861.

29. San Antonio *Alamo Express*, 2 March 1861. Also see Jacob De Cordova, *Texas: Her Resources and Her Public Men*, pp. 145–153; Samual Harman Lowrie, *Culture Conflict in Texas, 1821–1835*, pp. 120–181; Frederick C. Chabot, *With the Makers of San Antonio*, pp. 202–206; Charles W. Goldfinch and Jose T. Canales, *Juan Cortina: Two Interpretations*; James H. Thompson, "A Nineteenth-Century History of Cameron County, Texas" (M.A. thesis), p. 86; José María Rodríguez, *Rodríguez Memoirs of Early Texas*, p. 75.

30. For a discussion of the momentum generated by secessionists see Pot-

ter, *Impending Crisis*, pp. 485–513. Sam Houston sensed the advantages that appeals to action gave the secessionists. See Houston to J. M. Calhoun, 7 January 1861, *Writings* 8: 226–231; Houston, "Speech at Brenham, March 31, 1861," *Writings* 8: 295–300.

31. Urban commercial classes had been prominent in both the Whig and Opposition parties in part because of their more national orientation and their support of internal improvements. Among those who best articulated the views of the commercial classes were Ben H. Epperson, Ferdinand Flake, and William Pitt Ballinger. See Galveston *Die Union*, 17 November and 6 December 1850, 12, 31 January, and 7, 12, 19 February 1861; B. H. Epperson to James W. Throckmorton, 28 June 1859, Ben H. Epperson papers. Clarksville *Standard*, 22 December 1860; Ballinger, diary, 21, 30, 31 December 1860. Also see Thomas F. McKinney to Thomas Jack, W. P. Ballinger, and Guy M. Bryan, 22 November 1860, Bryan papers; G. D. Kingsbury to Dear Warren, June 1860, G. D. Kingsbury papers.

32. Throughout the secession crisis the Marshall *Texas Republican*, the mouthpiece for the planter class of East Texas, worked diligently for a stay law which would prevent the collection of debts until stability had been restored. See Marshall *Texas Republican*, 19, 26 January 1861. Little attention has been paid to manufacturing and trade in antebellum Texas by modern scholars. Some general information may be found in Vera Lee Dugas, "Texas Industry, 1860–1880," *SWHQ* 59 (October 1955): 151–183; Abigail Curlee Holbrook, "Cotton Marketing in Antebellum Texas," *SWHQ* 73 (April 1970): 431–455; Raymond E. White, "Cotton Ginning in Texas to 1861," *SWHQ* 61 (October 1957): 257–269; Leroy P. Graf, "The Economic History of the Lower Rio Grande Valley, 1820–1875" (Ph.D. dissertation). The Galveston *Civilian* often represented the views of business. See Galveston *Civilian*, 17, 24 November and 1, 8 December 1860.

33. Ballinger, diary, 30 December 1860.

34. Gulf Coast merchants like Thomas McKinney and editor-businessman Ferdinand Flake always seemed to have a clear perception of the value of the Union. See McKinney to Jack, Ballinger, and Bryan, 22 November 1860; Galveston *Die Union*, 24 January 1861. Also see Marshall *Texas Republican*, 24 November and 1, 15, 22, 29 December 1860, 5 January and 9, 23 February 1861.

35. Austin *Southern Intelligencer*, 5 September and 10 October 1860, 23, 30 January, 6, 13 February, and 6, 13, 20, 27 March 1861; San Antonio *Alamo Express*, 25 August, 3, 10, 17 September, and 1, 8, 22 October 1860, 9, 16, 23 February and 2 March 1861; John L. Haynes papers; Mary Whatley Clarke, *The Swenson Saga and the SMS Ranches*, pp. 61–71.

36. Some information on the commercial and manufacturing elements in antebellum Texas may be found in Margaret Sweet Henson, *Samuel May Williams: Early Texas Entrepreneur; Handbook of Texas* 1: 736, 2: 699, 792, 372; Ralph A. Wooster, "Ben H. Epperson: East Texas Lawyer,

Legislator, and Civic Leader," *ETHJ* 5 (March 1967): 29–42; San Antonio *Alamo Express*, 10, 17 September and 1 October 1860; Clarksville *Standard*, 22 December 1860, 19 January 1861; Marshall *Texas Republican*, 2 June and 1, 8 December 1860, 23 February 1861; Randolph B. Campbell, "Planters and Plain Folk: Harrison County, Texas as a Test Case, 1850–1860," *Journal of Southern History* 40 (August 1974): 369–398; Randolph B. Campbell and Richard G. Lowe, *Wealth and Power in Antebellum Texas*.

37. On the impact of the army on secession and the frontier economy see J. W. Latimer, "The Wheat Region and Wheat Culture in Texas," *Texas Almanac for 1859*, pp. 65–69; *N. B. Zeitung*, 10 October 1856; Austin *Texas State Gazette*, 11 June, 1859; 10 March and 17 November 1860, 5 January and 2 February 1861. Weatherford *Whiteman*, 13 September 1860; Dallas *Herald*, 18 May 1859; Clarksville *Standard*, 19 May and 20, 27 October 1860; Ramsdell, "The Frontier and Secession."

38. A list of the leaders of the secession movement and a description of their actions can be found in Ford, "Memoirs" 5: 942–984; Roberts, "Political, Legislative, and Judicial History of Texas," pp. 85–115. Also see Frank H. Smyrl, "Unionism in Texas, 1856–1861," *SWHQ* 68 (October 1964): 172–195; Maher, "Sam Houston and Secession," pp. 451–458; Marshall *Texas Republican*, 24 November 1860.

39. Dallas *Herald*, 16 January and 20 February 1861; *N. B. Zeitung*, 14, 21, 28 December 1860 and 4, 11, 18, 25 January 1861; Sandbo, "First Session."

8. LEGITIMIZING SECESSION

1. Houston, *Writings* 8: 226–227.

2. Private correspondence best reveals the attitudes of the leaders of secession. See John H. Reagan to O. M. Roberts, 1, 20 November and 7 December 1860, and F. B. Sexton to O. M. Roberts, 2 December 1860, Oran Milo Roberts papers.

3. The best sources on the Secession Convention of Texas are Anna Irene Sandbo, "First Session of the Secession Convention," *SWHQ* 18 (October 1914): 162–194; Ralph A. Wooster, *The Secession Conventions of the South*, pp. 121–135; idem., "An Analysis of the Membership of the Texas Secession Convention," *SWHQ* 62 (January 1959): 322–335; Ernest William Winkler (ed.), *Journal of the Secession Convention of Texas, 1861*.

4. Sandbo, "First Session," pp. 179–181; Frank H. Smyrl, "Unionism in Texas, 1856–1861," *SWHQ* 68 (October 1964): 185–190; E. L. Dohoney, *An Average American*, p. 76.

5. Llerena Friend, *Sam Houston: The Great Designer*, pp. 331–336; Sandbo, "First Session," pp. 182–185; Oran M. Roberts, "The Political, Legislative, and Judicial History of Texas for Its Fifty Years of Statehood, 1845–1895," *A Comprehensive History of Texas 1685–1897*, ed. Dudley G. Wooten, vol. 2: 85–99.

6. Sandbo, "First Session," pp. 183–185; Wooster, "Membership of the Texas Secession Convention," p. 322.

7. Wooster, "Membership of the Texas Secession Convention," pp. 323–327; Reagan to Roberts, 1 November 1860; La Grange *True Issue*, 31 January 1861.

8. Winkler (ed.), *Journal of the Secession Convention*, pp. 16–17. Also see ibid., pp. 15–19, and Sandbo, "First Session," pp. 185–186.

9. Winkler (ed.), *Journal of the Secession Convention*, p. 25. Also see ibid., pp. 19–27; Sandbo, "First Session," pp. 186–187; *The Handbook of Texas* 2: 889–890.

10. Winkler (ed.), *Journal of the Secession Convention*, pp. 35–36. Also see ibid., pp. 27–41; Roberts, "Political, Legislative, and Judicial History of Texas," pp. 101–103; Sandbo, "First Session," pp. 188–190.

11. Winkler (ed.), *Journal of the Secession Convention*, p. 36. Also see ibid., pp. 36–37; Sandbo, "First Session," pp. 188–189.

12. Winkler (ed.), *Journal of the Secession Convention*, p. 44.

13. Houston to a committee of the Secession Convention, 31 January 1861, *Writings* 8: 254. Also see Winkler (ed.), *Journal of the Secession Convention*, pp. 45–48.

14. Roberts, "Political, Legislative, and Judicial History of Texas," pp. 103–104; Sandbo, "First Session," pp. 190–194; Winkler (ed.), *Journal of the Secession Convention*, pp. 48–49.

15. Winkler (ed.), *Journal of the Secession Convention*, p. 35; La Grange *True Issue*, 7 February 1861. Also see Winkler (ed.), *Journal of the Secession Convention*, pp. 48–49; Francis Richard Lubbock, *Six Decades in Texas*, ed. C. W. Raines, pp. 305–306; Claude Elliott, *Leathercoat: The Life History of a Texas Patriot*, pp. 48–55.

16. John Salmon Ford, "The Memoirs of John Salmon Ford" (typescript) 5: 977. Also see Wooster, *Secession Conventions*, pp. 130–131, and Winkler (ed.), *Journal of the Secession Convention*, pp. 48–49.

17. Winkler (ed.), *Journal of the Secession Convention*, pp. 84–85.

18. Roberts, "Political, Legislative, and Judicial History of Texas," pp. 101, 113; "Address to the People of Texas," John L. Naynes papers, pp. 31–34; Winkler (ed.), *Journal of the Secession Convention*, pp. 8–9, n. 2; Houston, "Approval of the Joint Resolutions Concerning the Convention of the People of Texas, February 4, 1861," *Writings* 8: 257–258.

19. Winkler (ed.), *Journal of the Secession Convention*, p. 85.

20. Winkler (ed.), *Journal of the Secession Convention*, pp. 54–59.

21. Winkler (ed.), *Journal of the Secession Convention*, pp. 59–61; Sandbo, "First Session," p. 193; Lubbock, *Six Decades in Texas*, pp. 308–309.

22. Winkler (ed.), *Journal of the Secession Convention*, p. 66.

23. Winkler (ed.), *Journal of the Secession Convention*, p. 66.

24. Edward R. Maher, Jr., "Sam Houston and Secession," *SWHQ* 35 (April 1952): 448–458; Charles A. Culberson, "General Sam Houston and Secession," *Scribner's Magazine* 39 (May 1906): 584–591; Winkler (ed.), *Journal of the Secession Convention*, pp. 67–69.

25. Lubbock, *Six Decades in Texas*, pp. 305–306; Winkler (ed.), *Journal of the Secession Convention*, pp. 252–253.
26. Winkler (ed.), *Journal of the Secession Convention*, p. 256. Nationalism remains a difficult topic to analyze. This is especially true of a place like Texas where in modern times a good deal of importance is attached to its one-time nationhood. Two works whose views of the past seem particularly shaped by the present values are Mark W. Nackman, *A Nation within a Nation: The Rise of Texas Nationalism*, and Jimmie Hicks, "Texas and Separate Independence, 1860–1861," *ETHJ* 4 (October 1966): 85–106. One of the best works on nationalism in the South is John McCardell, *The Idea of a Southern Nation: Southern Nationalists and Southern Nationalism, 1830–1860*. Also important are Avery O. Craven, *The Growth of Southern Nationalism, 1848–1861*; Carlton J. H. Hayes, *Nationalism: A Religion*; Hans Kohn, *American Nationalism: An Interpretive Essay*; David M. Potter, *The Impending Crisis, 1848–1861*, pp. 448–554. On Texas itself, perhaps the most perceptive piece is D. W. Meinig, *Imperial Texas: An Interpretive Essay in Cultural Geography*. On unionist rhetoric see "Address to the People of Texas," San Antonio *Alamo Express*, 23 February 1861.
27. Winkler (ed.), *Journal of the Secession Convention*, p. 74. Also see ibid., pp. 73–79; Sandbo, "First Session," pp. 193–194.
28. Winkler (ed.), *Journal of the Secession Convention*, pp. 79–80.
29. Winkler (ed.), *Journal of the Secession Convention*, p. 85. Also see Sandbo, "First Session," pp. 193–194.
30. Winkler (ed.), *Journal of the Secession Convention*, p. 71; Edward R. Maher, Jr., "Secession in Texas" (Ph.D. dissertation), pp. 153–176; Julia Lee Hering, "The Secession Movement in Texas" (M.A. thesis), pp. 117–134.
31. For a list of the members of the Committee on Public Safety see Winkler (ed.), *Journal of the Secession Convention*, p. 404. For biographical material see *Handbook of Texas* 1: 225–226 and 617–618, 2: 89–90, 487; Wooster, "Membership of the Texas Secession Convention," pp. 328–335. On McCulloch see *Handbook of Texas* 2: 106.
32. Roberts, "Political, Legislative, and Judicial History of Texas," pp. 112–113; Lubbock, *Six Decades in Texas*, pp. 308–309; Charles W. Ramsdell, *Reconstruction in Texas*, pp. 17–19; Maher, "Secession in Texas," pp. 153–176; Winkler (ed.), *Journal of the Secession Convention*, pp. 262–308. On Twiggs see *Handbook of Texas* 2: 812.
33. Winkler (ed.), *Journal of the Secession Convention*, pp. 262–266.
34. Reagan to Roberts, 1 November 1860. Also see Galveston *Die Union*, 8 January 1861; Marshall *Texas Republican*, 3 November and 22 December 1860, 2, 23 February 1861; San Antonio *Alamo Express*, 2 March 1861.
35. The best source on the Knights of the Golden Circle in Texas is Roy Sylvan Dunn, "The KGC in Texas, 1860–1861," *SWHQ* 70 (April 1967): 543–573. Also see Ollinger Crenshaw, "The Knights of the Golden Circle: The Career of George Bickley," *American Historical Review* 47

(October 1941): 23–50; C. A. Bridges, "The Knights of the Golden Circle: A Filibustering Fantasy," *SWHQ* 44 (January 1941): 287–302.

36. Dunn, "The KGC in Texas," pp. 545, 555–561; Winkler (ed.), *Journal of the Secession Convention*, pp. 61, 261, 404.

37. Dunn, "The KGC in Texas," pp. 543, n. 1, 557–561; James P. Newcomb, *Sketch of Secession Times in Texas and Journal of Travel from Texas through Mexico to California*, pp. 6–13; Dale A. Somers, "James P. Newcomb: The Making of a Radical," *SWHQ* 72 (April 1969): 449–461.

38. Sandbo, "First Session," p. 175. Also see Dunn, "The KGC in Texas," pp. 558–562, 567–570; San Antonio *Alamo Express*, 2 March 1861. Dunn uses several numerical methods to hypothesize that the KGC were extremely influential in some counties, but because his basic assumption that all Germans were unionists is wrong his hypothesis is questionable. See Dunn, "The KGC in Texas," pp. 562–567; Walter L. Buenger, "Secession and the Texas German Community: Editor Lindheimer vs. Editor Flake," *SWHQ* 82 (April 1979): 379–381.

39. "Address to the People of Texas," Haynes papers, p. 34. Also see Newcomb, *Secession Times*, pp. 6–13; Claude Elliott, "Union Sentiment in Texas, 1861–1865," *SWHQ* 50 (April 1947): 449–477.

9. STILLING THE VOICE OF REASON

1. Alexis de Tocqueville, *Democracy in America*, ed. Richard D. Heffner, pp. 112–137; Clement Eaton, *The Freedom-of-Thought Struggle in the Old South*. Also see Frederick Law Olmsted, *A Journey through Texas; or, A Saddle-Trip on the Southwestern Frontier*, pp. 1–21; Austin *Texas State Gazette*, 24 November and 8 December 1860, 9, 23 February 1861.

2. John Salmon Ford, "The Memoirs of John Salmon Ford" (typescript) 5: 943–944; Marshall *Texas Republican*, 5, 12, 19, 26 January 1861; Austin *Texas State Gazette*, 5, 12, 19, 26 January and 9 February 1861.

3. John H. Reagan to Dr. Joseph Tyler, 23 December 1860, published in Marshall *Texas Republican*, 12 Janaury 1861; Reagan to the Nacogdoches *Chronicle*, reprinted in the Marshall *Texas Republican*, 9 February 1861; Ernest William Winkler (ed.), *Journal of the Secession Convention of Texas, 1861*, pp. 61–66; F. B. Sexton to O. M. Roberts, 2 December 1860, Oran Milo Roberts papers.

4. Houston, *Writings* 8: 295–299; *N. B. Zeitung*, 11 January 1861; Dallas *Herald*, 20 February 1861; Marshall *Texas Republican*, 15, 23 February 1861.

5. James P. Newcomb, *Sketch of Secession Times in Texas and Journal of Travel from Texas through Mexico to California*, pp. 6–13; Claude Elliott, *Leathercoat: The Life History of a Texas Patriot*, pp. 54–55; Thomas North, *Five Years in Texas*, pp. 90–92; Galveston *Die Union*, 8 January 1861; Marshall *Texas Republican*, 2 February 1861. Some counties formed special police or minutemen groups in the winter of 1860–1861. Their purpose was ostensibly to keep order and prevent slave rebellions, but they could have been used, as James Newcomb argued, to intimidate unionists. See Marshall *Texas Republican*, 22 De-

cember 1860, 5 January and 23 February 1861; San Antonio *Alamo Express*, 2 March 1861. For other examples of intimidation see Marshall *Texas Republican*, 3 November 1860 and 23 February 1861; Austin *Texas State Gazette*, 26 January 1861.

6. William Pitt Ballinger, diary, (typescript), 21, 31 December 1861; Maxwell Bloomfield, *American Lawyers in a Changing Society, 1776–1876*, pp. 280–285; San Antonio *Alamo Express*, 23 February and 2 March 1861.

7. *N. B. Zeitung*, 11 January 1861; Dallas *Herald*, 9 January 1861.

8. On southern nationalism see John McCardell, *The Idea of a Southern Nation: Southern Nationalists and Southern Nationalism, 1830–1860*; Avery O. Craven, *The Growth of Southern Nationalism, 1848–1861*. On the insistence upon southern solidarity see Austin *Texas State Gazette* 24 November and 8 December 1860, and 9, 23 February 1861; Dallas *Herald*, 2, 9 January and 20 February 1861; Marshall *Texas Republican*, 24 November and 1, 29 December 1860, and 16, 23 February 1861.

9. E. L. Dohoney, *An Average American*, pp. 71–88; Marshall *Harrison Flag*, 12 Janaury 1861; Galveston *Die Union*, 8, 12 January 1861; Ballinger, diary, 21, 30, 31 December 1861; Newcomb, *Secession Times*, pp. 6–14.

10. For a discussion of the importance of role models to a changing society see Thomas C. Cochran, *Social Change in America: The Twentieth Century*, pp. 11–29. For information on these non–Lower South regions during the secession crisis see Francis Richard Lubbock, *Six Decades in Texas*, ed. C. W. Raines, p. 314; Claude Elliott, "Union Sentiment in Texas," *SWHQ* 50 (April 1947): 449–453; Charles W. Ramsdell, "The Natural Limits of Slavery Expansion," *Mississippi Valley Historical Review* 16 (September 1929): 151–171; Benjamin H. Miller, "Elisha Marshall Pease: A Biography" (M.A. thesis); Hermann Speiss to Marie, 18 November 1860, Clyde H. Porter collection; Clarksville *Standard*, 9, 23 February and 2, 9 March 1861; Dallas *Herald*, 20, 27 February 1851; Austin *Southern Intelligencer*, 6, 13 February 1861; *N. B. Zeitung*, 22 February and 1 March 1861; San Antonio *Alamo Express*, 23 February 1861.

11. A copy of the "Address to the People of Texas" may be found in the John L. Haynes Papers, pp. 31–34.

12. "Address to the People of Texas," p. 34. Also see ibid., pp. 32–34.

13. One of the finest examples of unionist rhetoric was Andrew J. Hamilton, "Speech of Hon. Andrew J. Hamilton of Texas on the State of the Union, February 1, 1861." Also see San Antonio *Alamo Express*, 23 February 1861; Austin *Southern Intelligencer*, 13, 20 February and 13 March 1861. For an example of political phenomena explained as a reaction to events see Michael F. Holt, "The Politics of Impatience: The Origins of Know-Nothingism," *Journal of American History* 60 (September 1973): 309–331. For an example of arguments used by secessionists see "A Declaration of Causes which Impel the State of Texas to Secede

from the Federal Union," *Journal of the Secession Convention of Texas, 1861*, ed. Ernest William Winkler, pp. 61–66. For examples of how secessionists stressed action instead of talk see Marshall *Texas Republican*, 19, 26 January and 9, 16, 23 February 1861.

14. The Dallas *Herald* led the attack against those who argued that Texas should be loyal to the border states. See Dallas *Herald*, 2, 9, 16 January and 20, 27 February 1861. For an example of a man on the make from a central Texas county who supported secession see C. Alwyn Barr, "The Making of a Secessionist: The Antebellum Career of Roger Q. Mills," *SWHQ* 79 (October 1975): 129–144. Also, see Austin *Texas State Gazette*, 29 July 1854 and 29 February 1861.

15. Texans' nationalism is discussed earlier. On America and nationalism in general, see George Dangerfield, *The Awakening of American Nationalism, 1815–1828*; Carlton J. H. Hayes, *Nationalism: A Religion*; Hans Kohn, *American Nationalism: An Interpretive Essay*; idem., *The Idea of Nationalism: A Study in Its Origins and Background*; Rush Welter, *the Mind of America, 1820–1860*. Also still applicable are David M. Potter, *The Impending Crisis, 1848–1861*, pp. 448–554; Paul C. Nagel, *One Nation Indivisible: The Union in American Thought, 1776–1861*; Major L. Wilson, *Space, Time and Freedom: The Quest for Nationality and the Irrepressible Conflict, 1815–1861*. Also of interest are four recent works: McCardell, *The Idea of a Southern Nation*; James Oliver Robertson, *American Myth, American Reality*; Gary Wills, *Inventing America: Jefferson's Declaration of Independence*, pp. 323–362; Kenneth M. Stampp, *The Imperiled Union: Essays on the Background of the Civil War*. On Texas unionists' use of religious and psychological nationalism see Clarksville *Standard*, 28 June 1859; Marshall *Harrison Flag*, 15 September 1860; San Antonio *Alamo Express*, 5 November 1860; La Grange *True Issue*, 24 January 1861.

16. Potter, *Impending Crisis*, pp. 8–17; Nagel, *One Nation*, pp. 177–234. On the source of nationalism see Carlton J. H. Hayes, *The Historical Evolution of Modern Nationalism*; Frederick Hertz, *Nationality in History and Politics*, pp. 1–52, 182–187.

17. On the connection between mission and nationality see Nagel, *One Nation*, pp. 147–176; Nagel, *This Sacred Trust: American Nationality, 1798–1898*, pp. 3–193. For a romantic expression of mission see Austin *Texas State Gazette*, 2 March 1861. For two case studies of vigilantism and the drive for order in Texas see Donald E. Reynolds, "Vigilante Law during the Texas Slave Panic of 1860," (a paper given before the Southwest Social Sciences Convention, 1978); Paul D. Lack, "Slavery and Vigilantism in Austin, Texas, 1840–1860," *SWHQ* 85 (July 1981): 1–20.

18. Eugene C. Barker, *The Life of Stephen F. Austin, Founder of Texas, 1793–1836: A Chapter in the Westward Movement of the Anglo-American People*; Justin H. Smith, *The Annexation of Texas*; Llerena Friend, *Sam Houston: The Great Designer*, pp. 37–354; Rupert N. Richardson, Ernest Wallace, Adrian N. Anderson, *Texas: The Lone Star State*, pp. 57–219. Olmsted's travel books about the South are full of

comparisons between that region and his native environment. See, for example, Frederick Law Olmsted, *A Journey through Texas: Or, A Saddle-Trip on the Southwestern Frontier*, pp. 1–2.

19. Irving H. Bartlett, *Daniel Webster*, pp. 108–296; Richard N. Current, *Daniel Webster and the Rise of National Conservatism*; Glyndon G. Van Deusen, *The Life of Henry Clay*; Clement Eaton, *Henry Clay and the Art of American Politics*; John William Ward, *Andrew Jackson, Symbol for an Age*; Margaret L. Coit, *John C. Calhoun: American Portrait*.

20. For examples of the range of Texans' ideology see Austin *Southern Intelligencer*, 10 October 1860; San Antonio *Alamo Express*, 5 November 1860; Clarksville *Standard*, 22 December 1860; La Grange *True Issue*, 24 January 1861; Marshall *Texas Republican*, 24 November 1860; Austin *Texas State Gazette*, 17 November 1860.

21. As pointed out earlier, good examples of followers of Clay and Jackson from the non-Lower south regions of Texas were Ben Epperson and Charles De Morse. See Clarksville *Standard*, 22 December 1860; Ralph A. Wooster, "Ben H. Epperson: East Texas Lawyer, Legislator, and Civic Leader," *ETHJ* 5 (March 1967): 29–34.

22. Friend, *Sam Houston*, pp. 321–354; John L. Waller, *Colossal Hamilton of Texas: A Biography of Andrew Jackson Hamilton, Militant Unionist and Reconstruction Governor*, pp. 1–35.

23. Both Emory M. Thomas and John McCardell stress the influence of moderates and the continuity between the new Confederacy and the old United States. See McCardell, *The Idea of a Southern Nation*, pp. 315–394; Emory M. Thomas, *The Confederate Nation: 1861–1865*, pp. 37–66. One of those moderates was John Reagan. See Ben H. Procter, *Not without Honor: The Life of John H. Reagan*, pp. 99–161. For examples of the use of American symbols and the American political heritage by Texas secessionists see Austin *Texas State Gazette*, 1 September and 17 November 1860, 16 March 1861; Marshall *Texas Republican*, 1 December 1860 and 16 March 1861; Marshall *Texas Republican*, 1 December 1860; *To Our Fellow-Citizens of the State of Texas*, Secession Broadsides, William Harrison Hamman papers.

24. Bellville *Countryman*, 19 December 1860; Austin *Texas State Gazette*, 5, 12 January and 9 February 1861; Marshall *Texas Republican*, 19 January and 2, 9 February 1861; Dallas *Herald*, 16 January and 27 February 1861.

25. According to the Austin *Texas State Gazette*, 26 January 1861; the McKinney *Messenger* and Quitman *Clipper* were strong unionist newspapers. Unfortunately, no copies are available for this period. Also, see Marshall *Texas Republican*, 2, 9 February 1861. For examples of unionists appeals in the press see San Antonio *Alamo Express*, 23 February 1861; Austin *Southern Intelligencer*, 20 February 1861.

26. For information on Fayette, Bastrop, Van Zandt, and Angelina counties and their approach to secession, see Leonie Rummel Weyland and

Houston Wade, *An Early History of Fayette County*; Bill Moore, *Bastrop County, 1691–1900*; D. L. Vest, *Watterson Folk of Bastrop County, Texas*, pp. 78–82; Effie Boon, "The History of Angelina County" (M.A. thesis), pp. 40–75; Lufkin *Daily Times*, 27 January 1936; Angelina County Tax Records, Texas State Archives; Bastrop *Advertiser, In The Shadow of the Lost Pines: A History of Bastrop County and Its People*, pp. 5–7; W. S. Mills, *History of Van Zandt County*, pp. 9–155; Allan C. Ashcraft, "East Texas in the Election of 1860 and the Secession Crisis," *ETHJ* 1 (July 1963): 7–16; F. W. Grassmayer, *F. W. Grassmayer's Vindication* (broadside); La Grange *True Issue*, 7, 14 March 1861.

27. For election returns see Joe T. Timmons, "The Referendum in Texas on the Ordinance of Secession, February 23, 1861: The Vote," *ETHJ* 11 (Fall 1973): 15–16. For the reaction of unionists to the election see Austin *Southern Intelligencer*, 6 March 1861; San Antonio *Alamo Express*, 2, 9 March 1861; George W. Paschal to the Washington *National Intelligencer*, 23 March 1861; Houston "Speech at Brenham, March 31, 1861," *Writings* 8: 295–299.

28. Houston, "Speech at Independence, May 10, 1861," *Writings* 8: 302. Also see Elliott, *Leathercoat*, pp. 63–66; Dallas *Herald*, 27 March 1861; Galveston *Die Union*, 23 and 28 February 1861; Jimmie Hicks, "Texas and Separate Independence, 1860–1861," *ETHJ* 4 (October 1966): 85–106; Friend, *Sam Houston*, pp. 337–340; Austin *Southern Intelligencer*, 8 May 1861.

29. Houston, "Speech at Indepencence, May 10, 1861," *Writings* 8:302. Also see Elliott, "Union Sentiment in Texas"; Frank H. Smyrl, "Texans in the Union Army, 1861–1865," *SWHQ* 65 (October 1961): 234–250; Dale A. Somers, "James P. Newcomb: The Making of a Radical," *SWHQ* 72 (April 1969): 449–469; Jane L. Scarborough, "George W. Paschal: Texas Unionist and Scalawag Jurisprudent" (Ph.D. dissertation), pp. 69–94; Waller, *Colossal Hamilton*, pp. 35–152.

EPILOGUE: ACROSS THE RIVER

1. This quote is from *Texas v. White* (1869), a case argued by Paschal before the Supreme Court. See Alpheus Thomas Mason and William M. Beaney, *American Constitutional Law*, p. 131. Also see *The Handbook of Texas* 1:469–470, 759–760; 2:89, 148, 343–344; Harold M. Hyman, *A More Perfect Union: The Impact of the Civil War and Reconstruction on the Constitution*, pp. 517–518; Alvy L. King, *Louis T. Wigfall: Southern Fire-eater*, pp. 118–214; Ben H. Procter, *Not without Honor: The Life of John H. Reagan*, pp. 122–161; Claude Elliott, *Leathercoat: The Life History of a Texas Patriot*, pp. 58–178; Llerena Friend, *Sam Houston: The Great Designer*, pp. 339–354.

2. On Unionism during the war see Claude Elliott, "Union Sentiment in Texas, 1861–1865," *SWHQ* 50 (April 1947): 448–477; Frank H. Smyrl, "Texans in the Union Army, 1861–1865," *SWHQ* 65 (October 1961): 134–150.

3. Gilbert Kingsbury to Warren, June 1860, Gilbert Kingsbury to James R. Strong, 20 August 1862, Gilbert D. Kingsbury papers. Also see *Handbook of Texas* 2:961.

4. Sam Houston to Sam Houston, Jr., 6 November 1860, *Writings* 8:184–185.

5. Andrew J. Hamilton, "Speech of Hon. Andrew J. Hamilton of Texas on the State of the Union, February 1, 1861," pp. 15–16.

6. One of the clearest enunciations of the continuation of Unionism during and after the war came from James W. Throckmorton. See Throckmorton to Louis T. Wigfall, 30 December 1866, James Webb Throckmorton papers. On Texas after the war see Charles W. Ramsdell, *Reconstruction in Texas*.

Bibliography

PRIMARY SOURCES

Manuscript Collections

Austin Public Library, Austin–Travis County Collection. Austin, Texas.
—Brown, Frank. "Annals of Travis County and the City of Austin from the Earliest Times to the Close of 1875." Typescript. 12 volumes.
—Pease-Graham-Niles. Family papers.
Houston Metropolitan Research Center, Archives, Houston, Texas.
—Ballinger, William Pitt, and Thomas M. Jack. Papers.
Rice University, Fondren Library, Woodson Research Center. Houston, Texas.
—Hamman, William Harrison. Papers.
—Osterhout, John Patterson. Papers.
—Porter, Clyde H. Collection.
Rosenberg Library, Archives. Galveston, Texas.
—Ballinger, William Pitt. Diary.
—Ballinger, William Pitt. Papers.
—Flake, Ferdinand. "Register of 1864 of the Male and Female Inhabitants of Galveston City."
St. Mary's University, Academic Library. San Antonio, Texas.
—Laredo Archives.
Texas State Library, Archives, Austin, Texas.
—Eisenlaher, George W. Letters.
—Haas, Oscar. Collection.
—Houston, Sam. Governor's correspondence.
—Huson, Hobart. Collection.
—Seele, Herman H. Collection.
—Reagan, John H. Papers.
—Texas. Records of the Secretary of State. Election returns.
—Texas. Tax records of Texas counties.
—United States Census. Manuscript returns for 1850 and 1860.
University of Texas, Barker Texas History Center, Archives, Austin, Texas.
—Angelina County. Scrapbook.
—Brown, John Henry. Papers.
—Bryan, Guy M. Papers.
—Burleson, Edward. Letters, 1821–1876.
—Comal County. Scrapbook.
—Douai, Adolf. Papers.

—Epperson, Benjamin H. Papers.
—Ford, John Salmon. "The Memoirs of John Salmon Ford."
—Hamilton, Andrew Jackson. Papers.
—Haynes, John L. Papers.
—Kingsbury, Gilbert D. Papers.
—Maverick family. Papers.
—Reagan, John Henniger. Papers.
—Roberts, Oran Milo. Papers.
—Smith, Ashbel. Papers.
—Throckmorton, James Webb. Papers.
—Vandale, Earl. Papers.
—White, Francis Menefee. Papers.

Newspapers

Austin, Texas. *Southern Intelligencer.*
———. *Texas Democrat.*
———. *Texas State Gazette.*
———. *Texas State Times.*
Bastrop, Texas. *Advertiser.*
Bonham, Texas. *Era.*
Clarksville, Texas. *Standard.*
Corpus Christi, Texas. *Ranchero.*
Corsicana, Texas. *Navarro Express.*
Dallas, Texas. *Herald.*
Galveston, Texas. *Civilian and Galveston Gazette.*
———. *Journal.*
———. *News.*
———. *Die Union.*
———. *Zeitung.*

Hempstead, Texas. *Bellville Countryman.*
Houston, Texas. *Telegraph.*
La Grange, Texas. *True Issue.*
———. *Paper.*
Marshall, Texas. *Harrison Flag.*
———. *Texas Republican.*
Nacogdoches, Texas. *Chronicle.*
New Braunfels, Texas. *Neu Braunfelser Zeitung.*
San Antonio, Texas. *Alamo Express.*
———. *El Bejareno.*
———. *Herald.*
———. *El Ranchero.*
———. *Texas Staats-Zeitung.*
———. *Zeitung.*
Washington, Texas. *American.*
Weatherford, Texas. *Whiteman.*

Books

Acheson, Sam, and Julie Ann Hudson O'Connell (eds.). *George Washington Diamond's Account of the Great Hanging at Gainesville, 1862.* Austin: Texas State Historical Association, 1963.
Anderson, Charles. *Texas: Before and on the Eve of the Rebellion.* Cincinnati: Peter G. Thompson, 1884.
Barrett, Thomas. *The Great Hanging at Gainesville, Cooke County, Texas, October A.D. 1862.* Austin: Texas State Historical Association, 1961.
Bracht, Viktor. *Texas in Jahre 1848.* Elberfield and Iserlohn: Julius Baideker, 1849.
———. *Texas in 1848.* Translated by Charles F. Schmidt. San Antonio: Naylor Co., 1931.

Burnham, W. Dean. *Presidential Ballots, 1836–1892.* Baltimore: Johns Hopkins University Press, 1955.

Castro, Lorenzo. *Immigration from Alsace and Lorraine: A Brief Sketch of the History of Castro's Colony.* San Antonio: Herald, 1871.

Cazneau, Jane McManus, under the pseudonym of Cora Montgomery. *Eagle Pass: Or, Life on the Border.* New York: G. P. Putnam, 1852.

Cortés, Carlos E. (ed.). *The Mexican Experience in Texas.* New York: Arno Press, 1976.

De Bow, J. D. B. *De Bow's Review.* New Orleans, 1848–1860. Passim.

———. *Statistical View of the United States . . . Being a Compendium of the Seventh Census.* Washington, D.C.: Senate Printer, 1854.

De Cordova, Jacob. *Texas: Her Resources and Her Public Men.* Philadelphia: E. Crozet, 1858.

De Lono, A. *Galveston Directory for 1856–57.* Galveston: Galveston *News,* 1856.

Dohoney, E. L. *An Average American.* Paris, Tex.: privately published, 1907.

Dresel, Gustav. *Gustav Dresel's Houston Journal: Adventures in North America and Texas, 1837–1841.* Translated by Max Freund. Austin: University of Texas Press, 1954.

Dunt, Detlef. *Reise nach Texas, nebst Nachrichten von diesam Lande; für Deutsche, welche nach Amerika zu gehen beabschtigen.* Bremen: Carl W. Wiehe, 1834.

Ehrenburg, Herman. *With Milam and Fannin: Adventures of a German Boy in Texas' Revolution.* Austin: Pemberton Press, 1968.

Ford, John Salmon. *Rip Ford's Texas.* Edited by Stephen B. Oates. Austin: University of Texas Press, 1963.

Fröbel, Julius. *Aus Amerika: Erfahrungen, Reisen und Studien* (2 vols.). Leipzig: J. J. Weber, 1857–1858.

Goeth, Ottilie Fuchs. *Memoirs of a Texas Pioneer Grandmother, 1805–1915.* Translated by Irma Goeth Guenther. Austin: privately printed, 1969.

Green, Rena Maverick (ed.). *Samuel Maverick, Texan, 1803–1870: A Collection of Letters, Journals and Memoirs.* San Antonio: privately printed, 1952.

Halstead, Murat. *Three against Lincoln: Murat Halstead Reports the Caucuses of 1860.* Edited by William B. Hesseltine. Baton Rouge: Louisiana State University Press, 1960.

Haskew, Corrie Pattison (ed.). *Historical Records of Austin and Waller Counties.* Houston: Premier Printing, 1969.

Hayes, Rutherford Birchard. *Diary and Letters of Rutherford Birchard Hayes.* Edited by Charles Richard Williams. Columbus: Ohio State Archeological and Historical Society, 1922.

History of Texas together with a Biographical History of the Cities of Houston and Galveston. Chicago: Lewis Publishing Co., 1895.

Holley, Mary Austin. *Texas.* Lexington, Ky.: J. Clarke & Co., 1836.

Hollon, W. Eugene, and Ruth Lapham Butler (eds.). *William Bollaert's Texas.* Norman: University of Oklahoma Press, 1956.

Houston, Sam. *The Writings of Sam Houston, 1813–1863.* Edited by Amelia W. Williams and Eugene C. Barker (8 vols.). Austin: University of Texas Press, 1938–1943.

Huckabay, Ida Lasater. *Ninety-Four Years in Jack County, 1854–1948.* Austin: Steck Co., 1949.

Kennedy, Joseph C. G. *Agriculture of the United States in 1860.* Washington, D.C.: Government Printing Office, 1864.

———. *Manufactures of the United States in 1860.* Washington, D.C.: Government Printing Office, 1864.

———. *Population of the United States in 1860; Compiled from the Original Returns of the Eighth Census.* Washington, D.C.: Government Printing Office, 1864.

Lindheimer, Ferdinand J. *Aufsätze und Abhandlungen.* Frankfurt: Theodor Wentz, 1879.

Lubbock, Francis Richard. *Six Decades in Texas, or Memoirs of Francis Richard Lubbock, Governor of Texas in War Time, 1861–63: A Personal Experience in Business, War and Politics.* Edited by C. W. Raines. Austin: Ben C. Jones & Co., 1900.

McIntyre, Benjamin F. *Federals on the Frontier: The Diary of Benjamin F. McIntyre.* Edited by Nannie M. Tilley. Austin: University of Texas Press, 1963.

Menchaca, Antonio. *Memoirs.* San Antonio: Yanaguana Society, 1937.

Mills, William W. *Forty Years at El Paso, 1858–1898.* Edited by Rex W. Strickland. El Paso: Carl Herzog Press, 1962.

Moore, Ike. *The Life and Diary of Reading W. Black: A History of Early Uvalde.* Uvalde, Tex.: El Progresso Club, 1934.

Newcomb, James P. *Sketch of Secession Times in Texas and Journal of Travel from Texas through Mexico to California, including a History of the "Box Colony."* San Francisco: printed by the author, 1863.

North, Thomas. *Five Years in Texas; or, What You Did Not Hear during the War from January, 1861, to January, 1866: A Narrative of His Travels, Experiences, and Observations, in Texas and Mexico.* Cincinnati: Elm Street Printing Co., 1871.

Olmsted, Frederick Law. *A Journey through Texas; Or, A Saddle-Trip on the Southwestern Frontier.* New York: Dix, Edwards & Co., 1857.

Penniger, Robert. *Fest-Ausgabe zum fünfzigjahrigen Jubiläum der Grundung der Stadt Friedrichsburg.* Fredericksburg, Tex.: *Friedrichsburger Wochenblattes*, 1896.

Rankin, Melinda. *Texas in 1850.* Waco: Texian Press, 1966.

Reagan, John H. *Memoirs, with Special Reference to Secession and the Civil War.* Austin and New York: Pemberton Press, 1965.

Richardson, Willard. *Galveston Directory for 1859–60, with a Brief History of the Island.* Galveston: Galveston *News*, 1859.

Roberts, Oran M. "The Political, Legislative, and Judicial History of Texas for Its Fifty Years of Statehood, 1845–1895," *A Comprehensive History of Texas, 1685–1897* (2 vols.). Edited by Dudley G. Wooten. Dallas: William G. Scarff, 1898.

Rodríguez, José M. *Rodríguez Memoirs of Early Texas.* San Antonio: Standard Printing Co., 1961.

Roemer, Ferdinand. *Texas: Mit besonder Rüchsicht auf deutsche Auswanderung und die physischen Verhältnisse des Landes nach eigener Beobachtung geshildert.* Bonn: Adolph Marcus, 1849.

————. *Texas: With Particular Reference to German Immigration and the Physical Appearance of the Country.* Translated by Oswald Mueller. San Antonio: Standard Printing Co., 1935.

Scherpf, G. A. *Enstehungsgeschichte und Gegenwärtiger Zustand des Neuen, Unabhängigen amerikanischen Staates, Texas.* Augsburg: Matthew Rieger, 1841.

Seele, Herman. *Die Cypresse und Gesammelte Schriften.* New Braunfels, Tex.: *Neu Braunfelser Zeitung,* 1936.

————. *The Cypress and Other Writings of a German Pioneer in Texas.* Translated by Edward C. Breitenkamp. Austin: University of Texas Press, 1979.

Seguín, Juan N. *Personal Memoirs of Juan N. Seguín: From the Year 1834 to the Retreat of General Woll from the City of San Antonio in 1842.* San Antonio: Ledger Book and Job Office, 1858.

Siemering, August. *Ein Verfehltes Leben.* San Antonio: Freien Presse, 1876.

Solms-Braunfels, Prince Carl von. *Texas: Geschildert in Beziehung auf Seine geographischen, socilen und übrigen Verhältnisse mit besonder Rüchsicht auf die deutsche Colonisation.* Frankfurt: Johann David Sauerlander, 1846.

————. *Texas, 1844–1845.* Translated by Oswald Mueller. Houston: Anson Jones Press, 1936.

Spaight, A. W. *The Resources, Soil and Climate of Texas.* Galveston: A. H. Belo & Co., 1882.

Sprague, John T. *The Treachery in Texas, the secession of Texas, and the arrest of the United States Officers and soldiers serving in Texas.* New York: Rebellion Record, 1862.

Stevens, John W. *Reminiscences of the Civil War: A Soldier in Hood's Texas Brigade, Army of Northern Virginia.* Hillsboro: Hillsboro *Mirror* Printing Co., 1902.

Texas, State of. *Journals of the House of Representatives.* 5th–8th Legislatures. Austin: State Printer, 1855–1861.

————. *Journals of the Senate.* 5th–8th Legislatures. Austin: State Printer, 1855–1861.

————. *A Legislative Manual for the State of Texas.* Austin: E. W. Swindells, 1883.

Tocqueville, Alexis de. *Democracy in America.* Edited by Richard D. Heffner. New York: New American Library, 1956.

Urbantke, Carl. *Texas Is the Place for Me.* Translated by Ella Urbantke Fischer. Austin: Pemberton Press, 1970.

Wallace, Ernest, and Vigness, David M. (eds.). *Documents of Texas History.* Austin: Steck Co., 1963.

Wallis, Jonnie Lockhart, and Hill, Laurence L. *Sixty Years on the Brazos:*

The Life and Letters of Dr. John Washington Lockhart, 1824–1860. Los Angeles: privately printed, 1930.

War of the Rebellion: A Compilation of the Official Records of the Union and Confederate Armies (70 vols. in 127 and index). Washington, D.C.: Government Printing Office, 1880–1901.

Weeks, William F. *Debates of the Texas Convention*. Houston: J. W. Cruger, 1846.

Wilbarger, J. W. *Indian Depredations in Texas: Reliable Accounts of Battles, Wars, Adventures, Forays, Murders, Massacres, Etc., Etc., Together with Biographical Sketches of Many of the Most Noted Indian Fighters and Frontiersmen of Texas*. Austin: Hutchings Printing House, 1889.

Winfrey, Dorman H., and James M. Day (eds.). *The Indian Papers of Texas and the Southwest 1825–1916* (5 vols.). Austin: Texas State Library, 1960–1966.

Winkler, Ernest William (ed.). *Journal of the Secession Convention of Texas, 1861*. Austin: Austin Printing Co., 1912.

———. *Platforms of Political Parties in Texas*. Austin: University of Texas Press, 1916.

Zuber, William Physick. *My Eighty Years in Texas*. Austin: University of Texas Press, 1971.

Articles

Almonte, Juan N. "Statistical Report on Texas." Translated by Carlos E. Castañeda. *Southwestern Historical Quarterly* 28 (January 1925): 177–222.

Altgelt, Emma. "Emma Altgelt's Sketches of Life in Texas." Edited by Henry B. Dielman. *Southwestern Historical Quarterly* 43 (January 1960): 363–384.

Archer, Branch T. "Texas and Her Resources." *De Bow's Review* 19 (July 1855): 22–29.

Baker, William M. "A Pivotal Point." *Lippincott's Magazine* 26 (November 1880): 559–566.

Erath, George Bernard. "Memoirs of George Bernard Erath." Edited by Lucy A. Erath. *Southwestern Historical Quarterly* 27 (October 1923): 140–163.

Kettner, Franz. "Letters from a German Pioneer in Texas." Edited and translated by Terry G. Jordan and Marlis Anderson Jordan. *Southwestern Historical Quarterly* 49 (April 1966): 463–472.

Latimer, J. W. "The Wheat Region and Wheat Culture in Texas." *Texas Almanac for 1859*. Galveston: Galveston *News*, 1858.

Oldham, W. S. "Colonel John Marshall." *Southwestern Historical Quarterly* 20 (October 1916): 132–138.

Paschal, George W. "The Last Years of Sam Houston." *Harper's Magazine* 32 (April 1866): 630–635.

Reagan, John H. "A Conversation with Governor Houston." *Texas Historical Association Quarterly* 3 (April 1900): 279–281.

Sanchez, José Maria. "A Trip to Texas in 1828." Translated by Carlos E. Castañeda. *Southwestern Historical Quarterly* 29 (April 1926): 149–188.

Schmitz, Joseph (ed.). "Impressions of Texas in 1860." *Southwestern Historical Quarterly* 42 (April 1939): 334–350.

Terrell, Alexander W. "The City of Austin from 1839–1865." *Texas Historical Association Quarterly* 14 (October 1910): 113–128.

———. "Recollections of General Sam Houston." *Southwestern Historical Quarterly* 16 (October 1912): 113–136.

Printed Broadsides, Speeches, and Addresses

Grassmayer, F. W. "F. W. Grassmayer's Vindication." Broadside. La Grange, 1861.

Gray, Peter W. "Address to the Citizens of Houston on the African Slave Trade." Houston, 1859.

Hamilton, Andrew Jackson. "Speech of Hon. Andrew J. Hamilton of Texas on the State of the Union, February 1, 1861." Washington, D.C., 1861.

Haynes, John L. et. al. "Address to the People of Texas." Austin, 1861.

Reagan, John H. "Speech before the U.S. Congress." *Congressional Globe*, 36th Congress, 2nd Session, pp. 387–393.

Texas Convention, 1861. "A Declaration of the Causes which Impel the State of Texas to Secede from the Federal Union." Austin, 1861.

SECONDARY SOURCES

Books, Dissertations, Theses, and Booklength Manuscripts

Armstrong, James Curtis. "The History of Harrison County, Texas, 1839–1880." M.A. thesis, University of Colorado, 1930.

Arndt, Karl J. R., and May E. Olson. *German American Newspapers and Periodicals, 1735–1955*. Heidelberg: Quelle & Meyer, 1961.

Arnold, Marcus Llewellyn. "The Later Phases of the Secession Movement in Texas." M.A. thesis, University of Texas, Austin, 1920.

Ash, Bette Gay Hunter. "The Mexican Texans in the Civil War." M.A. thesis, East Texas State University, 1972.

Bailey, Leonard. "Unionist Editors in Texas during the Secession Crisis." M.A. thesis, Texas Southern University, 1973.

Barker, Eugene C. *The Life of Stephen F. Austin, Founder of Texas, 1793–1836: A Chapter in the Westward Movement of the Anglo-American People*. Nashville: Cokesbury Press, 1925.

———. *Mexico and Texas, 1821–1835*. Dallas: P. L. Turner Co., 1928.

Barkley, Mary Starr. *History of Travis County and Austin, 1839–1899*. Waco: Texian Press, 1963.

Barney, William L. *The Road to Secession: A New Perspective on the Old South*. New York: Praeger Publishers, 1972.

———. *The Secessionist Impulse: Alabama and Mississippi in 1860*. Princeton: Princeton University Press, 1974.

Bartholomew, Ed. *The Houston Story: A Chronicle of the City of Houston and the Texas Frontier from the Battle of San Jacinto to the War between the States, 1836–1865.* Houston: Frontier Press, 1951.

Bartlett, Irving H. *Daniel Webster.* New York: W. W. Norton & Co., Inc., 1978.

Bastrop *Advertiser. In the Shadow of the Lost Pines: A History of Bastrop County and Its People.* Bastrop, Tex.: Bastrop *Advertiser,* 1955.

Bates, Edward F. *History and Reminiscences of Denton County.* Denton, Tex.: McNitzky Printing, 1918.

Bell, William H. "Knights of the Golden Circle: Its Organization and Activities in Texas prior to the Civil War." M.A. thesis, Texas College of Arts and Industries, 1965.

Benjamin, Gilbert Giddings. *The Germans in Texas: A Study in Immigration.* Austin: Jenkins Publishing Company, 1974 (1910).

Bennett, Bob. *Kerr County, Texas, 1856–1956.* San Antonio: Naylor Co., 1956.

Biesele, Rudolph Leopold. *The History of the German Settlements in Texas, 1831–1861.* Austin: privately printed, 1930.

Billington, Ray Allen. *The Far Western Frontier, 1830–1860.* New York: Harper & Brothers, 1956.

———. *The Protestant Crusade, 1800–1860: A Study of the Origins of American Nativism.* New York: Rinehart, 1938.

Binkley, William Campbell. *The Expansionist Movement in Texas, 1836–1850.* Berkeley: University of California Press, 1925.

Blasig, Anne. *The Wends of Texas.* San Antonio: Naylor Co., 1954.

Bloomfield, Maxwell. *American Lawyers in a Changing Society, 1776–1876.* Cambridge, Mass., and London: Harvard University Press, 1976.

Bolton, Herbert Eugene. *Texas in the Middle Eighteenth Century: Studies in Spanish Colonial History and Administration.* Berkeley: University of California Press, 1915.

Boon, Effie. "The History of Angelina County." M.A. thesis, University of Texas, Austin, 1937.

Briggs, Richard Lee. "The Democratic Party in Early Texas." M.A. thesis, Lamar State College of Technology, 1970.

Bullard, Lucille Blackburn. *Marion County, Texas, 1860–1870.* Jefferson, Tex.: privately printed, 1965.

Burnham, W. Dean. *Presidential Ballots, 1836–1892.* Baltimore: Johns Hopkins University Press, 1955.

Burton, Margaret Sealy. *The History of Galveston, Texas.* Galveston: privately printed, 1937.

Caldwell, Lillie Moerbe. *Texas Wends: Their First Half-Century.* Salado, Tex.: Anson Jones Press, 1961.

Campbell, Mary E. *The Attitude of Tennesseans towards the Union, 1847–1861.* New York: Vantage Press, 1961.

Campbell, Randolph B., and Richard G. Lowe. *Wealth and Power in Antebellum Texas.* College Station and London: Texas A&M Press, 1977.

Carter, W. T. *The Soils of Texas.* College Station: Texas A&M College, 1931.

Caskey, Willie Malvin. *Secession and Restoration of Louisiana*. Baton Rouge: Louisiana State University Press, 1938.

Castañeda, Carlos E. (trans.). *The Mexican Side of the Texas Revolution, 1836*. Austin and Dallas: Graphic Ideas, 1970.

Cat Spring Agricultural Society. *The Cat Spring Story*. San Antonio: Lone Star Printing, 1956.

Chabot, Frederick C. *With the Makers of San Antonio: Genealogies of the Early Latin, Anglo-American, and German Families with Occasional Biographies, Each Group Being Prefaced with a Brief Historical Sketch and Illustrations*. San Antonio: privately published, 1937.

Channing, Steven A. *Crisis of Fear: Secession in South Carolina*. New York: Simon and Schuster, 1970.

Clarke, Mary Whatley. *The Swenson Saga and the SMS Ranches*. Austin: Jenkins Publishing Co., 1971.

———. *Thomas J. Rusk: Soldier, Statesman, Jurist*. Austin: Jenkins Publishing Co., 1971.

Cochran, Thomas C. *Social Change in America: The Twentieth Century*. New York: Harper & Row, 1972.

Coit, Margaret L. *John C. Calhoun: American Portrait*. Boston: Houghton Mifflin, 1850.

Cole, Arthur C. *The Whig Party in the South*. Washington, D.C.: American Historical Association, 1914.

Craven, Avery O. *The Growth of Southern Nationalism, 1848–1861*. Baton Rouge: Louisiana State University Press, 1953.

Crenshaw, Ollinger. *The Slave States in the Presidential Election of 1860*. Baltimore: Johns Hopkins University Press, 1945.

Crews, Litha. "The Know-Nothing Party in Texas." M.A. thesis, University of Texas, Austin, 1925.

Crocket, George L. *Two Centuries in East Texas: A History of San Augustine County and Surrounding Territory*. Dallas: Southwest Press, 1962.

Crook, Carland Elaine. "San Antonio, Texas, 1846–1861." M.A. thesis, Rice University, 1964.

Curlee, Abigail. "A Study of Texas Slave Plantations, 1822–1865." Ph.D. dissertation, University of Texas, Austin, 1932.

Current, Richard N. *Daniel Webster and the Rise of National Conservatism*. Boston: Little, Brown, 1955.

Curti, Merli. *The Roots of American Loyalty*. New York: Columbia University Press, 1946.

Dalzell, Robert. *Daniel Webster and the Trial of American Nationalism*. Boston: Houghton Mifflin, 1973.

Dangerfield, George. *The Awakening of American Nationalism, 1815–1828*. New York: Harper & Row, 1965.

Daniell, L. E. *Types of Successful Men of Texas*. Austin: Eugene Von Boeckmann, 1890.

Degler, Carl N. *The Other South: Southern Dissenters in the Nineteenth Century*. New York, Evanston, San Francisco, and London: Harper & Row, 1974.

De León, Arnoldo. "White Racial Attitudes toward Mexicanos in Texas, 1821–1900." Ph.D. dissertation, Texas Christian University, 1974.

Dick, Everett. *The Dixie Frontier: A Social History of the Southern Frontier from the First Transmontane Beginnings to the Civil War*. New York: Alfred A. Knopf, 1948.

Dickson, John B. "History of Gregg County, Texas." M.A. thesis, University of Texas, Austin, 1957.

Dixon, F. K. "A History of Gonzales County in the Nineteenth Century." M.A. thesis University of Texas, Austin, 1964.

Dobert, Eitel Wolf. *Deutsche Demokraten in America: Die Achteunger und ihre Schriften*. Gottinger: Vandenhoeck & Ruprect, 1958.

Dumond, Dwight L. *The Secession Movement, 1860–1861*. New York: Macmillan, 1931.

Dworaczyk, Edward J. *The First Polish Colonies of America in Texas*. San Antonio: Naylor Co., 1936.

Eaton, Clement. *The Freedom-of-Thought Struggle in the Old South*. New York: Harper & Row, 1964.

———. *Henry Clay and the Art of American Politics*. Boston: Little, Brown, 1957.

Elliott, Claude. *Leathercoat: The Life History of a Texas Patriot*. San Antonio: Standard Printing, 1938.

Ellis, Olin O. *Life in Uvalde, Texas, 1882–1903*. Baltimore: Harry S. Scott, Inc., 1963.

Ellison, Ronald C. "The Whig Party of Texas." M.A. thesis, Lamar State College of Technology, 1971.

Farber, James. *Fort Worth in the Civil War*. Belton, Tex.: Peter Hansbrough Press, 1960.

Farmer, Garland R. *The Realm of Rusk County*. Henderson, Tex.: Henderson *Times*, 1951.

Faulk, Odie B. *The Last Years of Spanish Texas, 1778–1821*. London, The Hague, Paris: Mouton & Co., 1964.

Foner, Eric. *Free Soil, Free Labor, Free Men: The Ideology of the Republican Party before the Civil War*. Oxford, London, New York: Oxford University Press, 1970.

Fornell, Earl W. *The Galveston Era: The Texas Crescent on the Eve of Secession*. Austin: University of Texas Press, 1961.

Friend, Llerena. *Sam Houston: The Great Designer*. Austin: University of Texas Press, 1954.

Gambrell, Herbert P. *Mirabeau Buonaparte Lamar: Troubadour and Crusader*. Dallas: Southwest Press, 1934.

Garrett, Julia Kathryn. *Fort Worth: A Frontier Triumph*. Austin: Encino Press, 1972.

Genovese, Eugene D. *The Political Economy of Slavery: Studies in the Economy and Society of the Slave South*. New York: Random House, 1961.

Geue, Ethel Hander. *New Homes in a New Land: German Immigration to Texas, 1847–1861*. Waco: Texian Press, 1970.

Glover, Robert W. (ed.). *Tyler and Smith County History: An Historical Appraisal.* Tyler, Tex.: Tyler/Smith County Bicentennial Committee, 1976.

Gold, Ella, and Esther Mueller. *Pioneers in God's Hills: A History of Fredericksburg and Gillespie County People and Events.* Austin: Von Boeckmann-Jones, 1960.

Goldfinch, Charles W., and Jose T. Canales. *Juan Cortina: Two Interpretations.* New York: Arno Press, 1974.

Gordon, Milton M. *Assimilation in American Life: The Role of Race, Religion and National Origins.* New York: Oxford University Press, 1964.

Graf, Leroy P. "The Economic History of the Lower Rio Grande Valley 1820–1875." Ph.D. dissertation, Harvard University, 1942.

Gray, Lewis C. *The History of Agriculture in the Southern United States to 1860* (2 vols.). Washington, D.C.: Carnegie Institution of Washington, 1933.

Haas, Oscar. *History of New Braunfels and Comal County, Texas, 1844–1946.* Austin: Steck Co., 1968.

Haimam, Miecilaus. *The Poles in the Early History of Texas.* Chicago: Polish RC Union of America, 1936.

Hall, Ada Marie. "Texas Germans in State and National Politics, 1850–1865." M.A. thesis, University of Texas, Austin, 1938.

Haltom, Richard W. *History and Description of Angelina County, Texas.* Austin: Pemberton Press, 1969.

Hamilton, Holman. *Prologue to Conflict: The Crisis and Compromise of 1850.* Lexington: University of Kentucky Press, 1964.

The Handbook of Texas. Volumes 1 and 2 edited by Walter Prescott Webb and H. Bailey Carroll. Austin: Texas State Historical Association, 1952. Volume 3 edited by Eldon Stephen Branda. Austin: Texas State Historical Association, 1976.

Harding, Jacobina B. "A History of the Early Newspapers." M.A. thesis, University of Texas, Austin, 1951.

Hasskarl, Robert A., Jr. *Brenham, Texas, 1844–1958.* Brenham: *Banner Press* Publishing Co., 1958.

Hatcher, Mattie Austin. *The Opening of Texas to Foreign Settlement, 1801–1821.* Austin: University of Texas Press, 1928.

Hawgood, John A. *The Tragedy of German-America: The Germans in the United States of America during the Nineteenth Century—and After.* New York: G. P. Putnam, 1940.

Hays, Carlton J. H. *The Historical Evolution of Modern Nationalism.* New York: Macmillan, 1931.

———. *Nationalism: A Religion.* New York: Macmillan, 1960.

Head, Nancy Ann. "State Rights in Texas, the Growth of an Idea, 1850–1860." M.A. thesis, Rice Institute, 1960.

Heintzen, Frank W. "Fredericksburg, Texas, during the Civil War and Reconstruction." M.A. thesis, St. Mary's University, 1944.

Henderson, Harry McCorry. *Texas in Confederacy.* San Antonio: Naylor Co., 1955.

Henson, Margaret Sweet. *Samuel May Williams: Early Texas Entrepreneur.* College Station: Texas A&M Press, 1976.

Hering, Julia Lee. "The Secession Movement in Texas." M.A. thesis, University of Texas, Austin, 1933.

Hertz, Frederick. *Nationality in History and Politics.* London: F. Paul, 1944.

Higham, John. *Strangers in the Land: Patterns of American Nativism, 1860–1925.* New York: Atheneum, 1975.

Hilliard, Sam B. *Hog Meat and Hoecake: Food Supply in the Old South, 1840–1860.* Carbondale and Edwardsville: Southern Illinois University Press, 1972.

Hogan, William Ransom. *The Texas Republic: A Social and Economic History.* Norman: University of Oklahoma Press, 1946.

Hohes, Pauline Buck. *A Centennial History of Anderson County, Texas.* San Antonio: Naylor Co., 1936.

Holland, G. A. *History of Parker County and the Double Log Cabin.* San Antonio: Naylor Co., 1936.

Horgan, Paul. *Great River: The Rio Grande in North American History* (2 vols.). New York and Toronto: Rinehart & Co., 1954.

House, Aline. *Big Thicket: Its Heritage.* San Antonio: Naylor Co., 1967.

Hudson, Estelle, and Henry R. Maresh. *Czech Pioneers of the Southwest.* Dallas: Southwest Press, 1934.

Hughes, W. J. *Rebellious Ranger: Rip Ford and the Old Southwest.* Norman: University of Oklahoma Press, 1964.

Hunter, J. Marvin. *The Lyman Wight Colony in Texas.* Bandera, Tex.: Bandera *Bulletin*, ca. 1940.

Huson, Hobart. *Refugio: A Comprehensive History of Refugio County from Aboriginal Times to 1953* (2 vols.). Woodsboro, Tex.: Rooke Foundation, 1953.

Hyman, Harold M. *A More Perfect Union: The Impact of the Civil War and Reconstruction on the Constitution.* New York: Alfred A. Knopf, 1973.

Jackson, Mary Susan. "The People of Houston in the 1850s." Ph.D. dissertation, Indiana University, 1974.

James, Marquis. *The Raven: A Biography of Sam Houston.* Indianapolis: Bobbs-Merrill, 1929.

Johnson, Elmer H. *The Natural Regions of Texas.* Austin: University of Texas Press, 1931.

Johnson, Frank W. *A History of Texas and Texans.* Edited by Eugene C. Barker. Chicago and New York: American Historical Society, 1916.

Johnson, William R. *A Short History of the Sugar Industry in Texas.* Houston: Texas Gulf Coast Historical Association, 1961.

Jordan, Terry G. "The German Element of Gillespie County, Texas." M.A. thesis, University of Texas, Austin, 1961.

———. *German Seed in Texas Soil: Immigrant Farmers in Nineteenth-Century Texas.* Austin: University of Texas Press, 1966.

Jurney, Richard Loyall. *History of Titus County, Texas, 1846 to 1960.* Dallas: Royal Publishing Co., 1961.

Kaufmann, Wilhelm. *Die Deutschen im amerikanischen Bürgerkriege, Sezessionkrieg, 1861–1865*. Munich and Berlin: R. Oldenburg, 1911.

Kemp, Louis Wiltz. *The Signers of the Texas Declaration of Independence*. Houston: Anson Jones Press, 1944.

Kimbrough, William Clayton. "A History of Clay County." M.A. thesis, Hardin Simmons University, 1942.

King, Alvy L. *Louis T. Wigfall: Southern Fire-eater*. Baton Rouge: Louisiana State University Press, 1970.

King, Irene M. *John O. Meusenbach: German Colonizer in Texas*. Austin: University of Texas Press, 1967.

Knight, Oliver. *Fort Worth: Outpost on the Trinity*. Norman: University of Oklahoma Press, 1953.

Kohn, Hans. *American Nationalism: An Interpretive Essay*. New York: Macmillan, 1957.

————. *The Idea of Nationalism: A Study in Its Origins and Background*. New York: Macmillan, 1944.

Landrum, Graham, and Allan Smith. *Grayson County: An Illustrated History*. Fort Worth: Historical Publishers, 1967.

Lathrop, Barnes F. *Migration into East Texas, 1835–1860: A Study from the United States Census*. Austin: Texas Historical Association, 1949.

Ledbetter, Barbara Neal. *Civil War Days in Young County, Texas, 1961–65*. Newcastle, Tex., 1965.

Ledbetter, Billy D. "Slavery, Fear and Disunion in the Lone Star State: Texans' Attitudes toward Secession and the Union, 1846–1861." Ph.D. dissertation, North Texas State University, 1972.

Lockhart, W. E. "The Slave Code in Texas." M.A. thesis, Baylor University, 1929.

Lonn, Ella. *Foreigners in the Confederacy*. Chapel Hill: University of North Carolina Press, 1940.

Lott, Virgil N., and Mercurio Martinez. *The Kingdom of Zapata*. San Antonio: Naylor Co., 1953.

Lowrie, Samuel Harman. *Culture Conflict in Texas, 1821–1835*. New York: Columbia University Press, 1932.

Loyd, Doyal T. *A History of Upshur County, Texas*. Waco: Texian Press, 1966.

Lucas, Mattie Davis, and Mita Holsapple Hall. *A History of Grayson County, Texas*. Sherman, Tex.: Scruggs Printing, 1936.

McCardell, John. *The Idea of a Southern Nation: Southern Nationalists and Southern Nationalism, 1830–1860*. New York and London: W. W. Norton & Co., Inc., 1979.

McConnell, Weston Joseph. *Social Cleavages in Texas: A Study of the Proposed Division of the State*. New York: Columbia University Press, 1925.

McCormack, Richard P. *The Second American Party System: Party Formation in the Jacksonian Era*. New York: Harper & Row, 1966.

McGrath, Sister Paul of the Cross. *Political Nativism in Texas, 1825–1860*. Washington, D.C.: Catholic University of America, 1930.

McWilliams, Carey. *North from Mexico: The Spanish Speaking People of the United States.* New York and Philadelphia: Lippincott, 1949.

Maher, Edward R., Jr. "Secession in Texas." Ph.D. dissertation, Fordham University, 1960.

Mason, Alpheus Thomas, and William M. Beaney. *American Constitutional Law.* Englewood Cliffs: Prentice-Hall, Inc., 1968.

Meinig, D. W. *Imperial Texas: An Interpretative Essay in Cultural Geography.* Austin: University of Texas Press, 1969.

Meyers, Marvin. *The Jacksonian Persuasion: Politics and Belief.* Stanford: Stanford University Press, 1957.

Miller, Benjamin H. "Elisha Marshall Pease: A Biography." M.A. thesis, University of Texas, Austin, 1927.

Mills, W. S. *History of Van Zandt County.* Canton, Tex., 1950.

Moore, Bill. *Bastrop County, 1691–1900.* San Angelo, Tex.: Educator Books, 1973.

Nackman, Mark W. *A Nation within a Nation: The Rise of Texas Nationalism.* Port Washington, N.Y.: Kennikat Press, 1975.

Nagel, Paul C. *One Nation Indivisible: The Union in American Thought, 1776–1861.* New York: Oxford University Press, 1964.

———. *This Sacred Trust: American Nationality, 1798–1898.* New York: Oxford University Press, 1971.

Nance, Joseph Milton. *After San Jacinto: The Texas-Mexican Frontier, 1836–1841.* Austin: University of Texas Press, 1963.

———. *Attack and Counterattack: The Texas-Mexican Frontier, 1842.* Austin: University of Texas Press, 1964.

Neville, A. W. *The History of Lamar County.* Paris, Tex.: North Texas Publishing Co., 1937.

Nevins, Allan. *Ordeal of the Union* (2 vols.). New York: Scribner's, 1947.

Newsome, Zoie Odom. "Antislavery Sentiment in Texas, 1821–1861." M.A. thesis, Texas Technological University, 1968.

Nicolay, John G., and John Hay. *Abraham Lincoln: A History* (10 vols.). New York: Century Co., 1917.

North, Douglas C. *The Economic Growth of the United States, 1790–1860.* Englewood Cliffs: Prentice-Hall, 1961.

Oates, Stephen B. *Visions of Glory: Texans on the Southwestern Frontier.* Norman: University of Oklahoma Press, 1970.

Oberste, William. *Texas Irish Empressarios and Their Colonies.* Austin: Von Boeckmann-Jones, 1953.

O'Connor, Richard. *The German-American: An Informal History.* Boston: Little, Brown, 1968.

Osburn, John D. "Secession and War in Red River County, Texas." Unpublished paper, Texas State Archives, 1960.

Overdyke, W. D. *The Know-Nothing Party in the South.* Baton Rouge: Louisiana State University Press, 1950.

Owsley, Frank L. *Plain Folk of the Old South.* Baton Rouge: Louisiana State University Press, 1949.

Park, Mance E. "Federal Forts Established in Texas, 1845–1861." M.A. thesis, Sam Houston State University, 1941.

Peterson, Merrill D. *The Jefferson Image in the American Mind.* New York: Oxford University Press, 1960.

Pierce, Burnett Cecil. "Titus County, Texas: Its Background and History in Ante-Bellum Days." M.A. thesis, University of Colorado, 1932.

Pierce, Frank Cushman. *A Brief History of the Lower Rio Grande Valley.* Menasha, Wis.: George Bantu Publishing Co., 1917.

Polk, Stella Gipson. *Mason and Mason County: A History.* Austin: Pemberton Press, 1966.

Potter, David M. *The Impending Crisis, 1848–1861.* Completed and edited by Don E. Fehrehbacher. New York: Harper & Row, 1976.

———. *Lincoln and His Party in the Secession Crisis.* New Haven and London: Yale University Press, 1942.

Procter, Ben H. *Not without Honor: The Life of John H. Reagan.* Austin: University of Texas Press, 1962.

Przygoda, Jacek. *Texas Pioneers from Poland: A Study in Ethnic History.* Waco: Texian Press, 1971.

Ramsdell, Charles W. *Reconstruction in Texas.* Austin: University of Texas Press, 1970.

Ransleben, Guido E. *A Hundred Years of Comfort in Texas: A Centennial History.* San Antonio: Naylor Co., 1954.

Rayburn, John C., and Virginia Kemp (eds.). *Century of Conflict, 1821–1913: Incidents in the Lives of William Neale and William A. Neale, Early Settlers in South Texas.* Waco: Texian Press, 1966.

Reed, S. G. *A History of the Texas Railroads and of Transportation Conditions under Spain and Mexico and the Republic and the State.* Houston: St. Clair Publishing, 1941.

Reynolds, Donald E. *Editors Make War: Southern Newspapers in the Secession Crisis.* Nashville: Vanderbilt University Press, 1970.

Richardson, Rupert Norval. *The Comanche Barrier to South Plains Settlement: A Century and a Half of Savage Resistance to the Advancing White Frontier.* Glendale, Calif.: Arthur Clarke, Co., 1933.

———. *The Frontier of Northwest Texas, 1846–1876.* Glendale, Calif.: Arthur Clarke, Co., 1963.

Richardson, Rupert Norval, Ernest Wallace, and Adrian N. Anderson. *Texas: The Lone Star State.* Englewood Cliffs: Prentice-Hall, 1981.

Riley, John Denny. "Santos Benavides: His Influence on the Lower Rio Grande, 1823–1891." Ph.D. dissertation, Texas Christian University, 1976.

Rippley, La Vern J. *The German-Americans.* Boston: Twayne Publishers, 1976.

Roach, Hattie Joplin. *A History of Cherokee County, Texas.* Dallas: Southwest Press, 1934.

Robertson, James Oliver. *American Myth, American Reality.* New York: Hill & Wang, 1980.

Robertson, Robert J. "The Texas Delegation in the National Congress, 1851–1861." M.A. thesis, Lamar State University, 1965.

Ryan, Dora. "The Election Laws of Texas, 1827–1875." M.A. thesis, University of Texas, Austin, 1922.

Santerre, George H. *White Cliffs of Dallas: The Story of La Reunion, The Old French Colony*. Dallas: Book Craft, 1955.

Scarborough, Jane L. "George W. Paschal: Texas Unionist and Scalawag Jurisprudent." Ph.D. dissertation, Rice University, 1972.

Scarbrough, Clara Stearns. *Land of Good Water: A Williamson County, Texas, History*. Georgetown: Williamson County *Sun* Publishers, 1973.

Sellers, Charles G., Jr. *James K. Polk* (2 vols.). Princeton: Princeton University Press, 1957–1966.

Shanks, Henry L. *The Secession Movement in Virginia, 1847–1861*. Richmond: Garrett and Massie, 1934.

Sibley, Marilyn McAdams. *Travelers in Texas, 1761–1860*. Austin: University of Texas Press, 1967.

Siegel, Stanley. *A Political History of the Texas Republic, 1836–1845*. Austin: University of Texas Press, 1956.

Simms, H. H. *A Decade of Sectional Controversy*. Chapel Hill: University of North Carolina Press, 1942.

Sinclair, Oran Lonnie. "Crossroads of Conviction: A Study of the Texas Political Mind, 1856–1861." Ph.D. dissertation, Rice University, 1975.

Smith, Justin H. *The Annexation of Texas*. New York: Barnes & Noble, 1911.

Snow, Laura. "The Poll Tax in Texas: Its Historical, Legal, and Fiscal Aspects." M.A. thesis, University of Texas, Austin, 1936.

Sonnichsen, C. L. *Pass of the North: Four Centuries on the Rio Grande*. El Paso: Texas Western Press, 1968.

Stabler, John B. "A History of the Constitutional Union Party: A Tragic Failure." Ph.D. dissertation, Columbia University, 1954.

Stambaugh, J. Lee, and Lillian J. Stambaugh. *A History of Collin County, Texas*. Austin: Texas Historical Association, 1958.

———. *The Lower Rio Grande Valley of Texas*. San Antonio: Naylor Co., 1954.

Stampp, Kenneth M. *The Imperiled Union: Essays on the Background of the Civil War*. New York: Oxford University Press, 1980.

Takaki, Ronald T. *A Pro-Slavery Crusade: The Agitation to Reopen the African Slave Trade*. New York: Free Press, 1971.

Tausch, Egon Richard. "Southern Sentiment among the Texas Germans during the Civil War and Reconstruction." M.A. thesis, University of Texas, Austin, 1965.

Taylor, Paul Schuster. *An American-Mexican Frontier: Nueces County, Texas*. Chapel Hill: University of North Carolina Press, 1934.

Thomas, Emory M. *The Confederate Nation: 1861–1865*. New York: Harper & Row, 1979.

Thompson, James H. "A Nineteenth-Century History of Cameron County, Texas." M.A. thesis, University of Texas, Austin, 1965.

Tilling, Moritz. *History of the German Element in Texas from 1820–1850 and Historical Sketches of the German Texas Singers' League and Houston Turnverein from 1853–1913.* Privately printed, 1913.

Tyler, George W. *The History of Bell County.* San Antonio: Naylor Co., 1936.

Tyson, Carl Newton. *The Red River in Southwestern History.* Norman: University of Oklahoma Press, 1981.

Van Deusen, Glyndon G. *The Life of Henry Clay.* Boston: Little, Brown, 1937.

Vandiver, Frank E. *The Southwest: South or West?* College Station: Texas A&M Press, 1975.

———. *Their Tattered Flags: The Epic of the Confederacy.* New York: *Harper's* Magazine Press, 1970.

Vaugh, Michael J. *The History of Cayuga and Cross Roads, Texas, and Related Areas in Anderson and Henderson Counties.* Waco: Texian Press, 1967.

Vest, D. L. *Watterson Folk of Bastrop County, Texas.* Waco: Texian Press, 1963.

Vigness, David M. *The Revolutionary Decades, 1810–1836.* Austin: Steck-Vaughan Co., 1965.

Von Rosenburg-Tomlinson, Alma. *The Von Rosenburg Family of Texas.* Boerne, Tex.: Toepperwein Publishing Co., 1949.

Wallace, Ernest. *Charles De Morse: Pioneer Editor and Statesman.* Lubbock: Texas Tech Press, 1943.

———. *Texas in Turmoil, 1849–1875.* Austin: University of Texas Press, 1965.

Wallace, Ernest, and E. Adamson Hoebel. *The Comanches: Lords of the South Plains.* Norman: University of Oklahoma Press, 1952.

Wallace, James Oldam. "San Antonio during the Civil War." M.A. thesis, St. Mary's University, 1940.

Waller, John L. *Colossal Hamilton of Texas: A Biography of Andrew Jackson Hamilton, Militant Unionist and Reconstruction Governor.* El Paso: Western Press, 1968.

Ward, John William. *Andrew Jackson: Symbol for an Age.* New York: Oxford University Press, 1955.

Waugh, Julia Nott. *Castro-Ville and Henry Castro, Empresario.* San Antonio: Standard Publishing Co., 1934.

Webb, Walter Prescott. *The Great Plains.* New York: Grosset & Dunlap, 1931.

———. *The Texas Rangers: A Century of Frontier Defense.* Boston: Houghton Mifflin, 1935.

Weber, David J. (ed.). *Foreigners in Their Native Land.* Albuquerque: University of New Mexico Press, 1973.

Welter, Rush. *The Mind of America, 1820–1860.* New York: Columbia University Press, 1975.

Weyland, Leonie Rummel, and Houston Wade. *An Early History of Fayette County.* La Grange, Tex.: La Grange *Journal*, 1936.

Wharton, Clarence R. *History of Fort Bend County.* San Antonio: Naylor Co., 1939.

Wheeler, Kenneth W. *To Wear a City's Crown: The Beginnings of Urban Growth in Texas, 1836–1865.* Cambridge, Mass.: Harvard University Press, 1968.

White, William W. "Migration into West Texas, 1845–1860." M.A. thesis, University of Texas, Austin, 1948.

Wilhelm, Hubert G. H. "Organized German Settlement and Its Effects on the Frontier of South-Central Texas." Ph.D. dissertation, Louisiana State University, 1968.

Wills, Gary. *Inventing America: Jefferson's Declaration of Independence.* Garden City, N.Y.: Doubleday & Co., 1978.

Wilson, Major L. *Space, Time, and Freedom: The Quest for Nationality and the Irrepressible Conflict, 1815–1861.* Westport, Conn.: Greenwood Press, 1974.

Winfrey, Dorman H. *A History of Rusk County, Texas.* Waco: Texian Press, 1961.

Wittke, Carl. *The German-Language Press in America.* Lexington: University of Kentucky Press, 1957.

———. *Refugees of Revolution, The German Forty-Eighters in America.* Philadelphia: University of Pennsylvania Press, 1952.

Wood, Thomas N. "Attitudes of Certain Texas Editors toward Secession." M.A. thesis, Baylor University, 1968.

Wooster, Ralph A. *The People in Power: Courthouse and Statehouse in the Lower South, 1850–1860.* Knoxville: University of Tennessee Press, 1969.

———. *The Secession Conventions of the South.* Princeton: Princeton University Press, 1962.

Zucker, A. E. (ed.). *The Forty-Eighters: Political Refugees of the German Revolution of 1848.* New York: Columbia University Press, 1950.

Articles

Addington, Wendell G. "Slave Insurrections in Texas." *Journal of Negro History* 35 (October 1950): 408–434.

Alexander, Thomas B. "Persistent Whiggery in the Confederate South, 1860–1877." *Journal of Southern History* 27 (August 1961): 305–329.

Ashburn, Karl E. "Slavery and Cotton Production in Texas." *Southwest Social Science Quarterly* 14 (December 1933): 257–271.

Ashcraft, Allan C. "East Texas in the Election of 1860 and the Secession Crisis." *East Texas Historical Journal* 1 (July 1963): 7–16.

Baggett, James Alex. "The Constitutional Union Party in Texas." *Southwestern Historical Quarterly* 82 (January 1979): 233–264.

Barker, Eugene C. "The Influence of Slavery in the Colonization of Texas." *Southwestern Historical Quarterly* 28 (July 1924): 1–33.

Barr, C. Alwyn. "The Making of a Secessionist: The Antebellum Career of Roger Q. Mills." *Southwestern Historical Quarterly* 79 (October 1975): 129–144.

Bender, Averam B. "The Texas Frontier, 1845–1861." *Southwestern Historical Quarterly* 33 (October 1934): 135–148.

Biesele, Rudolph Leopold. "The Texas State Convention of Germans in 1854." *Southwestern Historical Quarterly* 33 (April 1930): 247–261.

Blankinship, J. W. "Plantae Linheimerianae." *Missouri Botanical Garden Eighteenth Annual Report* (1907), 123–224.

Blount, Louis Foster. "A Brief Study of Thomas J. Rusk, Based on His Letters to His Brother, David, 1835–1856." *Southwestern Historical Quarterly* 34 (January 1931): 181–203; ibid. (April 1931): 271–293.

Bowen, Nancy Head. "A Political Labyrinth: Texas in the Civil War." *East Texas Historical Journal* 11 (Fall 1973): 3–11.

Breeden, James O. "Health of Early Texas: The Military Frontier." *Southwestern Historical Quarterly* 80 (April 1977): 357–398.

Bridges, C. A. "The Knights of the Golden Circle: A Filibustering Fantasy." *Southwestern Historical Quarterly* 44 (January 1941): 287–302.

Buenger, Walter L. "Secession and the Texas German Community: Editor Lindheimer vs. Editor Flake." *Southwestern Historical Quarterly* 82 (April 1979): 379–402.

———. "Unionism on the Texas Frontier, 1859–1861." *Arizona and the West* 22 (Autumn 1980): 237–254.

Bugbee, L. G. "Slavery in Early Texas." *Political Science Quarterly* 13 (September 1898): 389–412.

Campbell, Randolph B. "Human Property: The Negro Slave in Harrison County, 1850–1860." *Southwestern Historical Quarterly* 76 (April 1973): 384–396.

———. "Planters and Plain Folk: Harrison County, Texas, as a Test Case, 1850–1860." *Journal of Southern History* 40 (August 1974): 369–398.

———. "Texas and the Nashville Convention of 1850." *Southwestern Historical Quarterly* 76 (July 1972): 1–14.

———. "The Whig Party of Texas in the Elections of 1848 and 1852." *Southwestern Historical Quarterly* 73 (July 1969): 17–34.

Campbell, Randolph B., and Richard G. Lowe. "The Slave-Breeding Hypothesis: A Demographic Comment on the 'Buying' and 'Selling' States." *Journal of Southern History* 42 (August 1976): 401–412.

———. "Slave Property and the Distribution of Wealth in Texas, 1860." *Journal of American History* 63 (September 1976): 316–324.

———. "Some Economic Aspects of Antebellum Texas Agriculture." *Southwestern Historical Quarterly* 82 (April 1979): 351–378.

———. "Wealthholding and Political Power in Antebellum Texas." *Southwestern Historical Quarterly* 79 (July 1975): 21–30.

Connor, Seymour V. "The Evolution of County Government in the Republic of Texas." *Southwestern Historical Quarterly* 55 (October 1951): 163–200.

Cravens, John N. "Death of Thomas Jefferson Rusk." *East Texas Historical Journal* 4 (March 1966): 44–45.

Crenshaw, Ollinger. "The Knights of the Golden Circle: The Career of

George Bickley." *American Historical Review* 47 (October 1941): 23–50.

———. "The Speakership Contest of 1859–1860." *The Mississippi Valley Historical Review* 29 (December 1942): 323–338.

Crimmins, M. L. "Colonel Charles Anderson Opposed Secession in San Antonio." *West Texas Historical Association Year Book* 29 (October 1953): 67–68.

Culberson, Charles A. "General Sam Houston and Secession." *Scribner's Magazine* 39 (May 1906): 584–591.

Curlee, Abigail. "The History of a Texas Slave Plantation." *Southwestern Historical Quarterly* 24 (October 1922): 79–127.

Dew, Charles B. "Who Won the Secession Election in Louisiana." *Journal of Southern History* 26 (February 1970): 18–32.

Dugan, Frank H. "The 1850 Affair of the Brownsville Separatists." *Southwestern Historical Quarterly* 61 (October 1957): 270–287.

Dugas, Vera Lea. "Texas Industry, 1860–1880." *Southwestern Historical Quarterly* 59 (October 1955): 151–185.

Dunn, Roy Sylvan. "The KGC in Texas, 1860–1861." *Southwestern Historical Quarterly* 70 (April 1967): 543–573.

Elliott, Claude. "Union Sentiment in Texas, 1861–1865." *Southwestern Historical Quarterly* 50 (April 1947): 448–477.

Engerman, Stanley L. "A Reconsideration of Southern Economic Growth, 1770–1860." *Agricultural History* 49 (April 1975): 343–361.

Etzler, T. Herbert. "German-American Newspapers in Texas with Special Reference to the Texas Volksblatt, 1877–1879." *Southwestern Historical Quarterly* 57 (April 1954): 423–431.

Ewing, Floyd F. "Origins of Unionist Sentiment on the West Texas Frontier." *West Texas Historical Association Year Book* 32 (October 1956): 21–29.

———. "Unionist Sentiment on the North West Texas Frontier." *West Texas Historical Association Year Book* 33 (October 1957): 58–70.

Flanigan, Daniel J. "Criminal Procedure in Slave Trials in the Antebellum South." *Journal of Southern History* 40 (November 1974): 537–564.

Fornell, Earl W. "Agitation in Texas for Reopening the Slave Trade." *Southwestern Historical Quarterly* 60 (October 1956): 145–159.

———. "Ferdinand Flake: German Pioneer Journalist of the Southwest." *The American-German Review* (February–March 1955): 25–28.

Friend, Llerena. "The Texan of 1860." *Southwestern Historical Quarterly* 62 (July 1958): 1–17.

Gage, Larry Jay. "The City of Austin on the Eve of the Civil War." *Southwestern Historical Quarterly* 63 (January 1960): 428–438.

———. "The Texas Road to Secession and War: John Marshall and the *Texas State Gazette*." *Southwestern Historical Quarterly* 62 (October 1958): 191–226.

Geiser, Samuel Wood. "Naturalists of the Frontier, V: Ferdinand Jacob Lindheimer." *Southwest Review* 15 (Winter 1930): 245–266.

German, S. H., and Louilla Styles Vincent. "Governor George Thomas Wood." *Southwestern Historical Quarterly* 20 (January 1917): 260–276.

Green, Fletcher M. "Democracy in the Old South." *Journal of Southern History* 12 (February 1946): 3–23.

Griffin, Roger A. "Governor E. M. Pease and Texas Railroad Development in the 1850s." *East Texas Historical Journal* 10 (Fall 1972): 103–118.

———. "Intrastate Sectionalism in the Texas Governor's Race of 1853." *Southwestern Historical Quarterly* 76 (October 1972): 142–160.

Hart, James P. "George W. Paschal." *Texas Law Review* 28 (November 1949): 23–42.

Hicks, Jimmie. "Texas and Separate Independence, 1860–1861." *East Texas Historical Journal* 4 (October 1966): 85–106.

Holbrook, Abigail Curlee. "Cotton Marketing in Antebellum Texas." *Southwestern Historical Quarterly* 73 (April 1970): 431–455.

———. "A Glimpse of Life on Antebellum Slave Plantations in Texas." *Southwestern Historical Quarterly* 76 (April 1973): 361–383.

Holden, William Curry. "Immigration and Settlement in West Texas." *West Texas Historical Association Year Book* 5 (June 1929): 66–86.

Holt, Michael F. "The Politics of Impatience: The Origins of Know-Nothingism." *The Journal of American History* 60 (September 1973): 309–331.

Howren, Alleine. "Causes and Origin of the Decree of April 6, 1830." *Southwestern Historical Quarterly* 16 (April 1913): 378–422.

Jordan, Terry G. "The Imprint of the Upper and Lower South on Mid-Nineteenth-Century Texas." *Annals of the Association of American Geographers* 57 (December 1967): 667–690.

———. "The Origin of Anglo-American Cattle Ranching in Texas: A Documentation of Diffusion from the Lower South." *Economic Geography* 45 (January 1969): 63–87.

———. "Pioneer Evaluation of Vegetation in Frontier Texas." *Southwestern Historical Quarterly* 76 (January 1973): 233–254.

———. "Population Origins in Texas, 1850." *Geographical Review* 59 (January 1969): 83–103.

———. "The Texan Appalachia." *Annals of the Association of American Geographers* 60 (September 1970): 409–427.

Koch, Lena Clara. "The Federal Indian Policy in Texas, 1845–1860." *Southwestern Historical Quarterly* 28 (January 1925): 223–234; (April 1925): 259–286; 29 (July 1925): 19–25; (October 1925): 98–127.

Lack, Paul D. "Slavery and Vigilantism in Austin, Texas, 1840–1860." *Southwestern Historical Quarterly* 85 (July 1981): 1–20.

Leake, Chauncey. "Ashbel Smith, M.D., 1805–1886: Pioneer Educator in Texas." *Yale Journal of Biology and Medicine* 20 (January 1948): 224–232.

Ledbetter, Billy D. "The Election of Louis T. Wigfall to the United States Senate, 1859: A Reevaluation." *Southwestern Historical Quarterly* 77 (October 1973): 241–254.

McClellan, Waymon L. "1855: The Know-Nothing Challenge in East Texas." *East Texas Historical Journal* 12 (Fall 1974): 32–44.

McDonald, Forrest, and Grady McWhiney. "The Antebellum Southern Herdsman: A Reinterpretation." *Journal of Southern History* 41 (May 1975): 147–166.

Maher, Edward R., Jr. "Sam Houston and Secession." *Southwestern Historical Quarterly* 55 (April 1952): 448–458.

Maresh, Henry R. "The Czechs in Texas." *Southwestern Historical Quarterly* 50 (October 1946): 236–240.

Mering, John V. "The Slave-State Constitutional Unionists and the Politics of Consensus." *Journal of Southern History* 43 (August 1977): 395–410.

Muir, Andrew F. "The Destiny of Buffalo Bayou." *Southwestern Historical Quarterly* 47 (October 1943): 19–22.

———. "Railroads Come to Houston, 1857–1861." *Southwestern Historical Quarterly* 64 (July 1960): 42–63.

———. "Sam Houston and the Civil War." *Texana* 6 (Fall 1968): 282–287.

Nash, A. E. Keir. "The Texas Supreme Court and Trial Rights of Blacks, 1845–1860." *Journal of American History* 58 (December 1971): 622–642.

Norton, Wesley. "The Methodist Episcopal Church and the Civil Disturbances in North Texas in 1859 and 1860." *Southwestern Historical Quarterly* 68 (January 1965): 317–341.

Owsley, Frank L. "The Economic Basis of Society in the Late Ante-Bellum South." *Journal of Southern History* 6 (February 1940): 24–45.

Paxson, Frederic L. "The Constitution of Texas, 1845." *Southwestern Historical Quarterly* 18 (April 1915): 386–398.

Porter, Eugene O. "Railroad Enterprises in the Republic of Texas." *Southwestern Historical Quarterly* 59 (January 1956): 363–372.

Ramsdell, Charles W. "The Frontier and Secession." *Studies in Southern History and Politics.* New York: Columbia University Press, 1914, pp. 63–82.

———. "Internal Improvement Projects in Texas in the Fifties." *Proceedings of the Mississippi Valley Historical Association* 9 (1915–1916): 99–109.

———. "The Natural Limits of Slavery Expansion." *Mississippi Valley Historical Review* 16 (September 1929): 151–171.

Raunick, Selma Metzenthin. "A Survey of German Literature in Texas." *Southwestern Historical Quarterly* 33 (October 1929): 134–159.

Rippy, J. Fred. "Border Troubles along the Rio Grande, 1848–1860." *Southwestern Historical Quarterly* 23 (October 1919): 91–111.

Roper, Laura W. "Frederick Law Olmsted and the Western Texas Free-Soil Movement." *American Historical Review* 56 (October 1950): 58–64.

Rubin, Julius. "The Limits of Agricultural Progress in the Nineteenth-Century South." *Agricultural History* 49 (April 1975): 374–380.

Sandbo, Anna Irene. "Beginnings of the Secession Movement in Texas." *Southwestern Historical Quarterly* 18 (July 1914): 41–73.

———. "The First Session of the Secession Convention of Texas." *Southwestern Historical Quarterly* 18 (October 1914): 162–194.

Schott, Christine. "Gustavus Schleicher: A Representative of Early Emigration in Texas." *West Texas Historical Association Year Book* 28 (October 1952): 50–70.

Sellers, Charles G., Jr. "Who Were the Southern Whigs?" *American Historical Review* 59 (January 1954): 335–346.

Shook, Robert W. "The Battle of the Nueces, August 10, 1862." *Southwestern Historical Quarterly* 66 (July 1962): 31–42.

Smallwood, James. "Blacks in Antebellum Texas: A Reappraisal." *Red River Valley Historical Review* 2 (Winter 1975): 443–466.

Smyrl, Frank H. "Texans in the Union Army, 1861–1865." *Southwestern Historical Quarterly* 65 (October 1961): 234–250.

———. "Unionism in Texas, 1856–1861." *Southwestern Historical Quarterly* 68 (October 1964): 172–195.

Somers, Dale A. "James P. Newcomb: The Making of a Radical." *Southwestern Historical Quarterly* 72 (April 1969): 449–469.

Steen, Ralph W. "Texas Newspapers and Lincoln." *Southwestern Historical Quarterly* 51 (January 1948): 199–212.

Timmons, Joe T. "The Referendum in Texas on the Ordinance of Secession, February 23, 1861: The Vote." *East Texas Historical Journal* 11 (Fall 1973): 12–28.

Venable, Austin L. "The Conflict between the Douglas and Yancey Forces in the Charleston Convention." *Journal of Southern History* 8 (May 1942): 226–241.

Ward, James A. "A New Look at Antebellum Southern Railroad Development." *Journal of Southern History* 39 (August 1973): 409–420.

Watson, Judy. "The Red River Raft." *Texana* 5 (Spring 1967): 68–76.

White, Raymond E. "Cotton Ginning in Texas to 1861." *Southwestern Historical Quarterly* 61 (October 1957): 257–269.

White, William W. "The Texas Slave Insurrection in 1860." *Southwestern Historical Quarterly* 52 (January 1949): 259–286.

Williams, Frieda M. "German Pioneers in Texas." *Frontier Times* 13 (October 1935): 70–73.

Winfrey, Dorman H. "Mirabeau B. Lamar and Texas Nationalism." *Southwestern Historical Quarterly* 59 (October 1955): 184–205.

Wish, Harvey. "The Revival of the African Slave Trade in the United States in 1855–1860." *Mississippi Valley Historical Review* 27 (March 1941): 569–588.

Woodward, Earl T. "Internal Improvements in Texas under Governor Peter Hansborough Bell's Administration." *Southwestern Historical Quarterly* 76 (October 1972): 161–182.

Wooster, Ralph A. "An Analysis of the Membership of the Texas Secession Convention." *Southwestern Historical Quarterly* 62 (January 1959): 322–335.

———. "An Analysis of the Texas Know Nothings." *Southwestern Historical Quarterly* 70 (January 1967): 414–423.

———. "Ben H. Epperson: East Texas Lawyer, Legislator, and Civic Leader." *East Texas Historical Journal* 5 (March 1967): 29–42.

————. "Democracy on the Frontier: Statehouse and Courthouse in Ante-Bellum Texas." *East Texas Historical Journal* 10 (Fall 1972): 83–97.

————. "Early Texas Statehood: A Survey of Historical Writings." *Southwestern Historical Quarterly* 76 (October 1973): 121–141.

————. "Foreigners in the Principal Towns of Ante-Bellum Texas." *Southwestern Historical Quarterly* 66 (October 1962): 208–220.

————. "Notes on Texas' Largest Slaveholders, 1860." *Southwestern Historical Quarterly* 65 (July 1961): 72–79.

————. "Wealthy Texans, 1860." *Southwestern Historical Quarterly* 71 (October 1967): 163–180.

Mrs. Simon Baruch University Awards, 1927–1982

1927   Carpenter, Jesse Thomas, "The South as a Conscious Minority, 1789–1861." New York University, Washington Square, New York, 1930.

1929   Whitfield, Theodore M., "Slavery Agitation in Virginia, 1829–1832." Out of Print.

1931   Flanders, Ralph Betts, "Plantation Slavery in Georgia." Out of Print.

1933   Thompson, Samuel, "Confederate Purchasing Agents Abroad." Out of Print.

1935   Wiley, Bell Irvin, "Southern Negroes, 1861–1865." Yale University Press, New Haven, Connecticut, 1938.

1937   Hill, Louise Biles, "Joseph E. Brown and the Confederacy." Out of Print.

1940   Haydon, F. Stansbury, "Aeronautics of the Union and Confederate Armies." Out of Print.

1942   Stormont, John, "The Economic Stake of the North in the Preservation of the Union in 1861." Not Published.

1945   Schultz, Harold Sessel, "Nationalism and Sectionalism in South Carolina, 1852–1860." Duke University Press, Durham, North Carolina, 1950.

1948   Tankersly, Allen P., "John Brown Gordon, Soldier and Statesman." Privately Printed.

1951   Todd, Richard C., "Confederate Finance." University of Georgia Press, Athens, Georgia, 1953.

1954   Morrow, Ralph E., "Northern Methodism and Reconstruction." Michigan State University Press, 1956.
Cunningham, Horace, "Doctors in Gray." Louisiana State University Press, Baton Rouge, Louisiana, 1958.

1957   Hall, Martin H., "Sibley's New Mexico Campaign." University of Texas Press, Austin, Texas, 1960.

1960   Robertson, James I., Jr., "Jackson's Stonewall: A History of the Stonewall Brigade." Louisiana State University Press, Baton Rouge, Louisiana, 1963.

1969   Wells, Tom Henderson, "The Confederate Navy: A Study in Organization." University of Alabama Press, University, Alabama, 1971.

1970   Delaney, Conrad, "John McIntosh Kell, Luff of the Alabama." University of Alabama Press, University, Alabama, 1972.

1972   Dougan, Michael B., "Confederate Arkansas—The People and Politics of a Frontier State." University of Alabama Press, University, Alabama, 1976.

1974   Wiggins, Sarah W., "The Scalawag in Alabama Politics, 1865–1881." University of Alabama Press, University, Alabama, 1976.

1976   Nelson, Larry Earl, "Bullets, Ballots and Rhetoric." University of Alabama Press, University, Alabama, 1980.

1978   Franks, Kenny A., "Stand Watie and the Agony of the Cherokee Nation." Memphis State University Press, Memphis, Tennessee, 1979.

1980   Buenger, Walter L., "Secession and the Union in Texas." University of Texas Press, Austin, Texas, 1984.

1982   McMurry, Richard M., "John Bell Hood and the War for Southern Independence." University Press of Kentucky, Lexington, Kentucky, 1982.

Index